HOW TO MAXIMIZE TAX SAVINGS
IN BUYING,
OPERATING
AND SELLING
REAL PROPERTY

2nd Edition

HOW TO MAXIMIZE TAX SAVINGS

IN BUYING,

OPERATING

AND SELLING

REAL PROPERTY

Robert M. Weiss

Prentice-Hall, Inc.
Englewood Cliffs, N.J.

2nd Edition

Prentice-Hall International, Inc., *London*
Prentice-Hall of Australia, Pty. Ltd., *Sydney*
Prentice-Hall of Canada, Ltd., *Toronto*
Prentice-Hall of India Private Ltd., *New Delhi*
Prentice-Hall of Japan, Inc., *Tokyo*
Prentice-Hall of Southeast Asia Pte. Ltd., *Singapore*
Whitehall Books, Ltd., *Wellington, New Zealand*

© 1977 by

Prentice-Hall, Inc.

Englewood Cliffs, N.J.

This publication is designed to provide accurate and authoritative information in
regard to the subject matter covered. It is sold with the understanding that the
publisher is not engaged in rendering legal, accounting, or other professional service.
If legal advice or other expert assistance is required, the services of a competent
professional person should be sought.
... *From the Declaration of Principles jointly adopted by a Committee of the
American Bar Association and a Committee of Publishers and Associations.*

Library of Congress Cataloging in Publication Data

Weiss, Robert M
   How to maximize tax savings in buying, operating,
and selling real property.

   Includes bibliographical references and index.
   1. Real property and taxation--United States.
I. Title.
KF6535.W4 1977   343'.73'054   77-8962
ISBN 0-13-423798-6

Printed in the United States of America

DEDICATION

This book could not have been produced without the support of four outstanding women who made it possible—Joyce, Nancy, Elaine and Bernice. It is appropriate, therefore, that the book be dedicated to each of them.

A WORD FROM THE AUTHOR ABOUT
THE SECOND EDITION

Tax considerations play a critical role in every stage of a commercial real estate transaction. Before taking title to the site, the parties must create a business entity which not only meets their business requirements but also satisfies the diverse tax objectives of each of the participants in the group.

After the project is operating, the decisions relating to the depreciation method, the accounting method and the most appropriate treatment for various income and expense items are all tax-oriented.

Finally, when the time comes to dispose of the project the parties must determine how to qualify the sale as a capital gain, whether it is advisable to utilize the installment method, whether a tax-free exchange of the property for other real estate is appropriate, or whether some other form of disposition is preferable.

Of course, the importance of taxes in making business decisions is not unique to real estate. For a number of reasons, however, the tax considerations are particularly important in this area. First, the size of the potential tax liability or the potential tax saving—and, therefore, the penalty for error in case of an incorrect decision—is particularly great in most real estate projects. Second, in real estate investments the tax consequences are not merely one of the factors normally considered by the parties, they are frequently an overriding factor, outweighing in importance other business considerations; it is not unusual for high-bracket taxpayers to invest in a real estate venture for the primary purpose of obtaining the tax losses provided in the early years. Third, there is probably no area of tax law where the rules are more complex and confusing. For all of these reasons, a thorough understanding of the rules and the alternatives available is essential in order to properly structure, operate and dispose of a real estate project.

The first edition of this book attempted to present the tax law as it related to real estate operations in a manageable form for the benefit of developers, investors and their professional advisors. The large number of decisions and rulings which have been issued in the last six years makes a revised edition necessary in order for the book to continue to be a useful tool for the practitioner. Moreover, the Tax Reform Act of 1976, which was enacted October 4, 1976, made many additional changes affecting real estate and added more layers of complexity. For example, capital gains are now taxed at various rates, depending upon the amount of the gain realized, and in various forms, depending upon the status of the individual taxpayer. The rules relating to prepaid interest were changed. The rules relating to recapture of depreciation were tightened. The costs of organizing a partnership are no longer currently deductible although they may be amortized over a period of years. The rules governing allocation of partnership income and losses among the partners were clarified and some of the pre-1976 cases were rendered obsolete by the new Act. The minimum tax and the maximum tax which had relatively little impact on most real estate investors prior to 1976 have now become significant due to the increased rates and the reduced exemptions. In short, most areas of tax planning were affected and reliance on reference material which has not been updated to reflect the new provisions is dangerous.

This edition of the book, therefore, attempts to incorporate all of the important changes which have occurred through December 31, 1976—the cases, the rulings and the provisions of the 1976 Act. Also, in the seven years which have passed since publication of the first edition, a number of important new techniques have been developed and some of the old techniques have been refined or discarded. Throughout the book the approach has been a practical one—what is permitted under the tax law, what is clearly not permitted and what is the recommended procedure where the rules are not entirely clear.

The book is divided into three principal sections. The first section deals with selecting the form and organizing the entity which will be used to purchase and operate a real estate project or which will serve as the vehicle for syndicating a real estate investment. After reviewing the advantages and disadvantages of the various business forms in Chapter 1 we consider the specific problems of organizing the corporation in Chapter 2 and organizing the partnership in Chapter 3. This chapter, in addition to reviewing the case law on allocations of losses among the members of a partnerhsip, includes references to the Tax Reform Act of 1976. Chapter 4 covers a number of related problems involved in property acquisitions including the rules for determining the taxpayer's basis in the acquired property and a discussion of the question, most critical in real estate investments, of whether the mortgage can be included in the owner's basis.

The second section deals with the tax problems which arise during the period of ownership of property. Chapter 5 covers depreciation including the rules relating to recapture as modified under the 1976 Act. Chapter 6 covers the problems of leases—the tax consequences to landlords and tenants of their various receipts and disbursements in connection with leased property. Chapter 7 deals with miscellaneous problems in operating investment real estate such as how to handle prepaid interest, when to capitalize carrying charges and the accounting elections which are available for tax purposes.

The third section covers the problems of disposing of real estate. Chapter 8 discusses deferred payment sales including sales on the installment method—when is the installment election appropriate, what are the limitations on its use and what are the tax consequences of making the election. Chapter 9 deals with tax-free exchanges, a topic of particular importance in dispositions of real estate due to the fact that the tax losses produced in the early years, together with the appreciation in value which often occurs, result in a large potential gain. Moreover, due to the peculiarities of mortgage financing, the taxable gain on disposition often exceeds the cash realized on a sale. Chapter 10 discusses the important distinction between capital gains and ordinary income on sales of real estate. Where real estate is held in corporate form, a corporate liquidation is often a first step to disposing of the project and Chapter 11 discusses the various forms of corporate liquidations and the tax problems inherent in each of them. Finally,

Chapter 12 covers a number of difficult problems facing taxpayers who own projects where the tax losses have run out, continued ownership of the project has become impractical and the normal methods of disposition are inappropriate. For example, is it possible for the owners to make gifts of their interests in the project, either to family members or to a charity? The problems of disposition are particularly acute where the mortgage balance exceeds the depreciated basis of the owners, a situation which is fairly common in real estate projects.

In all cases the primary emphasis is on practical tax planning. Experience indicates that many of the most horrendous cases would have been avoided with proper planning early in the game. It is in this area—tax planning for the complex real estate transaction—that this book will have its greatest application.

Robert M. Weiss

CONTENTS

SHRINKING TAXES THROUGH DEFERRED PAYMENT SALES (*cont.*)
vs. Closed Transactions—Classification of Buyer's
Obligations

2   ESCAPING FROM A LEAKY SHELTER: SALES, GIFTS
     AND FORECLOSURES OF THE PROPERTY 187

Part 1

TAX PROBLEMS IN ACQUIRING REAL ESTATE:

Selecting the Form and Organizing the Entity

1

SELECTING THE MOST
PROFITABLE FORM
OF BUSINESS ENTERPRISE

Tax considerations are an important factor in the planning of any business enterprise. But in the field of real estate they are much more than that—tax benefits are frequently the prime reason for investor interest in the first place and in a sense they are often responsible for the very existence of the project. The high-bracket businessman or professional man, for example, may be willing to invest in depreciable real estate for a cash return which is less than he could realize elsewhere because he believes that the tax loss and the tax-free equity buildup will more than compensate for the inadequacy in current yield. When the tax losses run out he hopes for additional tax related benefits such as capital gain on the eventual sale or a tax-free exchange for other investment real estate.

Whether the investor will realize these benefits, however, depends to a large extent on the form of ownership utilized. A thorough understanding of the options available in taking title and operating the project and the tax consequences of each form of ownership is essential.

This chapter, after first analyzing the factors which favor investment in real estate, discusses the various forms of business enterprise and the suitability of each form to satisfy the investment objectives. The chapter is divided into the following sections:

1.1　Tax Factors in Real Estate Investments: An Overview
    (a)　Tax Loss and Cash Flow.
    (b)　Additional Benefits of Real Estate as a Tax Shelter.
    (c)　Some Qualifications of Tax Planning.

1.1   TAX FACTORS IN REAL ESTATE INVESTMENTS: AN OVERVIEW

(a) Tax Loss and Cash Flow.

Perhaps the principal attraction of real estate as an investment is the fact that the operation of a depreciable real estate project normally produces a loss for tax purposes. Of course, other business can also produce losses but the critical difference lies in the fact that in the real estate venture it is necessary to differentiate between an actual loss and a tax loss; there may be a surplus of cash receipts over cash disbursements—a positive cash flow—at the same time that the tax deductible expenses, including depreciation, exceed the income—a tax loss. There are two principal reasons for this, the tax law and the high leverage potential in real estate financing. Under the tax law, depreciation is a deduction even though it does not represent a cash outlay and since the basis which is used to compute depreciation normally includes the mortgage or other financing on the property, the amount of the deduction is not limited to the cash invested or to the income earned on the project. Under traditional real estate financing, the amount of leverage—that is, the proportion of borrowed funds to equity investment—far exceeds the financing normally available in other types of investment. Moreover, it is not unusual for such financing to be nonrecourse, i.e., without personal liability on the part of the borrower, but the absence of personal liability normally has no effect on the tax consequences of the transaction. The combination of these two factors—the availability of mortgage financing and the ability to include such mortgages in the depreciation base—can produce tax losses which are disproportionately large compared to the actual cash investment.

> *Example:* Assume a real estate investment requires $1,000,000 of capital. If an individual invests $100,000 of his own money and is able to borrow $900,000 to meet the capital requirement, or if he is able to purchase the property subject to a mortgage of $900,000, for tax purposes he is treated as having $1,000,000 in the investment. This means that if there are accelerated deductions of $200,000 in the first year, the investor, if he is in the 70% bracket, would be reducing his tax liability by $140,000. In this case, the deductions in the first year ($200,000) would be $100,000 more than the equity capital invested and the tax savings would be $40,000 more than the amount invested in that year. In effect, the investor is financing his investment with what amounts to an interest-free loan from the government.

The Tax Reform Act of 1976 imposed limitations on losses in excess of the amount "at risk" in certain specified kinds of business activities as well as in partnerships generally. See the discussion in Chapter 4, Section 2(c). However, investments in real estate (other than mineral leasing) are expressly excepted from these limitations and continue to be subject to the old rules.

We have seen in the above illustration that depreciation constitutes a tax deduction without a cash disbursement. Conversely, principal payments on a mortgage and capital improvements represent cash outlays which are not deductible for tax or accounting purposes. Therefore, the ideal combination of positive cash flows and tax losses will continue only so long as the depreciation (a tax deduction not involving a cash disbursement) exceeds the mortgage amortization (a nondeductible cash outlay).

Example: Investor is acquiring a new apartment building for $500,000 of which $50,000 is allocated to land and the balance represents the cost of the depreciable building. He is paying $50,000 down and taking title subject to a 9% 25-year mortgage for $450,000. He will depreciate the building over forty years on the double-declining method (a 5% rate on a declining balance). He anticipates a cash surplus before mortgage payments of $50,000 per year. Since the mortgage payments, including principal and interest, are $45,813 per year, the remaining cash flow is $4,187. The following schedule indicates the amount of tax loss at various points.

Year	Cash Surplus Before Debt Service	Mortgage Payments Interest	Mortgage Payments Principal	Depreciation	Tax Loss
1	$50,000	$40,500	$ 5,313	$22,500	$ 13,000
2	50,000	40,022	5,791	21,375	11,397
3	50,000	39,501	6,312	20,306	9,807
4	50,000	38,933	6,880	19,291	8,224
5	50,000	38,313	7,499	18,326	6,639
6	50,000	37,638	8,174	17,410	5,048
7	50,000	36,903	8,910	16,540	3,443
8	50,000	36,101	9,712	15,713	1,814
9	50,000	35,223	10,586	14,927	150
10	50,000	34,274	11,539	14,181	(1,545)
15	50,000	28,059	17,754	10,973	(10,968)
20	50,000	18,496	27,317	8,490	(23,014)
25	50,000	3,783	42,030	6,570	(39,647)

As the schedule indicates, in the early years, since the depreciation exceeds the principal payments, there is a tax loss. In later years, as the depreciation declines and the principal payments increase, there is taxable income. In Year 1, for example, depreciation exceeds the principal payments by $17,187 and deducting this amount from the cash flow of $4,187, produces a tax loss of $13,000. By Year 9 the tax loss has declined to only $150 and in year 10, the project begins to show taxable income. By Year 15 the taxable income of $10,968 actually exceeds the cash flow, i.e., the income reported by reason of the ownership of the project exceeds the cash received. At this point the tax-oriented investor will surely consider disposing of the project if he has not already done so.

(b)   Additional Benefits of Real Estate as a Tax Shelter.

In addition to the ability to generate tax losses even while a project is producing a positive cash flow, and the ability to obtain higher leverage through mortgage financing, real estate has a number of other characteristics which make it a particularly suitable tax-shelter investment. They include the following:

Ability to Syndicate the Investment—Real estate projects are particularly susceptible to syndication, i.e., to fragmenting of the investment into a number of units, each of which can be sold to individual investors. For one thing, the sheer size of the project frequently makes it impossible for an individual developer or group of developers to handle and they are, therefore, compelled to invite others to participate. Also, unlike most other businesses, it is possible to separate the investment function of a project from the management function. Thus, a number of individuals (investors) may be willing to make capital contributions because they find the project an attractive investment for their surplus funds. Other parties (developers with less capital) would prefer to handle the construction and management of the project. The syndicate or partnership can be structured so that each of these two groups receives diverse benefits which are consistent with their investment objectives and their respective contributions. Even within the investors' group it may be possible to allocate benefits in a manner consistent with individual objectives. Thus, some investors may prefer a high cash return while others in higher brackets may be happy to sacrifice cash returns for tax losses. Imaginative counsel will try to satisfy the objectives of all the participants.

Capital Gain and Depreciation Recapture—Under the Internal Revenue Code, as amended in 1969, all of the gain realized on a sale of personal property is "recaptured" as ordinary income to the extent of the depreciation claimed in prior years. However, in a sale of real estate, only depreciation in excess of straight-line depreciation is subject to such recapture rules and even this is reduced after a specified holding period in certain cases. Thus, the tax losses realized in the early years of a project which serve to shelter the owner's ordinary income do not always produce ordinary income upon eventual sale of the project at a gain. Moreover, in some cases it is possible to dispose of a project without the recognition of gain for tax purposes despite the realization of tax losses in early years, for example, by means of a tax-free exchange. While personal property may also qualify for such tax-free exchanges, the frequency of such transactions is considerably less, probably due to the shorter useful life of most items of personal property, which makes the exchange or trade-in value insignificant.

Ability to Control Tax Consequences—Unlike most other forms of investment, the parties involved in a real estate transaction can often tailor the flow of funds and other matters so as to suit their respective tax objectives, particularly where a cash-basis taxpayer is involved. For example, real estate taxes, management fees, and other operating expenses can be prepaid by the owner of the property. A landlord and a tenant can agree to have the rent under a lease prepaid or deferred, and they can agree as to which of them shall be responsible for the construction or demolition of leasehold improvements and other items involved in the operation of the property. A buyer of stock or bonds in a publicly held company, on the other hand, has no options as to his relationship with the corporation. Of course, the deductions created for one taxpayer normally result in simultaneous income to the other, but since there are so few parties involved in most real estate transactions, such differences can usually be negotiated.

Some Qualifications of Tax Planning—Before leaving this subject there are two important caveats to be noted. First, while all of the objectives outlined above are possible given the right set of circumstances, there are countless qualifications and exceptions which limit the taxpayer's ability to achieve these objectives. The rules of the game are found not only in the provisions of the Internal Revenue Code, but also in numerous Treasury Regulations, rulings of Internal Revenue Service, and judicial decisions. Therefore, only the well-informed can determine the limits of tax planning. It goes without saying that in this field a little knowledge is a dangerous thing and the principles set forth above should be treated as nothing more than objectives. Most of this book is intended to outline the rules and limitations governing these principles. Second, the price of most tax deductions is a reduction in the owner's tax basis in his property. Upon a sale or other taxable disposition gain is recognized to the extent that the sales price exceeds such reduced basis (although a portion of such gain is normally taxed at capital gain rates). In short, tax deductions in the early years normally produce taxable income in the year of sale. This is not to say that this is an unsatisfactory trade off—many taxpayers are more than willing to reduce their current taxes even at the risk of repaying some or all of the tax savings later on. The point is that the well-informed investor should be aware of the implications of his decisions. Any analysis of a project which deals only with the savings in the early years of ownership and ignores the long term consequences, is unrealistic.

1.2   THE CASE FOR PARTNERSHIPS

From the foregoing discussion it is clear that real estate, particularly when it is highly leveraged, offers great investment and tax opportunities. It is equally clear that the business entity utilized to own and operate the project should be one which insures that these benefits will be available to the participants and in most instances the corporate form will not meet this objective.

A corporation is not only an entity which is separate and distinct from its owners for most legal purposes, it is also a separate *taxable* entity. It files its own returns, pays its own taxes and claims its own deductions or losses. Consequently the tax loss in a corporate-owned real estate project is available only to the corporate owner, not to the individual shareholders. This often means that in the case of a new project the tax loss is deferred until such time as the project produces taxable income and the original losses can be offset against such income. In many cases because of the five-year limitation on corporate loss carry-forwards, the result is that the early years' depreciation and interest deductions are totally or partially wasted for tax purposes. Moreover, a distribution of cash by the corporation to its shareholders, to the extent that it exceeds their tax basis in capital stock, is a taxable distribution, notwithstanding the fact that it is made by a corporation which has no retained earnings or surplus.[1] This puts the shareholders in the unfortunate position of paying a tax on distributions of surplus rents which would have been received by them tax-free if the project had not been incorporated in the first place.

A partnership, on the other hand, is a conduit, not a taxpayer. The taxable income or loss is passed through to the partners directly, the partnership filing only an information return for reporting purposes.[2] Further, since the partnership is a conduit, the amounts distributed retain their character in the hands of the distributee partner— capital gain, tax-exempt interest, etc.—as contrasted with corporate distributions which are normally taxable as dividends at ordinary rates.

In view of these distinctions it is not surprising that it is the partnership form which is normally utilized in real estate projects, particularly where tax loses are anticipated.

Sometimes the parties take title to real estate as tenants in common without formally organizing a partnership. The tax treatment of tenants in common is similar to that of partnerships in that the tenancy in common is not an entity which is recognized for tax purposes. See Chapter 3, Section 1 for a discussion of tenancies in common.

1.3   THE CASE FOR CORPORATIONS

In view of the disadvantages of the corporate form, the question arises as to why corporations are ever utilized for real estate projects. Experience indicates that there are a number of reasons.

(a) *Habit*—Most businessmen customarily organize corporations for each new venture in which they are involved, thereby minimizing their personal liability and insulating the assets of each project from the creditors of other projects. This practice is frequently carried over to the organization of real estate projects as well; it is not until later in the game that the owners awake to the fact that they have created a difficult tax problem which may be impossible to rectify without great expense.[3]

(b) *Tax Considerations*—There are some cases where the corporate form presents certain tax advantages over the partnership. It permits effective estate and gift planning since it facilitates transfers of interests in the project in the form of corporate stock. Where it is anticipated that taxable income rather than losses will be realized, the ceiling on corporate rates may be considerably less than the top rate of tax which the individual stockholder would pay had he realized the same income personally.[4]

> *Observation:* Such an analysis is often short-sighted because the accumulated corporate income will eventually be subject to a second tax when it is distributed to the shareholders, either as a redemption of corporate stock, which may or may not qualify as a capital gain, or as a dividend. Careful analysis may indicate that this second tax may more than offset the short-run savings of the lower corporate rates.

It may be possible for an individual who is a dealer in real estate to transfer certain property to a corporation, thereby separating his investment property from property which is held for sale to customers in the ordinary course of his business. See Chapter 10, Section 10.2. Looking to eventual disposition of the property it may be possible to exchange the corporate stock for stock of another corporation in a tax-free reorganization where a like kind exchange of real estate may not be feasible. Finally, there are some corporations with surplus funds available for investment which acquire real estate anticipating a tax loss which will offset the other corporate income. In these cases the high-bracket corporation is motivated by the same investment objectives as the high-bracket individual.

(c) *Non-Tax Benefits*—Of course, the best reason for utilizing the corporate form is that it provides all of those non-tax benefits, the principal one being limited liability, which are traditionally characteristic of corporations. The real estate investor, like any other investor, wishes to avoid personal liability on the mortgage loan as well as other potential liabilities.[5] He wants a property interest which is freely transferrable to third parties. He frequently wants the benefits of professional, centralized management and he wants the entity owning the project to have perpetual existence which will not be affected by the death or incapacity of any of the participants. The corporation offers these benefits. Also, the mortgage lender sometimes prefers a corporate borrower since, under the laws of some states, a corporation cannot raise the defense of usury. As the following discussion will indicate, however, there are alternative techniques which can be utilized to accomplish some or all of these objectives without the tax disadvantages of the corporate form.

1.4   SUBCHAPTER S CORPORATIONS

Under Subchapter S of the Code (§ 1371-1378), corporations which meet certain prescribed requirements can elect to have their income taxed directly to the shareholders, thereby eliminating the double tax problem which exists in most corporations. Such corporations are commonly referred to as Subchapter S corporations.

The Subchapter S election is particularly useful to a real estate corporation during its initial stages, for example, during the period of construction or rentup, before the venture has realized any substantial profits. The Subchapter S election permits the shareholders to personally claim the operating losses which are incurred during this period, such as losses resulting from the payment of interest, property taxes, and similar expenses.

However, after a project begins to produce rental income, the corporation will normally not qualify as a Subchapter S corporation. The Subchapter S election terminates if the corporation's rental income exceeds 20% of its gross receipts.[6] For all practical purposes this precludes the election in the case of corporations which are operating shopping centers, apartment buildings or office buildings. Where substantial services are also provided in connection with the use of the property, however, the income is not considered rent and this prohibition would not apply. Thus, income from the operation of a hotel or motel is not rent because changing the linen and cleaning the rooms constitutes substantial services.[7] Taxpayers have been relatively unsuccessful to date in persuading the courts that services rendered in connection with rental projects take the corporate income out of the passive rent category. For example, where a taxpayer owned and operated an office building and also leased space to tenants for the operation of a barber shop, a drugstore and a lunch counter, and provided incidental services for the repair of machines and furniture which belonged to the tenants, the rent received was held to be for the use of property, not for "significant services," and Subchapter S status was not available.[8] Similarly, where a corporation owned and maintained several large buildings and derived its income from leasing parts thereof, the landlord's activities in maintaining the public restrooms, sweeping the sidewalks and alleys surrounding the building, repairing equipment, etc., were not enough to qualify the corporation under Subchapter S.[9]

An equally serious problem is that the losses which can be claimed by a Subchapter S stockholder cannot exceed in the aggregate the basis of his capital stock and loans to the corporation.[10] This must be contrasted with the tax treatment accorded partners who, since mortgages are normally included in the basis of partnership interests, can deduct tax losses far in excess of their actual investment.

See Chapter 2, Section 4, for a discussion of the requirements for qualification as a Subchapter S corporation.

The following chart summarizes the tax treatment of partnerships, regular corporations and Subchapter S corporations. It is obvious that only the partnership provides all of the tax benefits listed.

COMPARISON OF TAX BENEFITS OF VARIOUS BUSINESS FORMS

TAX BENEFIT	PARTNERSHIP	REGULAR CORPORATION	SUBCHAPTER S CORPORATION
1. Income taxed directly to individual investor (partner or stockholder) without tax on the operating entity.	Yes	No	Yes
2. Tax losses of project deductible by individual investor against his other income.	Yes	No	Partially*
3. Distributions by operating entity retain their character (e.g., capital gain) in the hands of the distributee.	Yes	No	Yes
4. Excess losses can be carried forward by individual investor if they exceed his other income.	Yes	No	Partially*

*Stockholders of Subchapter S corporations can deduct corporate losses but not in excess of the basis for their stock and their loans to the corporation. This normally does not include mortgage loans on corporate property.

ALTERNATIVE TECHNIQUES

Since the corporation has certain business advantages (such as limited liability and transferable interests), while the partnership has certain tax advantages, the objective of the participants in real estate projects has frequently been to get the best of both possible worlds, that is, to utilize an entity which provides the benefits of both forms without their disadvantages. Various techniques, some successful and some unsuccessful, have been used to achieve these objectives.

1.5 THE STRAW CORPORATION

A tempting solution to the dilemma is to organize a corporation (referred to as a straw, or nominee, or sham corporation) which takes title to the property and executes the mortgage and mortgage note, thereby insulating the shareholders from personal liability. The straw corporation then conveys the real estate to its shareholders, subject to the mortgage, permitting them as the record owners to claim the tax loss and cash flow without being personally liable on the mortgage. The corporation which has then served its purpose terminates its business activities at least insofar as the specific project is concerned. There are also other reasons for utilizing straw corporations, such as obscuring the true owners of the project; avoiding problems generally inherent in large partnerships such as death of an owner or cumbersome execution problems; and avoiding a usury problem, since a high-interest loan may be the only available financing, and corporations are often exempt from the application of the usury laws.

The danger is that while the participants may consider the corporation a nominee, for tax purposes it may be treated as a viable and a taxable entity in which case any income realized from the project during the period of corporate ownership will be taxed to it and then taxed again to the shareholders as a distribution of earnings. Even more serious, the conveyance of the property from the corporation to its shareholders or principals would constitute a taxable event often resulting in recognition of capital gain or ordinary income.

In a decision going back to 1943, the U.S. Supreme Court refused to ignore the existence of a corporation which was allegedly a nominee or straw acting on behalf of its sole stockholder. The Court stated:

> Whether the purpose be to gain an advantage under the law of the state of incorporation or to avoid or to comply with the demands of creditors, or to serve the creator's personal or undisclosed convenience, so long as that purpose is the equivalent of business activity or is followed by the carrying on of business by the corporation, the corporation remains a separate taxable entity.[11]

The Court continued to utilize this "business activity" test in a number of later cases involving real estate corporations,[12] but probably the most graphic illustration of the danger of utilizing a corporation which engages in any business activity whatever is the case of *Paymer v. Comm'r.*[13] In that case there were two corporations established under almost identical circumstances. One of them was held to be a mere nominee while the other was recognized as a separate taxable entity. The latter corporation, as partial security for a $50,000 loan, executed an assignment of its rights in two leases and covenanted that it was the sole lessor and that the leases were in full force and effect. Although this corporation held no meetings after the first one, where the minutes stated that the corporation was acting as a nominee only and that beneficial interest remained in the stockholders, the Court held that the corporation was

> . . . active enough to justify holding, that it did engage in business in 1938. The absence of books, records and officers and the failure to hold corporate meetings are not decisive on that question.

Even though a corporation is formed only for the purpose of avoiding the usury laws, it may be recognized for tax purposes. A 1976 decision by the Tax Court involved the following facts:

In 1967, Mr. Strong and a group of other investors decided to form a partnership to develop an apartment complex. Under the New York usury laws, they could not get the financing they needed as individuals but they could as a corporation. Accordingly, they formed Heritage Village, Inc. in order to get loan commitments. The partnership transferred three parcels of land to the corporation and the corporation executed mortgages and rent assignments and engaged in other transactions related to the financing. It issued no stock, held no meetings and had no employees. Except for receipt and disbursement of advancement on the loans, the corporation had no income and paid no expenses. All income and expenses relating to construction were carried on the partnership books. The operating losses were reported on the partnership returns and passed through to the individual partners. The corporation filed returns but showed no income or loss reporting its business as "nominee corp." The Tax Court held that although the corporate business activities were minimal, the degree of corporate purpose and activity needed for recognition of a corporation as a separate taxable entity is extremely low and it found the activities of Heritage Village were adequate to meet this standard. Avoiding usury laws is a business purpose and the corporate activities in connection with the financing were enough to require recognition of its separate existence.[13(a)]

If a straw corporation must be utilized, there are two possible approaches to be considered and the distinctions between them are important. At the outset of the transaction, therefore, the parties must decide which of these approaches they wish to follow and then create a record which will support the position selected.

(a) Nominee Status; Absence of Business Activity.

First, the parties may take the traditional approach that the corporation is nothing more than a nominee. Although taxpayers have lost most of the cases, there have been some victories. For example, in the *Paymer* case discussed above, although most discussions focus on the corporation which was held to be a taxable entity, there was another corporation owned by the same stockholders which did not transact business and which was held to be a nominee only. (The corporation in question was intended to serve only as a blind to deter the creditors of one of the parties.) In *Louis Steinmetz*[14] two taxpayers discovered that their properties were to be condemned and were advised that a greater condemnation award could be obtained if their adjacent parcels were owned by a single entity. Accordingly, they both transferred their properties to a corporation. The corporation did not engage in any business activity and the properties were operated in the same manner as they had been prior to the conveyances; the rental income was received by the individuals and the expenses were paid by them. The net profits realized from the operation of the properties were reported on the individual tax returns. However, the corporation did maintain a bank account into which the condemnation award was deposited and from which withdrawals were made and divided between the parties. The Tax Court held that the corporation was no more than a nominee, holding naked title to the properties.

In short, to establish the nominee status of a corporation the corporate activities must be restricted so as to prevent it from doing any more than is absolutely necessary to close a transaction and hold title. Despite the lack of success of taxpayers in this area, the fact remains that there appears to be no case holding that a corporation constitutes a taxable entity if it merely acquires property in a nominee status and immediately reconveys that property without engaging in any other activity relating to it.[15] The absence of such a clear precedent may result from the fact that the Internal Revenue Service has at least unofficially accepted nominee status when corporate activities are so restricted. However, the fact that taxpayers may simply fail to report such transactions on the assumption that nominees have nothing to report may also have a bearing on the recorded cases. Of course, such an assumption hardly constitutes a satisfactory basis for proper tax planning.

(b)   Agency Status; Business Activity on Behalf of a Principal.

In view of the minimal amount of activity required for a corporation to lose its status as a mere nominee, an alternative approach is to recognize and admit the separate existence of the corporation but to establish that the activities are carried on by the corporation in its status as an agent acting on behalf of a specified principal or principals. In *National Carbide Corp. vs. Comm'r.*[16] the U.S. Supreme Court expressly recognized this principle and stated as follows:

> What we have said does not foreclose a true corporate agent or trustee from handling the property and income of its owner-principal without being taxable therefor. Whether the corporation operates in the name and for the account of the principal, binds the principal by its actions, transmits money received to the principal, and whether the receipt of income is attributable the services of the employees of the principal and to assets belonging to the principal are some of the relevant considerations in determining whether a true agency exists. If the corporation is a true agent, its relations with its principal must not be dependent upon the fact that it is owned by the principal, if such is the case. Its business purpose must be the carrying on of the normal duties of an agent.

The principal-agent theory has not been advanced by taxpayers as frequently as the nominee theory and probably presents a more realistic position. In *Carver v. United States*[17] a corporation was utilized by an attorney to handle real estate transactions over a substantial period of years. He maintained that the corporation should be disregarded for tax purposes. Although the agency theory was rejected for those transactions were the corporation was acting solely in his (the stockholder's) behalf, the agency theory was accepted when applied to one transaction where the corporation acted for both the attorney and his client in holding title "for the use and benefit of" the parties. Apparently, the crucial factor was that Mr. Carver's client, an unrelated third party who was the motivating force behind the transaction, did not own any capital stock in the corporation which held title to the property.

The *Carver* decision should be contrasted with a later decision from the same court, *Harrison Property Management Co., Inc. v. U.S.*[18] In that case, the corporation was taxed on profits from oil leases, even though it had entered into a formal agency agreement with the beneficial owners of the property. The Court noted that the alleged principals were also corporate shareholders and concluded that the corporation would not have made the agency contract had the beneficial owners not been shareholders of the corporation.

It can be reasonably concluded from these two decisions that where a corporation is to be utilized as an agent it is better practice if the beneficial owners of the property are not also shareholders of the corporation. Corporations organized by law firms, title companies, and others which serve as agents for the clients or customers of the firms controlling such corporations, stand a better chance of being recognized as agents for tax purposes.

In Revenue Ruling 75-31[19] a conduit corporation was organized by the corporate general partner of a limited partnership. The conduit corporation executed various instruments when it acquired title to the property setting forth its agency relationship and the duties of the parties. The lender, the New York State Housing Finance Agency, received from the conduit corporation letters stating that it would be liable for the loan and incorporating the various documents by reference. All of the relevant partnership documents stated that the corporation held record title for the benefit of the partnership (principal). The Internal Revenue Service held that even though the corporate general partner owned the stock of the conduit corporation, it was the agent of the partnership and such agency relationship should be recognized "by reason of the unique facts and circumstances described." Although this ruling demonstrates again the possibilities of having a corporation treated as an agent, it is limited to its facts, and may be unique to the area of public housing in view of a number of factors, including the general public benefit derived from permitting such public financing arrangements.

Guidelines Indicating Agency Relationship—The following guidelines set forth the steps to be followed where the taxpayer proposes to rely upon an agency theory.

1. As indicated above, the beneficial owners (principals) should not own any of the capital stock of the corporate agent.

2. All of the corporate documents such as certificate of incorporation, corporate resolutions, contracts, etc., should clearly reflect that the corporation is an agent acting on behalf of principals.

3. Written agreements between the agent and the principals are advisable. Obviously, such agreements should make it clear that the agent will take such action as the principal may specify from time to time.

4. The agent should be paid a fee for its services and, of course, should be compensated by the principal for all expenses incurred in the performance of its duties.

5. The agent should file tax returns indicating that it is engaged in the business of being an agent. It should also file Form 56, Notice to District Director of Fiduciary Relationship, indicating agent status. The corporation should also file Form 1087 as to income received on behalf of the principal.

6. If the corporation was organized to serve as agent in one transaction only, it should be dissolved upon the conclusion of that transaction, thus clarifying its limited status.

7. Title to the real estate in question should be held for as short a time as possible. For example, if the lender requires that a corporation be organized to execute a mortgage note so as to avoid a usury problem, then title to the property should be transferred to the principals as soon as possible after the closing of the loan transaction. Where the lender insists that the corporation existence be continued—for example, during the construction of a project—the taxpayer's position is weakened. (Of course, the corporation which continues to take mortgage draws,

pay subcontractors and engage in other construction activities, has an almost hopeless case of claiming status as a nominee for the reasons indicated above.)

1.6   ASSOCIATIONS TAXABLE AS CORPORATIONS

Since operating through a corporation has such a serious tax impact it is not surprising that many developers have attempted to create organizations which, although not formally incorporated under state law, possess some or all of the traditional corporate attributes, particularly limited liability. Such organizations have taken the forms of partnerships, trusts or hybrid forms which defy definition, but the objective is the same, namely, to achieve the non-tax corporate advantages without suffering the tax disadvantages of the corporate form. An unincorporated business which has more corporate than non-corporate attributes is designated as an "association" for federal tax purposes and both the U.S. Supreme Court[20] and the Treasury[21] hold that such associations may be taxed as corporations. The simple failure to formally incorporate will not be determinative.

There are six basic characteristics which count in determining whether a business will be classified as an association and, therefore, taxed as a corporation. They are:

1. The presence of associates.
2. The intention to conduct business.
3. Limited liability.
4. Continuity of life.
5. Centralized management.
6. Free transferability of interests.

The regulations establish a mechanical criterion to determine if an unincorporated business will be classified as an association, namely, if the organization in question has more corporate than non-corporate characteristics. Since all businesses other than a sole proprietorship have the first two attributes—associates and an intention to conduct business—these factors can be ignored, leaving only four relevant characteristics to measure in determining whether corporate status exists. Accordingly, under the "majority rule" test of the regulations, if 0 or 1 or 2 of these characteristics are present, the organization is treated as a partnership or other unincorporated form; however, if 3 or 4 (that is, more corporate than non-corporate) of these characteristics are present, the organization is treated as a corporation for tax purposes.

> *Example:* A group of 25 persons forms an organization to invest in real estate. Each member has the power to dissolve the organization at any time. Management control is vested in a five man executive committee elected by the members. Each member's liability is limited to paid and subscribed capital. A member can transfer his interest to third parties subject to a first right of the organization to acquire the interest proposed to be transferred. Such an organization is an association taxable as a corporation. Although it lacks continuity of life, it has 3 of the 4 crucial corporate characteristics (limited liability, centralized management, and a modified form of free transferability of interests) in addition to associates and an objective to carry on business and divide the gains therefrom. Example 6, Reg. 301 7701-(g).

Since the "majority rule" test of the regulations is fairly well spelled out, there have been relatively few cases on the question of whether a particular organization should be taxed as a corporation. Most practitioners have apparently been able to draft the partnership agreements so as to avoid this attack. Recently, however, there were two decisions involving limited partnerships having a corporate sole general partner where the courts found it necessary to apply the regulation to actual sets of facts. The courts' approach to these cases is, therefore, illuminating.

> *The Court of Claims Case.*[22] Towne House was formed as a limited partnership under the Missouri Limited Partnership Law which was substantially similar to the Uniform Limited Partnership Act. The sole general partner was a corporation that owned 51% of the partnership interests. The corporation was capitalized at $500, had no substantial assets other than its interests in the partnership and engaged in no activities other than management of the partnership. The Court looked at the four factors mentioned above to determine if Towne House more closely resembled a partnership or an association and concluded that it lacked all four corporate characteristics. IRS argued that Towne House possessed corporate characteristics which were not expressly described in the Regulations but should be considered in determining if it were a partnership or an association. However, the Court refused to consider additional factors. It held that the fact that Towne House lacked all four of the corporate characteristics expressly treated in the Regulations was more than sufficient to warrant partnership treatment.

The Tax Court Case[23]-This case involved two limited real estate partnerships which had a California corporation as their sole general partner. The corporation had a small capital of $21,000. There were some 44 limited partners in the larger partnership and 8 in the smaller one. Both partnerships were commercially sponsored. The general partner made no investment in the partnerships and its cash flow participation was subordinated to the repayment to the limited partners of their after-tax investments. The partnership agreements provided for dissolution by vote of the limited partners and for the removal or election of a new general partner. The partnership interests were transferable without affecting the continuity of the enterprise. The Tax Court originally held in favor of the Commissioner. In a most unusual action, however, it withdrew that decision for reconsideration and subsequently held in favor of the partnership. The Tax Court felt that in making its determination, it was required to follow the Regulations under §7701 since neither party questioned their validity. The Court found that the partnerships had only two of the four corporate characteristics—centralized management and free transferability of interests. The partnerships lacked continuity of life because under California law the bankruptcy of the general partner would result in a technical legal dissolution; the fact that a replacement general partner could be elected was not determinative. Also, since the corporate general partner was not a "dummy" the partnership did not have limited liability. In short, since the regulations require equal weighting of each characteristic, the two-two tie resulted in a decision in favor of the taxpayer. (It may be important to note that six dissenting judges wrote five dissenting opinions ranging from total disregard of the regulations to a finding that even under the regulations the partnerships should be classified as a corporation. Caution in relying on this decision therefore, is obviously called for.)

See Chapter 3, Section 2, for a discussion of the requirements which must be met where a partnership wishes to obtain an advance ruling that it will be classified as a partnership rather than as an association.

1.7 REAL ESTATE INVESTMENT TRUSTS

A clear exception to the "association taxable as a corporation" rule is expressly sancioned by the Code. A series of Code sections (§ 856-858) provides for the creation of Real Estate Investment Trusts (REIT's). These are generally large organizations which, if they satisfy the statutory requirements, are exempt from corporate tax. Thus, while the trust resembles a corporation for state law purposes, it resembles a partnership for purposes of federal income tax. However, in order to qualify for this unique treatment, the REIT must meet all of the statutory requirements including the following:

1. *Ownership Test.* The REIT must have at least 100 shareholders and no five persons may own, directly or indirectly, more than 50% of the shares of the trust during the last six months of the tax year.

2. *Management by Trustees.* Management of the affairs of the REIT must be committed to trustees who, in turn, hold title to the trust property.

3. *Income Test.* The REIT cannot actively engage in business. At least 90% of its income must be passive. Of the REIT income, at least 75% must be derived from investment in real estate.

4. *The Asset Test.* Of the trust's assets, at least 75% must be in real estate, government securities and cash items. Investments in the securities of any one corporation cannot exceed 5% of the trust's assets or 10% of the outstanding voting securities of the issuer.

5. *Limitation on Gains.* Gains from the sale of real estate held less than four years and gains from the sale of stock or securities held less than six months must amount to no more than 30% of the trust's gross income.

6. *Distribution Requirement.* At least 90% of the trust's current REIT taxable income must be distributed to its shareholders each year.

It is obvious from the foregoing discussion that REIT's are of limited use as vehicles for real estate transactions. Where large amounts of capital are being raised from large numbers of investors, the REIT may be appropriate but the typical syndication will fail to meet one or more of the requirements. Moreover, even if the requirements could be met, the REIT lacks much of the flexibility which is available through other forms of organization such as the Subchapter S corporation and the limited partnership. For example, capital losses and operating losses are not passed through to the trust beneficiaries and the trust itself has no right to carry such losses forward or backward. It is not surprising, therefore, that except for the large publicly held REIT's, this device has not found much popularity with real estate developers.

1.8 LIMITED PARTNERSHIPS

The Uniform Limited Partnership Act defines a limited partnership as follows:

> A limited partnership is a partnership formed by two or more persons . . . having as members one or more general partners and one or more limited partners. The limited partners as such shall not be bound by the obligations of the partnership.

Where there is at least one party (the general partner) who is willing to assume the risk of liability for debts of the partnership, all of the others involved in the project may be limited partners who have no personal liability for partnership obligations. In the typical real estate project involving a developer and a group of passive investors who seek only a yield on their investment and a tax loss, the limited partnership provides the most convenient and practical form. The developer is normally the one most familiar with the details of the project, the most confident about the ability of the project to carry the mortgage loan and pay the other debts of the partnership, and the one who will probably be involved in managing the project. Accordingly, he is the logical party to assume the obligations of the general partner. The passive investors can become limited partners and if the technicalities of the Uniform Limited Partnership Act are carefully followed they are assured of limiting their liability to their actual investment including the amounts of capital committed by them under their subscription agreements. At the same time, a properly drafted partnership agreement can avoid association status and assure each of the participants that he will receive his prorata share of tax loss and cash flow.[24] The Treasury has issued a number of regulations which specify the requirements to be met if an advance ruling on partnership status is requested, particularly if a corporation is being utilized as a sole general partner. These regulations are discussed in Chapter 3, Section 2. Although there are a number of limitations on the ability of the participants to control the tax consequences of their investment, the fact remains that the partnership is the most flexible form for holding and operating real estate projects. For this reason, virtually all of the large syndications as well as many smaller ones have been organized as limited partnerships.

FOOTNOTES FOR CHAPTER ONE

[1]§ 301(c) (3).

[2]§ 704.

[3]Conveyance of the property from the corporation to its shareholders normally constitutes a taxable liquidation under Section 331. Also, if the corporation is held to be collapsible, the gain will usually be taxed as ordinary income and real estate development corporations are particularly vulnerable to the collapsible taint.

[4]The Tax Reform Act of 1976 extends corporate tax cuts through December 31, 1977. Corporations continue to pay 20% on the first $25,000 of taxable income; 22% on the next $25,000; and 48% on taxable income over $50,000. Individual rates of tax on the other hand go as high as 70% although earned income is subject to a 50% maximum tax.

[5]An exculpatory provision in the mortgage note whereby the lender agrees to look only to the property as security for the loan, waiving any rights against the borrowers individually, is a simple and effective means of solving the liability problem without incorporating the venture. Unfortunately many lenders refuse to accept such provisions although a shell corporation as borrower gives the lender no greater security without personal guaranties.

[6]§ 1372 (e) (5).

[7]Reg. 1.1372-4(b)(5)(vi).

[8]*Bramlette Building Corp., Inc. v. Comm.* 424 F. 2d 751,25 AFTR 2d 70-1061 (CA5, 1970).

[9]*City Markets, Inc. v. Comm.* 433 F. 2d 1240,26 AFTR2d 70-5760 (CA6, 1970). See also *H & L Reid, Inc. v. U.S.,* 33 AFTR2d 74-447 (E.D. Mich., 1973).

[10]§ 1374 (c) (2).

[11]*Moline Properties, Inc. v. Comm.,* 319 U.S. 436,30 AFTR 1291 (1943).

[12]e.g., *Comm. v. State-Adams Corp.*, 283 F2d 395,6 AFTR2d 5752 (CA2, 1970). See annotations, P-H 1976 Fed Tax ¶41,020 (Corporate entity) and ¶41,023 and ¶41,025 ("dummy" real estate corporations.)

[13]150 F2d 334, 33 AFTR 1536 (CA-2, 1945).

[13(a)]*William B. Strong, et al.,* 66 TC 12 (1976).

[14]1973 P-H Memo T.C. ¶73,208.

[15]Baker & Rothman, "Nominee & Agency Corporations: Grasping for Straws" 33 NYU Inst. on Fed. Taxation 1255 (1975, 1282). The Tax Court has sanctioned the reverse situation, i.e., an individual holding title as nominee of his controlled corporation. *Manuel M. Koufman,* ¶76,330 P-H Memo T.C.

[16]336 U.S.422, 37 AFTR 834 (1949). The Court held against the taxpayer on the facts of the case despite its acceptance of the principal-agent possibility.

[17]412 F.2d 233,23 AFTR2d 69-1701 (Ct. Claims, 1969).

[18]475 F.2d 263, 31 AFTR2d 946 (Ct. Claims, 1963) cert. denied.

[19]1975-1 C.B.10. See also Rev. Rul. 76-26, 1976-1 C.B. 10

[20]*Morrisey v. Comm.,* 296 U.S. 344, 16 AFTR 1274 (1935). See McGee, "Problems of the Unintentional Corporation: The Association Taxable as a Corporation" 29 NYU Institute on Federal Taxation 853 (1971).

[21]Reg. 301.7701-2(a)(3). This is the same regulation which was held invalid in a number of cases to the extent that it imposed special requirements on professional corporations in order for them to be recognized as corporate entities. Eventually, the Treasury conceded the point and agreed to amend the Regulation.

[22]*Zuckman v. U.S.,* 524 F.2d 729, 36 AFTR 2d75-6193 (Court of Claims, 1975).

[23]*Phillip G. Larson,* et al, 66 T.C. 159 (1976), on appeal by government to 9th Circuit.

[24]The regulations expressly recognize partnership tax treatment for limited partnerships created under the Uniform Limited Partnership Act. Reg. 301.7701-3 (b).

2

ORGANIZING
THE CORPORATION

As noted in the previous chapter the corporate form is not normally suitable for the operation of a real estate venture for a number of reasons. The cash flow is subjected to a double tax burden if it is distributed as a dividend; the tax loss is wasted unless the corporation has other income available to absorb it; withdrawal of the project from corporate form is itself a taxable event in most cases; Subchapter S status is not available if more that 20% of the gross receipts are derived from rents or other passive sources; and the corporation simply does not offer the flexibility of the partnership in terms of allocating duties and benefits among the participants. Also, where an owner of depreciable property transfers it to a corporation, even pursuant to a tax-free transfer, the corporation does not qualify for any of the accelerated methods of depreciation as the original use of the property did not commence with the corporation.[1] Despite these limitations, however, there are many instances where real estate projects are held in corporate form. Sometimes this results from defective tax planning of the parties or their advisors. There are other cases, however, where even well informed taxpayers conclude that corporate ownership is most desirable. Sometimes it is the only way to avoid personal liability on the mortgage loan or other obligations of the venture. Occasionally there is a corporation which has surplus funds, pays a high rate of tax on profits derived from another business and, therefore, is itself a proper candidate for acquisition of a tax shelter. Other considerations are discussed in Chapter 1, Section 3.

The point is that despite the general rule militating against corporate ownership of depreciable real estate, there are enough exceptions that attention should be given to the problems of organizing a corporation which will engage in real estate development or will be a transferee of an interest in a real estate project.

This chapter, after comparing the consequences of a taxable incorporation with a tax-free transaction, discusses the tax rules of organizing a corporation, particularly one involving a real estate venture. The chapter is divided into the following sections:

2.1 TAXABLE VS. TAX-FREE INCORPORATIONS

§351 is intended to eliminate any tax on the incorporation of a new business or a business which was formerly operated as a proprietorship or partnership. The section is short and its objective is clear, namely, that the incorporation of a business is not an event having any tax significance. Incorporation is merely a change in the legal form of the business with the former proprietor or partners receiving corporate stock or securities in exchange for their interests in the property transferred to the corporation. In a practical sense no gain or loss has been realized on the conveyance of the property, the stock or securities being nothing more than "pieces of paper—stock certificates—representing their net value."[2]

As is customary under the Code, however, the price of a tax-free transfer is a carryover of basis to the transferee. Thus, where real estate (or any other property) is conveyed to a closely held corporation in exchange for corporate stock or securities, and where the conveyance is tax-free under §351, the corporate transferee is required to adopt a basis for the transferred property equal to the transferor's basis. If the conveyance is partially taxable the corporate transferee can step up its basis to the extent that gain was recognized by the transferor. §362.

> *Example:* A and B are the owners of a tract of land having a cost to them of $50,000. They acquired the tract many years ago and today its fair market value has increased to $200,000. If A and B transfer the land to their controlled corporation, receiving in exchange all of the capital stock, the corporation has a basis for tax purposes of only $50,000.

Since tax-free incorporation results in a carryover of basis, it may be preferable to pay a tax on the conveyance to the corporation, thereby reducing corporate income at a later stage of development.

> *Example (Cont.):* Refer to the above example involving land with a $50,000 basis and a $200,000 value. If it is intended to subdivide this land, the corporation will eventually be taxed on the $150,000 increment in the value at ordinary income rates.

However, if the initial conveyance could be cast as a *taxable* transaction, A and B may be subject to only a capital gains tax on this amount. The corporation would have its basis in the property stepped up to $200,000 and would be taxed at ordinary rates only to the extent that the selling price of the lots exceeded that stepped up basis.

A realistic approach is to recognize that the potential tax resulting from increments in values is normally not *eliminated* in a tax-free transfer, but merely *deferred* until the time that the corporation disposes of the property. Therefore, whether tax-free treatment of the transfer is desirable is a question of simple mathematics: is it more economical to have the unrealized gain taxed at the time of conveyance to the corporation or to postpone the taxable event until there is a sale or other disposition by the corporate transferee? This depends upon a comparison of the tax brackets of the transferors and the corporations, on whether the same type of gain (capital or ordinary, installment or non-installment) is realized at each stage, on the use that can be made of the funds which are saved by deferring payment of the tax, and various other factors.

Remember that the deferral of tax consequence under §351 applies to both gains and losses. Thus, where property has declined in value, §351 will preclude a deduction of the loss incurred on the transfer, for example, where the stock and securities received are worth less than the transferor's basis in the property transferred. Avoidance of the statutory tests, on the other hand, permits immediate recognition of the loss on the exchange.

> *Observation:* Note that §351 is not an elective section—if its requirements are met, then neither gain nor loss is recognized to the transferors and the carryover of basis follows. If any of the requisite elements of §351 are absent, gain or loss is recognized and the carryover of basis rules are modified accordingly.

It is not surprising to find that the Internal Revenue Service and the taxpayers frequently switch positions in arguing for or against application of §351. The requirements for tax-free incorporation may be viewed as a two-edged sword to be complied with or avoided depending upon the taxpayer's objectives.

2.2 THE REQUIREMENTS OF §351

§351(a) is a short, relatively well-written section which has been in the Code since 1921. It provides as follows:

> No gain or loss shall be recognized if property is transferred to a corporation . . . by one or more persons solely in exchange for stock or securities in such corporation and immediately after the exchange, such person or persons are in control . . . of the corporation. For purposes of this section, stock or securities issued for services shall not be considered as issued in return for property.

The requirements of this section may be summarized as follows:

(a) A transfer of property to a corporation;

(b) Solely in exchange for stock or securities in the corporation; and

(c) Immediately after the exchange, the transferors are in control of the corporation. Each of these requirements will be discussed in greater detail.

(a) Transfer of Property to a Corporation.

The term "property" is defined broadly for purposes of this provision and includes cash, real estate and personal property. It does not include services, however. In real estate transactions, it is not uncommon for the owning entity, whether corporation or partnership, to consist of two separate groups—investors who contribute their capital and developers who contribute their services, experience and know-how. Are the developers taxable on the stock which they receive upon the organization of the enterprise? The answer is important not only to the developer, but to the investors as well: if the stock is received for services and if such stock accounts for more that 20% of the total, the transfer is disqualified under Section 351 and even the investors will be taxable on the exchange transaction to the extent of any gain realized.

The Service has ruled in at least one instance that "know-how" is "property" for purposes of §351 and that a manufacturer, therefore, realizes no gain or loss on the stock which it receives when it assists a newly organized foreign corporation to enter a business of making and selling the same kind of product as that made by the manufacturer.[3] In furnishing its know-how, the manufacturer has made a transfer of "property" (tax-free) rather than being compensated for "services" (taxable).

Whether such tax-free treatment would be granted a real estate developer is doubtful. Compensation paid for services rendered or to be rendered is taxable and it makes little difference if the payment takes the form of money or some other form, such as a bargain purchase of a corporate interest.

> *Example:* Investors who owned land entered into an agreement with Developer whereby he undertook to get the necessary FHA commitment and financing to construct an apartment project. If Developer was successful, Investors would transfer their land to a corporation in exchange for one-half of the stock and Developer would get the other half. After Developer obtained the necessary commitments, the corporation was organized and each group received its half of the issued stock. The Court held that the commitments which Developer got for the corporation were not his "property rights." Therefore, he received his stock in exchange for services and the entire transaction was disqualified under §351. Not only did the Developer realize taxable income, but Investors had taxable gain to the extent that the value of their stock exceeded their basis in the land transferred.[4]

> *Example:* Frazell was a geologist. He entered into an agreement with Investors whereby he was to seek out oil leases and if the sites were approved by all of the parties, he would attempt to acquire the properties, taking title in the names of Investors. Although he was to receive compensation in an agreed amount, plus specified interests in the property acquired, he was not to be entitled to own any interest in the properties until Investors had recovered all of their costs and expenses. Four years later when it was evident that the venture would be successful, the contract was revised and a corporation was organized. Frazell received 13% of the corporate stock having a fair market value of $91,000, subject to a provision that Investors were entitled to the first profits from the venture until their capital investment had been fully recovered. The Court held that Frazell did not receive his stock tax-free under §351(a), but as compensation for services rendered by him despite the fact that Investors reserved the right to take the first profits from the venture until their capital investment had been recovered.[5]

As the above decisions indicate, any stock interest granted to a developer for services jeopardizes a Section 351 transaction. An alternative procedure might be to organize the corporation in two stages. In the first stage, the developer invests some money or other property for capital stock. The corporation then acquires an option or engages in other activities. In the second stage, the corporation sells additional stock to the investors at a higher cost per share. For example, Developer may buy one-fourth of the stock for $10,000 in stage 1 and Investors buy three-fourths of the stock for $90,000 in stage 2, recognizing the increases in value which have occurred in stage 1. Such an arrangement has been sustained as a tax-free transaction.[6]

(b) Exchange Solely for Stock or Securities.

§351(a) provides that a conveyance to a corporation is tax-free if it is "solely" in exchange for "stock or securities." On the other hand, §351(b) provides that if, in addition to the stock or securities which are permitted to be received tax-free, the transferors receive "other property or money" (commonly referred to as "boot"), then gain will be recognized but not in excess of the amount of the boot. This rule thus creates three possibilities for transfers to controlled corporations: *a tax-free* transfer to the corporation in exchange for only stock or securities; a *taxable* transfer with no stock or securities being issued to the transferors (for example, a sale to the corporation or a transfer where the entire consideration takes the form of boot, such as short-term notes); or a *partially taxable* transfer involving some of the amount of gain realized. Naturally, to the extent that the transferors recognize gain upon the transfer, the corporation has a step-up in the basis of the property transferred.

Where the transfer of property is made to a corporation controlled by the transferors, the parties obviously have considerable latitude in deciding what the corporate transferee will issue in exchange for the property acquired. Certain tax consequences follow if the corporation issues stock and other consequences follow if the corporation issues promissory notes or other forms of debt. Consider the following distinctions:

(i) If the corporation issues stock, the transferor's basis will carry over to the corporation, while if the corporation issues debt there may be a step-up in basis to the extent of fair market value. (However, if the debt qualifies as "securities" it is treated the same as stock for this purpose and there will be a carryover of basis.)

(ii) If the corporation issues stock, the transferors will normally recognize no gain or loss, while if the corporation issues debt, the transaction may be taxable to the transferors.

(iii) The corporation is entitled to a deduction for interest paid on debt, thus avoiding the double tax problem, whereas dividends paid on capital stock are not deductible. Tax treatment to the payee, on the other hand, is virtually the same regardless of whether he is receiving interest or dividends.

(iv) Payment of the principal amount of the debt will ordinarily constitute a tax-free return of capital to the payee or may result in capital gain under §1232 if the collections exceed the basis of the debt. On the other hand, retirement of capital stock, particularly where there is not a complete termination of the stockholder's interest in the corporation, will normally be treated as payment of a taxable dividend.

(v) The Internal Revenue Code imposes limits on the amount of retained earnings which a corporation may accumulate without being subjected to a penalty tax. §531. Payment of corporate debt at maturity may constitute a "reasonable business need" which will justify the accumulation of earnings and, thereby, avoid the penalty tax. §533(a). However, accumulating earnings for the purpose of redeeming corporate stock will normally not qualify to avoid the penalty tax. (§537 is an exception and permits accumulations to redeem the stock of a deceased stockholder under §303).

For all of these reasons, the issue of whether a particular instrument qualifies as stock or debt is one which is frequently litigated. Because the body of law is so large and complex, no attempt will be made here to outline tax rules in this area.[7] It should be noted, however, that the Tax Reform Act of 1969 added §385 to the Code which authorizes the Commissioner to define corporate stock and debt by regulations for all purposes under the Code. Such regulations have not yet been issued and there is no indication as to when that will occur. However, the section lists a number of factors which may be considered by the Commissioner in issuing his regulations. Taxpayers are well advised to consider these factors when setting up corporate-stockholder instruments since in one form or another they will undoubtedly be relevant in determining the status of the instrument as stock or debt.

(c) Control in the Transferors Immediately After the Exchange.

In order for §351 to apply, the transferors must be in control of the corporation "immediately after the exchange." For purposes of this section, control means ownership of at least 80% of the voting stock and 80% of all other classes of stock.[8]

What happens when the original transferors of the property sell or otherwise transfer some of their corporate stock to third parties, for example, where developers who own land which is to be the site of a project, convey that land to a corporation for its capital stock, and, immediately or shortly thereafter, they sell a portion of that stock to other investors. If the sale to the investors is disregarded for purposes of measuring control "immediately after the exchange," the original conveyance to the corporation is tax-free; otherwise it may be taxable.

The Regulations state that:

> The phrase "immediately after the exchange" does not necessarily require simultaneous exchanges by two or more persons, but comprehends the situation where the rights of the parties have been previously defined and the execution of the agreement proceeds with an expedition consistent with orderly procedure.[9]

Where there is no legal obligation requiring the original transferors (the developers in our example) to dispose of their capital stock, a tax-free incorporation results. Even momentary control existing immediately after the conveyance of the property to the corporation is sufficient to meet the control requirement and to effect a tax-free transaction.[10] On the other hand, where there is a pre-existing legal obligation on the part of the controlling stockholders to make transfers of at least 20% of their stock, or a pre-existing contract to have outsiders acquire an interest in the newly organized corporation, or where the corporation is planning a simultaneous public offering of at least 20% of its stock, the requisite control is not truly present and a taxable transfer results upon incorporation.[11]

Comment: Most of the decided cases appear to involve ambiguous fact situations which do not fit neatly into the recognized categories, probably due to a lack of planning by the taxpayers involved. Actually, the ground rules for each of the requirements for a tax-free transfer are fairly well spelled out. Once the taxpayers decide which type of transaction—taxable, partially taxable, or tax-free—is most desirable, they can usually structure the incorporation and related steps so as to achieve the intended result.

2.3 SALES TO THE CONTROLLED CORPORATION

A stockholder sometimes attempts to bypass all of the technical requirements of §351 by simply "selling" the property in question to his corporation. This technique permits the owner of land which has appreciated to realize a capital gain on the increment in value, possibly spread over a period of years by means of an installment sale,[12] while the corporate buyer gets a stepped-up basis which obviously reduces its ordinary income from eventual subdivision or other utilization of the land. In short, when this technique is successfully utilized, it permits the conversion of ordinary income to capital gain. It is not surprising to find that the courts examine such transactions carefully to insure that they are not disguised contributions to capital, in which case the normal consequences of a tax-free incorporation follow.

There are a great variety of factual possibilities, of course, but the following decided cases give some guidelines as to the factors which influence the courts in distinguishing between sales and capital contributions.

(1) Corporation was organized at the end of August. In mid-September of the same year, stockholder sold a warehouse to the corporation for $125,000, payable $4,000 semi-annually. Purchase payments were made out of rents realized from the warehouse operation. *Held:* This was a bona fide sale. Although "business purpose" is essential to support certain transactions, it is not necessary to substantiate a sale.[13]

(2) A partnership sold land to a controlled corporation for $250,000, payable $9,000 down, $49,000 by assumption of a mortgage and the balance of $192,000 payable over five years. *Held:* This was a tax-free capital contribution, not a sale. The same court which decided case (1) distinguished the two fact situations according to the character of the property involved. The first case, said the Court, involved an income-producing warehouse, thus indicating a reasonable expectation of repayment of the note; but the second case involved raw land which was at the risk of the business and which could support only capital stock.[14]

(3) A corporation with a total paid-in capital of $60,000 purchased from its stockholders options to buy land. The corporation gave its note for most of the purchase price. The corporation then exercised the options and commenced selling lots from the land acquired. *Held:* The sale of the options to the corporation was recognized. Although unimproved land was involved, the Court felt this case was controlled by case (1) above rather than case (2). The notes were unconditional promises to pay with fixed maturity dates bearing reasonable interest rates and conferring no voting rights. Moreover, the facts indicated some degree of certainty as to the financial success of the venture, thereby refuting the Commissioner's contention that the land in question was placed as equity at the risk of the business.[15]

(4) The developers owned a tract of land at a cost of $100,000. They purportedly sold it to a corporation owned by their nominees for $360,000 payable by means of notes and reported capital gains on the transaction. However, the notes were renewed from time to time and were still partially unpaid at the time the case came to trial several years later. *Held:* This was a contribution to capital. Substance controls

over form and this transaction lacked the essential characteristics of a sale as claimed by the taxpayers.[16]

(5) Husband and wife owned 55% of Gyro Engineering Corp., the balance of the stock being owned by their children and by the husband's brother. The corporation had only $30,000 of assets. Husband and wife sold to the corporation for $3,200,000 an apartment house which they owned personally and which they had depreciated down to $800,000. The downpayment was only $30,000 but the corporation agreed to pay the balance of $2,300,000 (after crediting mortgages) in $30,000 semi-annual installments. The balance was evidenced by non-interest-bearing promissory notes issued by the corporation. The corporation claimed a large step-up in basis and sellers claimed capital gain since they did not own more than 80% of the total value of the stock. *Held:* This was not a paper tax device or "gimmick" but a real sale in form. The corporation had sufficient assets to make the downpayment and the anticipated rentals appeared to be sufficient to meet the installment payments under the note. The fact that the corporation's capitalization was thin "has no force, for that condition would not tend to show that Gyro's agreement to pay was fictitious, unrealistic or beyond its ability to perform."[17]

(6) Transferors, A and B, bought two tracts of land and sold them to their controlled corporation at twice their cost. Payment by the corporation was spread over a period of years. The corporation developed and sold the land in individual lots. *Held:* The gain realized by A and B on the sale of land to the corporation is taxable as ordinary income rather than capital gain. It is well settled that a person may engage in business via an agent in which case the activities of the agent will be imputed to the principal. The Court concluded that the controlled corporation here was simply used by A and B to develop the land for them so they could take the profits out of the venture as capital gain. Looking through the form of the arrangement to the substance, A and B were real estate dealers with respect to the land.[18]

2.4 TAX CONSEQUENCES OF THE TRANSFER OF PROPERTY SUBJECT TO A MORTGAGE.

Normally, the assumption of a mortgage debt by the corporate transferee or the transfer of property subject to a mortgage does not create a taxable transaction. §357(a). There are, however, two important exceptions to this rule which are particularly applicable to transfers of real estate because real estate is so frequently subject to high levels of mortgage debt.

First Exception—The entire mortgage will be treated as boot and taxable to the transferors if the principal purpose of the taxpayer in making the conveyance was tax avoidance or was not a bona-fide business purpose. §357(b). Obviously, where this possibility exists it is advisable that the opening corporate minutes which authorized the acquisition should recite the business purpose assuming that one is present.

Second Exception—Even without the prohibited tax avoidance purpose referred to above, where the mortgage debt exceeds the transferor's basis for the property, the transferors are subject to tax on the transfer to the extent of such excess.

> *Example:* A has property which originally cost him $100,000 but by reason of depreciation deductions, has been written down to $50,000. He is able to obtain a current appraisal showing a value of $150,000. In January, he places a $100,000 mortgage loan on the property and retains the proceeds thereof. In February, he conveys the property subject to the mortgage to a controlled corporation solely in

exchange for stock or securities. Under §357(c) he must recognize gain to the extent that the mortgage exceeds basis, or $50,000 in this example.

The gain recognized under §357(c) is reported as ordinary income, long term capital gain or short term capital gain, according to the nature of the property transferred. The Code section does not attempt to characterize the nature of the gain but merely to provide an exception to the normal nonrecognition rules of §351.

2.5   SUBCHAPTER S CORPORATIONS.

Subchapter S (§1371-1379) of the Internal Revenue Code provides that certain so called small business corporations may file an election to avoid corporate taxation. If a corporation qualifies and the election is properly filed, the corporation is not taxed at all. Instead, the corporate taxable income is reported by its stockholders pro rata, according to the number of shares held by each of them. Losses are also passed through to the stockholders. It makes no difference whether the profits are actually distributed; each stockholder reports his share just as partners report their distributive shares of partnership profits. In a subsequent year, when the cash is available, such profits may be distributed without tax consequence to the stockholders.

Subchapter S provides the following tax benefits: (1) Avoidance of corporate income tax; (2) Passing through of losses to stockholders to the extent of their basis in corporate stock and loans, thus permitting them to offset such losses against their other income; (3) Pension plans, profit sharing plans and other fringe benefits become available to shareholders if they are also corporate employees; (4) Greater flexibility in selecting a fiscal year is possible since the corporate year may differ from that of its stockholders (something not permitted to partnerships); (5) It is possible to divide income among family members by having some of the corporate stock held in the names of children or custodians for children, who will each report their shares of corporate income; and (6) The tax on unreasonable accumulations of corporate earnings is eliminated since there are no accumulations.

Requirements for Qualification—In order for a corporation to be eligible for treatment under Subchapter S it must meet all of the following requirements: (1) It must be a domestic corporation. (2) It must not be a member of an affiliated group (where a parent corporation owns at least 80% of a subsidiary corporation). (3) It must have no more than ten shareholders except that under the Tax Reform Act of 1976, effective after December 31, 1976, after a corporation is in existence for five years it is permitted to have up to 15 shareholders. Also, if the number of shareholders goes above ten during the first five years solely because of new shareholders who inherited their stock, the additional shareholders will be permitted although the number can never exceed 15. (4) All of the shareholders must be individuals or estates; stock held by corporations or trusts will disqualify Subchapter S status. Under the Tax Reform Act of 1976, however, certain trusts can be shareholders of Subchapter S corporations after 12/31/76. These trusts are: Trusts that are treated as owned by the grantor under the grantor trust rules; trusts that are created primarily to vote the stock transferred to them; and any trust that receives stock under a will, but only for 60 days after the stock is transferred to the trust. (5) There must be no nonresident alien shareholders. (6) The corporation can have only one class of stock. (7) The corporation cannot derive more than 80% of its gross receipts from sources outside the U.S. (8) The corporation cannot derive more than 20% of its gross receipts from passive sources such as rents, royalties, dividends, interest or sales of securities.

As indicated in Chapter 1, Section 4, it is often difficult or impossible for a corporation engaged in certain aspects of the real estate business to qualify under Subchapter S because of the passive income rule. Where the corporate income consists primarily of rent from an apartment project, office building, or other rental project, Subchapter S is simply not available. There will, of course, be some cases where real estate corporations can qualify. For example, a developer who anticipates subdivision of a parcel of land and sale of the lots and who wishes to utilize the corporate form for business reasons may avoid the double tax problem by qualifying the corporation under Subchapter S. A construction business is normally operated in corporate form in order to avoid liability to third parties. In such cases, a Subchapter S election will virtually eliminate questions relating to unreasonable compensation and unreasonable accumulations of earnings.

If it is determined that Subchapter S status is no longer desired, the election can be terminated in a number of ways. Once terminated, however, the corporation cannot again qualify under Subchapter S for five years unless IRS permission is given.

> *Warning:* In order to qualify under Subchapter S the election must be made during the first month of the taxable year or during the last month of the prior taxable year. A new corporation wishing to elect for its first year of existence must make its election by the end of its first month of existence. It is, therefore, the duty of the attorneys involved in organizing the corporation to discuss the advisability of qualifying under Subchapter S and to properly and timely file the election if appropriate.

2.6 MISCELLANEOUS CONSIDERATIONS.

A number of other factors in corporate organization should be noted although they will not be discussed in detail.

(a) Sales of Depreciable Property to Controlled Corporations.

When gain is recognized upon the transfer of depreciable property to a controlled corporation, (for example, where boot is received pursuant to the transfer or where the property is sold to the corporation) §1239 provides that the gain will be taxed as ordinary income if 80% or more in value of the corporate stock is owned by the transferor or by certain related individuals or entities. Note that the test relates to 80% of the *value* of the stock, not to the number of shares. Therefore, it is possible that 80% of the outstanding shares represents more than 80% of the value of the corporate stock, particularly when the minority shares are subject to restrictions which have the effect of reducing their value.[19] Remember, also, that if any gain is recognized, §1250, relating to recapture of depreciation, may apply.

(b) Multiple Corporations.

Under the Tax Reform Act of 1969, the rules relating to multiple corporations were tightened. Following the expiration of a six year transition period in 1974, a controlled group of corporations is limited to one $25,000 surtax exemption and one $100,000 accumulated earnings credit. §1561. The definition of multiple corporations subject to this rule includes parent-subsidiary corporations (corporations where the parent owns 80% or more of the stock of the subsidiary) and brother-sister corporations. A brother-sister group includes two or more corporations which are owned 80% or more by five or fewer persons provided that these five or fewer persons identically own more than 50% of each corporation. §1563(a)(2). Also, there are certain attribution of ownership rules whereby a stockholder is deemed to own stock owned by certain members of his family as well as by certain entities (partnerships, corporations, trusts) in which he has an interest. The net effect of these rules is that the practices formerly followed by some taxpayers whereby each building in a project, or each division or activity of a business, were divided into separate corporations will no longer work; all of such corporations will normally be taxed as a single entity. The primary reason for utilizing multiple corporations is now related to business considerations, such as limiting the liabilities of each entity, rather than tax considerations.

(c) Allocation of Income and Deductions.

Under §482, IRS has the power to apportion or allocate income, deductions, credits or allowances between corporations or businesses that are controlled, directly or indirectly, by the same interests. The purpose of §482 is to prevent controlled corporations from evading taxes and to assure that each return clearly reflects the income of the reporting entity. §482 is particularly important to persons involved in the real estate business who control a number of corporations. Often, what appears to be an innocent transaction will be restructured by IRS. For example, it is necessary to charge interest on intercorporate loans, to charge a reasonable rate of rent where one property uses a corporation which belongs to another, and generally, to attempt to treat controlled entities at arms length. Moreover, §482 is not limited to corporations—in some cases IRS has successfully alleged that individuals who control corporations are included in the parties among whom the allocation can be made.

> *Example:* The Coopers owned a construction company which they operated as a proprietorship. They organized a corporation (presumably in order to get limited liability) to carry on the business. However, they retained the building and various other depreciable assets necessary for successful construction operations. They agreed that the corporation could gratuitously use the assets until it became profitable. IRS allocated the fair rental value of the assets to the Coopers and taxed them on the constructive rental income relying on §482. The Court agreed. Although §482 is limited to "organizations, trades or businesses" the Court felt that the Coopers were conducting a business enterprise within the purview of that section.[20]

FOOTNOTES FOR CHAPTER TWO

[1]Rev.Rul. 56-256, 1956-1 C.B. 129.

[2]*Est. of Heinz Schmidt v. Comm.,* 355 F.2d 111, 17 AFTR 2d 242 (CA-9, 1966).

[3]Rev.Rul.64-56, 1964-1 C.B. 133.

[4]*William A. James v. Comm.,* 53 T.C. 63 (1970).

[5]*U.S. v. Frazell,* 355 F.2d 487, 14 AFTR 2d 5378 (CA-5, 1964) cert. denied.

[6]*Bruce Berckmans,* ¶61,100 P-H Memo TC.

[7]See Bittker & Eustice: "Federal Income Taxation of Corporations and Shareholders" Chapter 4. For a recent Tax Court decision differentiating between corporate stock and corporate debt, see: *Robert W. Adams,* 58 T.C. 41 (1972).

[8]§368(c).

[9]Reg.1.351-1(a)(1).

[10]*American Bantam Car v. Comm.,* 11 TC 397, (1948), aff'd. *per curiam* 177 F. 2d 513,38 AFTR 820 (CA-3, 1949), cert. denied.

[11]P-H Fed. Taxes ¶18,025. See *Intermountain Lumber Co.,* 65 T.C. 1025 (1976).

[12]*Dennis v. Comm.,* 473 F.2d 274, 31AFTR 2d 73-646 (CA5, 1973) held that if the initial transfer is tax-free under Section 351 (a) because the debt instruments received are securities, then installment sales treatment is not available to the transferor.

[13]*Sun Properties, Inc. v. U.S.,* 220 F.2d 171, 47, AFTR 273 (CA-5, 1955).

[14]*Aqualane Shores, Inc. v. Comm.,*269 F.2d 116, 4 AFTR 2d 5346 (CA-5, 1955). Also, *Stanley, Inc. v. Schuster,* 23 AFTR 2d 60-715 (DC Ohio, 1969) where sale treatment was denied where corporation issued $240,000 of short-term notes and $4,500 of capital stock.

[15]*The Piedmont Corp.,* 388 F.2d 886, 21 AFTR 2d 534 (CA-4, 1968).

[16]*Burr Oaks v. Comm.,* 365 F.2d 24, 18 AFTR 2d 5018, (CA-7, 1966).

[17]*Gyro Engineering Corp. v. U.S.,* 417 F.2d 437 24 AFTR 2d, 69-5797 (AA-9, 1969).

[18]*Boyer v. Comm.,* 58 T.C. 316 (1972). Compare *Ralph E. Gordy v. Comm.,* 36 T.C. 855 (1961), where the taxpayer was permitted to report the gain from the sale of an option to his controlled corporation as a capital gain.

[19]*U.S. v. Parker,* 376 F.2d 402, 19 AFTR 2d, 1281 (CA5, 1967).

[20]*R.D. Cooper v. Comm.,* 64 T.C. 576 (1975).

3

ORGANIZING

THE PARTNERSHIP

Most real estate projects are operated as partnerships. As demonstrated in Chapter 1, the corporate form serves to insulate the individual owners (stockholders) from the property and precludes direct realization by them of the tax loss and cash flow generated by the project. The partnership, on the other hand, is essentially a conduit—the tax loss and cash flow are passed through to the individual owners (partners) without the intervention of a taxable entity. A thorough understanding of the tax rules relating to partnerships is, therefore, essential in setting up real estate ventures.

This chapter analyzes the tax factors in organizing a partnership which will engage in the business of operating a real estate project. The following topics will be covered:

3.1 Definitions
3.2 Associations Taxable as Corporations—Advance Rulings
    (a) Corporate General Partners—Stock Ownership and Net Worth Requirements
    (b) Uneconomic Limited Partnerships
    (c) Information to be Furnished with Ruling Requests
3.3 Transfers of Property to the Partnership
3.4 Compensating the Developer
    (a) Receipt of an Interest in Partnership Capital
    (b) Receipt of an Interest in Partnership Profits
    (c) Granting the Developer an Option to Purchase an Interest in the Project or the Partnership
    (d) Granting the Developer's Partnership Interest at an Early Stage
    (e) Deductions by the Partnership for Payments to a Partner

3.1   DEFINITIONS

For income tax purposes, the term "partnership" is defined quite broadly and includes any:

> ... syndicate, group, pool, joint venture, or other unincorporated organization through ... which any ... venture is carried on, and which is not ... a trust or estate or a corporation ...[1]

Thus, where two or more persons are jointly involved in a business activity, such as the operation of a real estate project, they will generally be classified as a partnership for tax purposes even though they hold their undivided interests in their own names. Where no business activities are carried on, however, there is no partnership for tax purposes. For example, tenants in common may hold unimproved land or make a passive real estate investment, such as net leased realty requiring no management.[2] The tenancy in common is a cumbersome device compared to the partnership, however, and rarely fills the bill where income properties are involved.

The distinction between a tenancy in common and a partnership can have considerable tax significance. Although a partnership does not pay taxes, it is a reporting entity. Consequently, certain elections and tax determinations are made at the partnership (entity) level and apply equally to all members of the partnership rather than being made at the individual partner level. If a co-ownership arrangement is held to constitute a joint venture or partnership, the capital gain potential for an individual co-owner may be destroyed even though he would qualify for capital gain treatment absent the partnership classification.[3] Also, a short-term partner (one who holds his partnership interest for less than six months) is entitled to long-term capital gain treatment where the property sold is a long-term asset to the selling partnership.[4] The election to defer recognition of the gain on an involuntary conversion of property, or to report income as capital gain rather than ordinary income, or to report a sale on the installment method, are all made at the partnership level.[5]

3.2   ASSOCIATIONS TAXABLE AS CORPORATIONS—ADVANCE RULINGS

Remember that a partnership which has more corporate than non-corporate characteristics becomes an association taxed as a corporation notwithstanding the fact that it has not been formally incorporated under state law. See Chapter 1, Section 6 for a discussion of the rules relating to association status.

Sometimes the organizers of a partnership desire an advance ruling to the effect that the organization in question will be classified as a partnership and not as an association. Of course, the Internal Revenue Service issues rulings on such questions just as it does in most other areas of tax law. Accordingly, the Internal Revenue Service has established a number of guidelines or revenue procedures which must be met if a favorable ruling is to be issued. These procedures, therefore, create certain "safe harbors" in the sense that businesses which meet the established criteria can anticipate a favorable ruling at least on the issues to which the procedures are addressed. Although compliance with these revenue procedures is not mandatory, the fact is that most Revenue Agents will consider the failure or inability to satisfy these rules as an important factor in evaluating the tax status of the organization in question.

(a)   Corporate General Partners—Stock Ownership and Net Worth Requirements.

In Revenue Procedure 72-13, 1972-1 CB 735, the IRS established conditions which must be satisfied before it will rule that a limited partnership with a sole corporate general partner will be classified as a partnership for federal income tax purposes. These conditions are:

Stock Ownership Test—The limited partners must not own, directly or indirectly, more than 20% of the capital stock of the corporate general partner. The normal attribution of ownership rules are applied to determine if the 20% stock ownership test has been met.

Net Worth Test—The sole corporate general partner must have a net worth of at least $250,000, or 15% of the capital contributions of the limited partners, whichever is less. (Where capital contributions exceed $2,500,000, the corporate net worth must be at least 10% of the contributions.) The net worth of the corporate general partner is based on the current fair market value of its assets. Moreover, the value of any interest which the corporate general partner has in any limited partnership as well as its accounts and notes receivable from and payable to any limited partnerships in which it has an interest, will be disregarded.

> *Warning:* Some times a corporation acts as general partner in a number of limited partnerships. In such cases the corporate net worth must be at least equal to the net worth requirements for each separate limited partnership. For example, if a corporation is the sole general partner of limited partnership A wherein the limited partners invested $500,000, and also of limited partnership B wherein the limited partners invested $500,000, then the corporation must have a net worth of at least $150,000 or 15% of the capital contributions in both partnerships.

(b)   Uneconomic Limited Partnerships.

Revenue Procedure 74-17, 1974-1 CB 438 contains several guidelines which IRS will use in deciding whether or not to issue a requested ruling where it appears that the partnership may not be organized for the purpose of making a profit. The requirements are as follows:

Minimum Interest of General Partners—The interests of all general partners, taken together, in each material item of partnership income, gain, loss, deduction or credit must be equal to at least 1% of each such item at all times during the existence of the partnership. Limited partnership interests owned by general partners don't count for this computation.

Limit on Deductions in First Two Years—Aggregate deductions claimed by partners as distributive shares of partnership losses for the first two years of operation cannot exceed the amount of equity capital invested by the limited partners.

Loans Convertible to Partnership Interest—Creditors making nonrecourse loans to the limited partnership cannot acquire, as a result of the loan, any direct or indirect interest in the profits, capital or property of the partnership other than as a secured creditor.

(c) Information to be Furnished with Ruling Requests.

In Revenue Procedure 75-16, 1975-1 CB 676, IRS has listed the detailed information that must accompany requests for advance rulings that organizations qualify as partnerships for tax purposes. The checklist covers advance rulings for both general and limited partnerships. Among other items, the request for a ruling must contain the following information: the partnership agreement and all amendments; the partnership certificate filed or to be filed; the registration statement filed or to be filed with SEC, and if a registration statement is not required to be filed with SEC, then the documents filed or to be filed with any federal or state agency engaged in the regulation of securities and any private offering memorandum; a description of arrangements regarding the marketing of the partnership interests; a representation of the net worth of the general partners; an outline of promotional material used to sell interests in the organization, particularly including statements regarding the possible tax consequences of the arrangement; a detailed description of all creditors' interests other than security interests and rights to repayment; a statement indicating the amount of the capital contributions to be made by the general partners and the limited partners, and a detailed explanation of the participation of general partners and limited partners in profits and losses; a statement indicating whether there will be a shift in the proportion of profit and loss sharing ratio during the operation of the partnership and the details of same; a statement as to whether any negative capital balance of a general partner or a limited partner will be paid by him to the partnership upon termination of the entity; and a statement describing the manner and method of proposed distributions to the partners.

3.3   TRANSFERS OF PROPERTY TO THE PARTNERSHIP

§721 of the Internal Revenue Code provides that a contribution of property to a partnership is not a taxable event. This section reads as follows:

> No gain or loss shall be recognized to a partnership or to any of its partners in the case of a contribution of property to the partnership in exchange for an interest in the partnership.

As is typical in the Internal Revenue Code, a tax-free transfer results in a carryover of basis. Therefore, the basis of the transferor's interest in the partnership is equal to the amount of money and the basis of any property transferred by him. §722. The basis of the transferred property to the partnership is the same as it was in the hands of the transferor. §723.

> *Example:* A and B form a partnership with A contributing real estate worth $50,000 but which has a basis in A's hands of only $20,000. B contributes real estate which also has a value of $50,000 but which has a basis to B of $60,000. A and B agree that they will be equal partners. On the partnership books, the basis of the individual partners is carried over and the real estate, therefore, has a basis of $20,000 and $60,000 respectively. Similarly, A has a $20,000 basis for his partnership interest and B has a $60,000 basis for his partnership interest.

Where the partnership assumes responsibility for the payment of a transferor partner's obligations, he is deemed to have received a cash distribution equal to the liability for which he has been relieved. §752(b). The constructive distribution is first applied against the partner's basis and if it exceeds basis, he is deemed to have realized a gain notwithstanding the general rule of §721 referred to above which provides for non-recognition of gain on transfers to partnerships. Moreover, §752(c) provides that a liability to which property is subject shall, to the extent of the fair market value of the property, be considered a liability of the owner. (This appears to be consistent with the rule of the *Crane* case, discussed in Chapter 4, Section 2, which provides that in a purchase of mortgaged property, the amount of the mortgage, whether or not assumed, is added to basis and in a sale of mortgaged property the amount of the mortgage must be included in the sale price, whether or not assumed.) Therefore, the transfer of mortgaged property by a partner to his partnership can produce gain even where there is no personal liability by the transferor and the partnership does not assume the mortgage debt.[6]

The holding period of the partnership for the transferred property includes the period of time that the property was held by the transferor partner.[7] The transferor partner has a holding period for his partnership interest which includes the time that he held the transferred property provided that the property is either a capital asset or property used in a trade or business qualifying under §1231(b).[8]

Where the transfer from partner to partnership was a tax-free exchange—the typical case—there will not be any recapture of depreciation.[9]

Whether there will be a recapture of the investment credit upon a conveyance of property from a partner to a partnership is a more complicated question. Recapture of investment credit is not required because of a mere change in the form of conducting the business provided that (1) the §38 property, property which was subject to the investment credit remains in the same business; (2) the taxpayer retains a "substantial interest" in the business; (3) substantially all of the property, whether or not it is §38 property, is transferred in connection with the change of form; and (4) the basis of the §38 property is carried over in whole or in part.[10] Thus, no adjustment is required if a sole proprietor transfers his §38 property to a partnership and retains a substantial interest in the business. (However, the partnership by making an early disposition of the property can cause recomputation of the transferor's credit or such a recomputation could be required on a sale of his interest or upon his failure to retain a substantial interest in the partnership.)[11] The taxpayer is considered to have retained a substantial interest only if, after the change, his interest is (1) substantial in relation to the total interest of all of the owners; or (2) is equal to or greater than his interest prior to the change. For example, a taxpayer having a 5% interest in property who retains at least a 5% interest after the transfer is considered to have retained a substantial interest in the business.[12] It is also possible, of course, that the formation of a partnership will represent a merger of several existing businesses or the creation of a new business which would not qualify as a "mere change in form."

3.4 COMPENSATING THE DEVELOPER

The developer is the individual who will normally organize the partnership. Typically, he utilizes his time and experience as well as his contacts to acquire the site, to negotiate the purchase of the land or the project, to obtain the financing, to organize the partnership and to handle the construction and rental of the project. Naturally, he expects to be compensated for these services. It is possible, of course, to pay him a fee for his services but this is usually unsatisfactory to both parties. From the standpoint of the developer the receipt of a fee represents ordinary income and from the standpoint of the investor, the payment of a fee represents a financial commitment which he is reluctant to make before the project has been proved to be successful. A number of alternative techniques have, therefore, been developed for compensating the developer.[13] The following examples illustrate some of the methods which have been utilized to satisfy the objectives of both parties.

(a) Receipt of an Interest in Partnership Capital.

Although it is clear that a partnership interest obtained in exchange for a contribution of money or other property does not produce taxable income, assuming no "bargain purchase" element is present, the Code contains no provision covering the acquisition of a partnership interest in exchange for services rendered or to be rendered. However, the regulations recognize that, normally, a partner is entitled to be repaid his capital contribution; and if he relinquishes any part of that right in favor of another partner as compensation for services, the service partner receives ordinary income in the amount of the fair market value of the capital interest transferred.[14]

> *Example:* Investor contributes $100,000 to the partnership and receives a 1/2 interest. Developer, in recognition of his services in acquiring the site, etc., makes no capital contribution but receives a 1/2 interest in the partnership. Result: Developer has realized $50,000 of ordinary income having been, in effect, compensated for his services.

For many years, it was assumed that if instead of receiving a present interest in partnership capital the service partner received a future interest in partnership capital, for example, a capital interest which was deferred until such time as the other partners had recovered an amount equal to their capital contributions, there was no immediate tax consequence to the service partner. However, the *Frazell* case[15] reached the opposite result. Mr. Frazell was a geologist who formed a partnership with two investors to develop oil and gas properties. His only contribution consisted of some maps but he agreed to supervise the exploration and development activities and render other services to the partnership. The other two partners invested approximately $1,000,000 in cash. The parties agreed that the first $1,000,000 in cash receipts was to be distributed to the investors and, thereafter, Frazell was to receive a share of the profits. The joint venture was successful and after approximately four years, most of the $1,000,000 had been returned to the investing partners. At that time the partnership was incorporated and Frazell received 13% of the capital stock as his interest in the venture. He claimed that the receipt of stock was non-taxable because he had transferred his partnership interest to the corporation under §351. The Court held, however, that the incorporation of the partnership represented a transer of 13% of the capital accounts from the investing partners to Frazell and that the value of this account, after subtracting the nominal value of the maps he contributed, was taxable to him as ordinary income. The point is that it was not the transfer to the corporation that created the taxable event but the constructive distribution by the partnership in liquidation. In order to be entitled to participate in the liquidating distribution, the capital would have to be credited to Frazell on the partnership books. That constructive transfer of capital apparently produced the taxable event even though Frazell received no cash or property in his own name (other than the capital stock) upon the incorporation of the business.

The *Frazell* case involved a transaction prior to 1969. However, if a transfer occurs after June 30, 1969, §83 applies. Under that section, the fair market value of property received by a taxpayer for services rendered is taxed immediately unless the property is forfeitable and non-transferrable. Assuming that the property received meets these tests, then the transfer is taxable when the property (partnership interest) first becomes non-forfeitable or transferrable. §83(h) provides that the person for whom the services are rendered may deduct any amount that is taxed as ordinary income to the transferee.

(b)   Receipt of an Interest in Partnership Profits.

Since the *Frazell* case was decided in 1964, most tax practitioners were aware of the tax problems inherent in the receipt of an interest in partnership *capital*. It was generally assumed, however, that if, instead of an interest in capital, the service partner received only an interest in partnership *profits* there was no immediate tax to him upon the organization of the partnership. This assumption was based upon the language of Treasury Regulation 1.721-1(b)(1) which provides as follows:

> To the extent that any of the partners gives up any part of his right to be repaid his contributions (as distinguished from a share in partnership profits) in favor of another partner as compensation . . . Section 721 does not apply.

Note that the parenthetical phrase quoted above appears to make a distinction between an interest in capital and an interest in profits. However, in the case of *Sol Diamond*[16] the Court came to the opposite conclusion. Mr. Diamond performed services for a Mr. Kargman by obtaining a mortgage loan for an office building which Kargman was purchasing. For these services, Diamond received an interest in a partnership which was formed to acquire the property. Diamond's interest entitled him to 60% of the profits over a 24-year period. Three weeks after the closing, Diamond sold his 60% interest back to Kargman for $40,000 and reported the amount received as a short term capital gain. Since he had short term losses resulting from other transactions, he paid no tax on the $40,000 received. The Commissioner alleged that Diamond's gain should be taxed as ordinary income. The Tax Court agreed with the Commissioner, holding that the parenthetical phrase in the regulation quoted above distinguishing between an interest in capital and an interest in profits was "obscure." Although the Tax Court decision was widely criticized by commentators, it was affirmed by the U.S. Court of Appeals for the 7th Circuit in 1974.

(c) Granting the Developer an Option to Purchase an Interest in the Project or the Partnership.

It may be possible to defer the taxability of the interest or potential interest to be granted to the developer or service partner by granting him an option to purchase a partnership interest rather than giving him an immediate interest in the partnership. Mr. Fraser was an attorney engaged in real estate development. One of the projects in which he was involved included the construction and development of apartment projects in San Francisco and Hawaii. Due to financial difficulties, he was unable to participate in a particular project but he did bring the matter to the attention of another developer, Bakar, and together, they negotiated for the purchase of the property. Such negotiations eventually resulted in an agreement between the seller and Bakar. Although Fraser was not a party to the purchase agreement, it was agreed that he would be entitled to a one third participation in the transaction. Bakar formed a partnership which did not include Fraser as one of its partners and the transaction eventually was closed. Although he did not contribute any funds, Fraser did participate in the negotiations with lenders and other parties and for all practical purposes, played the same role as Bakar did in the development. He received no compensation for such services. Eventually, he sold his option for $175,000 reporting the gain as a long term capital gain. The Commissioner alleged that the payment was actually compensation for services and was taxable as ordinary income. The Tax Court held in favor of Fraser despite the fact that the sale was actually made to the other partners.[17]

> *Warning:* The Court distinguished another option case involving a taxpayer by the name of Saunders.[18] In that case, the partners had reserved the alternative right to pay Saunders a specified sum in lieu of permitting him to become a partner, thereby changing the character of his so-called option. When Saunders attempted to exercise his option to become a partner, the other parties paid him off in cash. Therefore, according to the Circuit Court, the purported option did not create a "privilege or option" entitled to be accorded capital gains treatment under §1234. The Court stated that "that Section is limited to unilateral agreements which are inflexibly binding upon the purported vendor." In short, if the parties wish to insure favorable treatment under the *Fraser* case, it is essential that the other partners not have the right to terminate the developer's option by means of a cash payment.

(d) Granting the Developer's Partnership Interest at an Early Stage.

Most of the problems discussed above result from the fact that the developer or service partner is receiving his interest at a time when such interest clearly has value. In the *Diamond* case this value was easy to measure because of the fact that it was sold shortly after formation of the partnership. Even where the value of the interest is not that clear, however, there remains the problem of reporting the receipt of an interest in partnership capital or an interest in profits for tax purposes.

It would appear that this danger can be minimized by bringing the developer into the partnership at the earliest possible stage. For example, if the parties form the partnership before any significant capital contributions are made and the developer receives his partnership interest at that point, it may have only nominal value. It might also be possible for the developer himself to organize the business with the other parties coming in later. Assume, for example, that in stage one, the developer acquires a site and commences development of a projcet. At stage two an invitation is made to outside investors to participate in the project, contributing the funds necessary to complete construction to the extent that such funds are not provided from mortgage loans. The new participants make capital contributions to an entity which becomes a partnership or an expanded partnership. Of course the partnership realized no income on contributions to its capital. Note that the developer has not received any fees, nor has he realized a bargain purchase. The result, however, is to permit him to get in on the ground floor with a minimum capital contribution and minimum tax consequences until his partnership interest is actually sold or distributions are actually made to him from the partnership.

(e) Deductions by the Partnership for Payments to a Partner.

(1) Trade and Business Expenses—It is clear that payments by a partnership of trade and business expenses which are normally deductible under the Code do not lose that status merely because they are paid to a partner. In fact, §83(h) provides expressly that the party for whom services are rendered (the partnership) may deduct any amount that is taxed to the payee as ordinary income. (The proposed regulations add the qualification that such items must be otherwise deductible.)[19] It follows that where the developer has rendered services to the partnership and has received in payment therefor an interest in partnership capital or profits, the partnership will be entitled to a deduction to the same extent as if it had paid cash for such services. Further, a partnership is permitted to allocate deductions among its members within certain prescribed limits. See Chapter 3, Section 5 below.

> *Suggestion:* The tax planning implications of these rules are fairly obvious. Where the developer may be compelled to recognize income by reason of his receipt of an interest in partnership capital or an interest in partnership profits under the rules discussed above, it may be possible for the partnership agreement to allocate to him the partnership deduction relating to that item. The net effect will be that the developer will be deemed to have realized income to the extent of the value of the interest received for his services but simultaneously will be allocated a partnership deduction in exactly the same amount; the income item and the expense item will offset one another and the unfavorable tax consequence will be nullified.

(2) Organization and Syndication Costs and Other Capital Items—In the past some partnerships took the position that payments made by a partnership to a partner were deductible if they were "guaranteed payments" under §707(c). It is now clear, however, that this section does not override the normal rule that in order for any payment to be deductible, it must be an ordinary and necessary business expense.

Example: A real estate partnership was formed to build an office-showroom complex. The partnership agreed to pay the managing partner a $110,000 management fee for his services in advising, supervising and managing the partnership. The Court found that "No portion of the management fee was for managing the property after it was completed." Rather it was for work done at the inception and during the development of the office-showroom complex. The deduction to the partnership was disallowed, the Tax Court holding that the payment must qualify as an ordinary and necessary currently deductible business expense in order to be deductible.[20]

Example: A limited partnership was formed to acquire, develop and sell property. One of the general partners was responsible for handling all of the matters and paying all of the costs pertaining to the organizing of the limited partnership and the sale of the limited partnership interests. Immediately after the organization was completed, he was to be paid an amount specified in the agreement as compensation for his services in organizing the partnership. IRS ruled that even though the payment qualified under §707, it was not deductible by the partnership because it constituted a capital expenditure in organizing the partnership.[21]

Suggestion: Where some of a partner's services relate to capital items such as organization expenses and some of his services relate to deductible items such as management fees, it is advisable to have him submit an invoice specifying the nature of the services and making a reasonable allocation of the total fee among the various categories of services rendered.

The Tax Reform Act of 1976 prohibits a partnership as well as its partners from deducting the partnership's organization and syndication costs in the year paid. Organization costs may, by election of the partnership, be amortized over 60 months although the items eligible for this election are limited (similar to existing corporate rules), and syndication costs are never deductible. The Act provides that guaranteed payments to partners are subject to the same rules as payments to other parties; thus, if such guaranteed payments are for the purpose of organizing the partnership or syndicating interest in it, they must be capitalized. §709.

This provision is effective for partnership years beginning after December 31, 1975. However, amortization of organization costs may be elected only for costs paid or incurred in years beginning after December 31, 1976. Prior years are left for the courts to dispose of under prior law.

Comment: One approach which was utilized prior to the Tax Reform Act of 1976 and which continues to be available is to demonstrate that the general partner's services in earning its fee involved activities other than organization of the partnership and syndication of the limited partnership interests. For example, some publicly held syndications pay "rent-up fees" for the services of the general partner in renting the apartments of the project. Some partnerships pay a fee to a partner for his guaranty of loans or other services. Careful documentation of the services performed is obviously required.

(3) Time for Deduction by Partnership—Supposing that a partnership is on the accrual basis of accounting while the developer or service partner is on the cash basis of accounting. Assume further that both the partnership and the partner report on a calendar year basis. Can the partnership accrue the fee payable to the partner and claim a deduction in the year of accrual while the partner-payee defers reporting the item until a later accounting period when the payment is actually made? Such a practice is ex-

pressly sanctioned for corporations by §267 of the Code provided that the payment complies with the two and a half month rule if it is made to a major stockholder. However, in the case of partnerships, the regulations expressly provide that a payee-partner must include the payment as income for his taxable year which corresponds with the partnership year in which the partnership claimed the deduction for the payment under its method of accounting. A 1977 decision held that this rule applies only to accrued payments to a partner for services in his capacity as a partner. Where the payment is for interest or for services as an outsider (such as accounting or legal services) such consistency is not required and deferral of the income by the payee is permitted.[22]

3.5   ALLOCATION OF PROFITS AND LOSSES AMONG THE PARTNERS

One of the most common questions faced by taxpayers in connection with the organization of real estate partnerships is how to allocate the profits and losses among the members of the partnership. Frequently, the partnership group includes a developer who has contributed services and who hopes to be paid for such services in the form of a distribution of cash flow. The group will probably include high-bracket investors who contributed capital and who would be willing to receive the bulk of their return in the form of tax losses to be offset against their other income, although they hope to recover their capital investments and a profit upon the eventual sale or other disposition of the project. Can the partnership agreement make such disproportionate allocations giving the cash flow to the developer and the tax losses to the investors? IRS will typically take the position that the partnership, like spumoni ice cream, cannot be split into separate components; each partner must include in his slice of partnership allocations a uniform share of each item such as capital gain, profits, losses, etc. Taxpayers, on the other hand, will often attempt to create a structure which accomplishes the objectives of each of the parties, inconsistent as they may be, allocating benefits and burdens according to the tax and financial situation of each partner.

(a)   The General Rule.

The general rule is simplicity itself—a partner's distributive share of the gains, losses, deductions or credits is determined by the partnership agreement.[23] Moreover, §761(c) provides that the "partnership agreement" includes all modifications of the agreement which are made prior to the due date of the partnerships's tax return. Thus, not only is the partnership agreement an instrument of considerable flexibility but it can be modified, within limits, to accomodate the situations of the individual partners as they develop during the taxable year.

Section 704(b) provides that if the partnership agreement does not provide for allocation of any particular item, the distributive shares of such item are determined in accordance with the ratio in which the partners divide the general profits or losses of the partnership. However, the agreement may also provide for a non prorata allocation of specific items as the following examples indicate.

> *Example:* G and H, each of whom is engaged as a sole proprietor in the business of developing and marketing electronic devices, enter into a partnership agreement to

develop and market electronic devices. H contributes $2500 cash and agrees to devote his full-time services to the partnership. G contributes $100,000 cash and agrees to obtain a loan for the partnership of any additional capital needed. The partnership agreement provides that the full amount of any research and experimental expenditures and any interest on partnership loans are to be charged to G. It also provides that G's distributive share is to be 90% of partnership income or loss computed without reduction by such research and experimental expenditures and such interest, until all loans have been repaid and G has received through his 90% share of income an amount equal to the full amount of such research and experimental expenditures, of such interest and his share of any partnership operating losses. During this time H's distributive share will be 10%. Thereafter, G and H will share profits and losses equally. Since all of the research and experimental expenditures and interest specially allocated to G are in fact borne by G, the allocation will be recognized in the absence of other circumstances showing that its principal purpose was tax avoidance or evasion.[24]

Example: To finance the development of a parcel of real estate, a partnership obtained a $900,000 construction loan on December 28, 1970. One of the partners paid a non-refundable loan fee of $36,000 and prepaid interest of $44,000 to be applied against interest to accrue on the loan the following year. After concluding that the loan fee and interest were properly deductible in the year paid, the Tax Court held further that the deduction for these items could be specially allocated to the partner paying for same since he would bear the economic burden of the expenditure underlying the deduction.[25]

(b) First Exception: The Substantial Economic Effect Rule.

§702(a) requires each partner to take into account separately his "distributive share" of various categories of income, gain, loss, deduction, or credit, together with his distributive share of the partnership's general taxable income or loss exclusive of the items requiring separate computation. §704(b)(2) provides that a special allocation of any particular item will be ignored and that each partner's distributive share of such item will be determined in accordance with the general profit and loss ratio if the principal purpose of the allocation is tax avoidance or evasion. The Treasury Regulations include a number of factors to consider in determining whether the principal purpose of an allocation is tax avoidance or evasion, such as whether there is a business purpose for the allocation; whether related items from the same source are subject to the same allocation; whether the allocation was made without recognition of normal business factors and only after the amount of the specially allocated item could reasonably be estimated; the duration of the allocation; the overall tax consequences of the allocation; and whether the allocation has "substantial economic effect." Although all of these factors are relevant, most commentators have concluded that the "substantial economic effect" test is the principal one, and that an allocation which does not have substantial economic effect will normally not be recognized for tax purposes.

Example: In *Stanley C. Orrisch,*[26] a partnership agreement was amended so as to allocate 100% of the partnership's depreciation to the taxpayer-partner. A reading of the agreement indicated, however, that the partners actually contemplated an equal distribution of the partnership's assets at all times including any distribution upon liquidation of the partnership. Thus, the special allocation would never affect the taxpayer's right to share equally with the other partners in the partnership assets. Accordingly, the Court concluded that the special allocation had no substantial economic effect and would not be recognized.

The teaching of the above case is clear. If the taxpayers expect the government to recognize their allocation, it must have some effect other than providing tax deductions. As a minimum, the tax loss which is allocated to a particular partner must also be charged to his capital account so that upon the eventual disposition of the property, the allocation will affect that partner's gain or loss on sale as well as the amount payable to him upon liquidation of the partnership. As the Court said itself in the *Orrisch* case, "to find any economic effect of the special allocation agreement aside from its tax consequences, we must, therefore, look to see who is to bear the economic burden of the depreciation if the buildings should be sold for a sum less than their cost."

Changes Under the Tax Reform Act of 1976. The Tax Reform Act of 1976 amends §704(b) to provide that the test of whether a special allocation will be permitted is one of substantial economic effect. This replaces the broader tax avoidance purpose test of which substantial economic effect was only one consideration. Also, the Act places the requirement on allocations of *net* income or loss, as well as on special allocation of individual items of income, gain, loss, deduction or credit. Under the prior law, it was not clear whether an allocation of *net* income or loss was required to meet any test of this sort, although in one case the Tax Court had upset such an allocation by finding that it was not a genuine allocation on the particular facts.[27] In short, under the current law it no longer makes any difference whether there is a so-called bottom line allocation of net income or an allocation of individual items of income or loss; in either case, the allocation must have substantial economic effect if it is to be recognized for tax purposes.

The Tax Reform Act of 1976 also makes a change in the manner in which the disallowed item is reallocated among the partners. In the past, Treasury Regulations required that when a special allocation of an item was upset, it would be shared by the partners in the same proportion as they shared in partnership net income or loss. The Act provides that, if either a special or net allocation does not have substantial economic effect, or if the partnership agreement makes no provision for sharing of the item in question, it will be shared in accordance with the partners' respective "interests in the partnership" determined by taking into account all "facts and circumstances." The House and Senate Committee reports indicate that the relevant facts and circumstances would include a partner's relative interest in cash flow and his relative rights to distributions of capital upon liquidation.

This provision is effective for partnership taxable years beginning after December 31, 1975.

(c)   Second Exception: The Contributed Property Rule.

For assets which are contributed to the partnership by a partner, the partnership's basis is the same as the basis for such assets in the hands of the contributing partner. §723. Since depreciation cannot exceed basis it follows that the contributing partner's basis becomes a ceiling on the amount of depreciation deductions. This is true even where the parties agree that the property has a value in excess of basis.

However, where there is a disparity between basis and fair market value the partners can agree to a special allocation of the depreciation on the contributed property to reflect such disparity subject, of course, to the rule that in no event can total depreciation deductions exceed basis.[28]

> *Example:* A and B form a partnership to which A contributes $100,000 and B contributes property which is worth $100,000 but which has an adjusted basis of only $75,000. The property is depreciable at the rate of 10% per year. The allowable depreciation for the first year is $7500 (10% of $75,000 basis). However, depreciation on the basis of book value would be $10,000 (10% of $100,000 agreed value). Assuming that the partnership earnings for the year are $60,000 before deducting depreciation, the net taxable income after depreciation is $52,500. In the absence of an agreement to the contrary, the depreciation for tax purposes will be allocated between the partners equally and each partner will have $26,250 of taxable income for the year. However, the partnership agreement may provide that Partner A shall receive the benefit of a sufficient portion of the depreciation to offset the economic depreciation to his interest in the property. In that case, the allowable deduction would be allocated $5,000 to A (1/2 of the $10,000 depreciation based on book value) and the balance of $2,500 to B. In that case, the partnership income would be divided $25,000 to A and $27,500 to B. Reg.1.704-1(c)(2).

(d) Third Exception: Losses Limited to Partner's Basis.

The previous section dealt with the basis of property to the partnership treating the partnership as an entity. An entirely different question, however, is the amount of the individual partner's basis in his partnership interest. It is clear that irrespective of the amount of partnership losses allocated to a particular partner, he cannot claim a deduction for such losses in excess of the amount of the basis of his partnership interest. The amount of such basis is a ceiling on the amount of losses which can be passed through to the partner. Understanding the rules which define such basis is, therefore, essential.

Generally speaking, the original basis for a partner's interest in the partnership equals the amount of cash contributed by him to the partnership plus the basis of any property contributed by him. §722. However, his basis as so determined must be adjusted to take into account the partner's share of partnership liabilities and, thereafter, basis is subject to continuous readjustment to reflect partnership income and losses regardless of whether distributed to him or not. The basis for a partner's partnership interest is increased by his distributive share of partnership income and gain and decreased by his distributive share of the partnership's losses.

> *Warning:* Amounts advanced by a partner to the partnership as a loan, rather than as a capital contribution, are not included in the computation of the basis of the lending partner's interest in the partnership. In such cases, a partner may lose the right to claim partnership losses on his personal return because of inadequate basis whereas he would have been able to claim such losses had he made a capital contribution rather than a loan.[29]

The basis to a partner of his partnership interest is increased to reflect his share of partnership liabilities. §752. It is this rule, of course, which makes the partnership form a particularly attractive vehicle in real estate venture because the liabilities generally exceed the capital contributions. Generally, partnership liabilities (such as the mortgage loan utilized to construct a building) are allocated among the partners in accordance with their ratio for sharing partnership losses. Since limited partners are normally not responsible for partnership losses, this rule, without qualification, would present a serious problem. However, the Regulations provide that where none of the partners have any personal liability with respect to a partnership liability (such as a mortgage loan where the note is not personally guaranteed by any of the partners) then all of the partners, including limited partners, are considered as sharing such liability in the same proportion as they share partnership profits.[30] This distinction is crucial in the organization of real estate partnerships since it is axiomatic that the liabilities, principally in the form of real estate mortgage loans, are intended to be included in the depreciation base. In the absence of qualifying under this rule, a partner's share of losses is limited to his capital contribution adjusted as indicated above.

> *Example:* Developer, the general partner, and Investor, the limited partner, form a partnership. Each of the partners makes contributions of cash. Pursuant to the partnership agreement, they will share profits and losses equally but Investor's obligations are limited to his actual capital contribution. The partnership purchases real estate for $1,000,000 paying $100,000 down and taking title subject to a $900,000 mortgage. Neither the partnership nor any of the partners assume any liability on the mortgage note. Under these circumstances, the basis of the property to the partnership is $1,000,000. Both Developer and Investor can increase the basis of their partnership interests by $450,000 since each partner's share of the liability has been increased by that amount. The liability is allocated in accordance with the profit sharing ratio because neither partner has any personal liability on the note.

> *Warning:* In view of this rule it is important to the limited partners upon entering a limited partnership to make sure not only that they have no personal liability on the mortgage note but also that the general partner has not personally guaranteed the note. This can be accomplished either by taking the property "subject to" the mortgage but without an assumption of liability, or a non-recourse mortgage can be negotiated wherein the lender agrees that it will accept the proeprty as the sole security for the loan and that no deficiency will be claimed against any partner.

The IRS has issued a number of rulings limiting the ability of the parties to create such non-recourse liabilities. For example, in 1969 IRS ruled that an agreement by the limited partners to indemnify the general partner does not create a liability which the limited partners share for basis purposes. The liability of limited partners must be enforceable by the outside creditors of the partnership.[31] Similarly, the making of a non-recourse loan by a general partner to the limited partners or to the limited partnership constitutes a capital contribution by the general partner.[32] Finally, IRS has ruled that a non-recourse "loan" to the limited partnership by a third party, secured only by unproven oil and gas leases and coupled with an option to convert the loan at any time into an interest in partnership profits, constituted an equity investment by the third party rather than a debt. Accordingly, the purported liability cannot be utilized to increase basis of the partners.[33]

Although these Revenue Rulings require careful attention in organizing partnerships, the fact remains that their significance can be overstated. All Revenue Rulings are limited to the specific facts involved. Moreover, the last two rulings discussed above both involved partnerships engaged in the oil and gas business. Most ventures in the oil and gas field result in drywells and, therefore, a non-recourse loan to the partnership is highly speculative. In real estate partnerships, by way of contrast, there is normally considerably more security for the loan and a greater opportunity to establish that the loan is bonafide. Finally, §707(a) of the Code specifically provides that a transaction between a partner, general or limited, and the partnership in which he is a member, will be treated as "occurring between the partnership and one who is not a partner," and the regulations specifically provide that loans between a partner and the partnership will be included within the purview of this section. Reg. 1.707-1(a). In short, it should not be concluded from these rulings that all loans by a member of a partnership will necessarily be classified as equity contributions.

The Tax Reform Act of 1976 imposed limitations on losses in excess of the amount "at risk" in certain specified kinds of business activities as well as in partnerships generally. See the discussion in Chapter 4, Section 2(c). However, investments in real estate (other than mineral leasing) are expressly excepted from these limitations and continue to be subject to the old rules.

(e) Fourth Exception: Retroactive Allocations of Profits and Losses.

Prior to the Tax Reform Act of 1976 many partnerships followed the practice of allocating a large share of the full year's income, gain or loss, to a new partner despite the fact that he became a partner toward the end of the year. The taxpayers relied on §761(c) which provides that a partnership agreement can be amended retroactively even after the close of the partnership year. However, this practice was of questionable validity. First, §706(c)(2)(b) provides that the taxable year of a partnership shall not close with respect to a partner who sells or exchanges less than his entire interest in the partnership or with respect to a partner whose interest is reduced but such partner's distributive share of items of income, expense, etc. shall be determined by taking into account his varying interests in the partnership during the year. One appellate court has expressly rejected the ability of a partnership to retroactively allocate to a partner who was admitted late in the year.[34]

The Tax Reform Act of 1976, effective for partnership years beginning after 12/31/75, clarifies the situation by providing that partnership income or loss will be allocated to a partner only for the portion of the year he is a member of the partnership. §706(c)(2)(B) as amended. The partnership will either allocate among its partners on a daily basis, or separate the year into two or more segments and allocate items among partners who participated during each segment.

> *Comment:* The ability to divide the year into segments continues to present a possibility of allocating losses to partners admitted late in the year even without retroactive allocations. For example, assume the case of a partnership with $100,000 of losses, $20,000 of which occur prior to November 30 and the remaining $80,000 of which occur during December. A large portion of the December loss could be allocated to a partner entering the partnership on December 1. The House Ways and Means Committee report of November 12, 1975, specifically sanctions this result. Another consequence of the Tax Reform Act of 1976 provision referred to above will, undoubtedly, be to cause new partnerships to be formed late in the year so that the partners who enter after formation can obtain a larger portion of the loss of the initial year. Where this is not possible, i.e., where the losses are incurred earlier in the year, it will simply be necessary to market the partnership interests early in the year.

One other point should be emphasized in connection with the subject of newly admitted partners. A partnership is considered to terminate if, within a 12-month period, there is a sale or exchange of 50% or more of the total interests in partnership capital and profits. §708(b)(1)(B). (Termination of a partnership can have serious consequences such as disqualifying the partnership from first user depreciation. Termination also has a number of other consequences including closing of the partnership taxable year, termination of elections made by the old partnership which are not binding upon the new partners, possible changes in basis, etc.) Accordingly, where new major partners (more than 50%) are being admitted, it is often advisable to have them contribute capital to the partnership rather than buy the interests of existing partners. Such a contribution does not constitute a sale or exchange of partnership interests and the partnership does not terminate, even though there is a 50% or more change in capital and profits.[35] Of course, where the existing partners insist on being "cashed out", tax planning may have to give way to business requirements.

3.6   LIMITED PARTNERSHIPS

As the foregoing discussion demonstrates, the limited partnership is a form which can satisfy the objectives of all of the parties. In large syndicates, it is a common device for this reason and it is surprising that it is not used more frequently in smaller groups. Part of the reason may be due to the lack of familiarity with this form of business organization.

Section 1 of the Uniform Limited Partnership Act provides:

> A limited partnership is a partnership formed by two or more persons under the provisions of Section 2, having as members one or more general partners and one or more limited partners. The limited partners as such shall not be bound by the obligations of the partnership.

§7 of the Uniform Act then goes on to state:

> A limited partner shall not become liable as a general partner unless, in addition to the exercise of his rights and powers as a limited partner, he takes part in the control of the business.

In short, if they carefully avoid becoming involved in the control or management of the project—a position consistent with the objectives of most investors—the limited partners can limit their liability to their actual agreed investment. This limitation should be stated in the subscription agreement and Certificate of Limited Partnership (similar to Articles of Incorporation) which is filed as a part of the public records, there-by putting potential creditors on notice of the limited partner status of the investors. Moreover, if none of the partners, general or limited, are personally liable on the mortgages on the partnership property, such mortgages may be added to basis and allocated in part to the limited partners in accordance with their profit-sharing ratio. In short, the limited partner-investors achieve the best of both possible worlds, the non-tax advantages of limited liability normally associated only with corporations and the tax benefits of depreciation deductions available in partnerships.[33]

3.7 THE PARTNERSHIP AGREEMENT

There are a number of excellent formbooks which contain illustrative agreements readily adaptable to most business partnerships. Real estate partnerships have some unique characteristics, however, requiring special comment. The following list, although not intended as exhaustive, includes some points which should be carefully considered in the drafting of real estate partnership agreements in addition to those provisions covered in partnership agreements generally.

(a) Definition of Terms—Since the parties do not participate uniformly in the various partnership benefits, it is particularly important that the terms be defined as clearly as possible. For example, is "cash flow," which presumably will be distributed principally to the working partner, computed after deduction for mortgage payments? After compensation payable to partners? After establishment of a working capital fund or contingency fund and, if so, how are the amounts of such funds determined? Similarly, is the bookkeeping "loss," which presumably will be allocated principally to the investing partner, computed based on straight-line or accelerated depreciation? Are interest, taxes and other carrying costs during construciton to be deducted (thereby increasing the loss) or capitalized? Who is to make the accounting judgments on matters not covered in the agreement?

(b) Capital Investments—If additional funds are invested to complete construction or to cover mortgage payments or for other partnership purposes, do such amounts constitute permanent capital contributions or loans to the partnership? Assuming the latter, how are such loans to be repaid—do they constitute a prior charge on available cash flow before payments to the working partner? If cash flow is insufficient to repay them after a specified period, are the non-contributing partners obligated to repay the advances in a pro rata fashion? Do such advances bear interest and, if so, how is the rate determined? While the investors are normally prepared to carry the project within the limits, these matters should be covered in advance.

(c) Defaults—What sanctions are imposed on a partner who fails to meet his capital obligations? A lawsuit to compel payment is of academic value only, since the other partners may be compelled to make up his deficiency in order to avoid a default on the mortgage and loss of the project. It may be possible to provide that a partner who pays more than his required share has a continuing lien on the interest of the defaulting partner, including a right to his share of cash flow and eventually a right to terminate the defaulted interest and succeed to his share of tax loss and equity as well.

(d) Management—Although the investors normally wish to avoid becoming involved in management problems (and in a limited partnership the limited partners lose that status if they do participate in management), there are normally some limits imposed on the powers of the working partners. For example, they may be prohibited from selling the property, refinancing the mortgage or incurring debt in excess of a specified amount without the consent of a specified percentage of the partnership interests.

(e) Transfers of Partnership Interests—For non-tax purposes a partnership is nor-

mally terminated by death of a partner or lifetime transfers of partnership interests. Where real estate is involved, however, such a result seems unnecessarily harsh, particularly with respect to the interests of the investing partners. Therefore, the agreement may permit the transfers of the interests of certain partners under certain conditions, such as after a period of time (say 60 days) within which the other partners have the right to meet the terms of any offers to purchase the interest of the selling partner. The buyer of an interest should be required to assume the seller's obligations under the agreement and unless the buyer can demonstrate financial ability the seller may not be released from his obligations to the partnership.

(f) Partnership Elections—The Code provides for certain elections available to partnerships. The interests of the parties may be adverse with respect to the question of whether such elections should be made. Therefore, to the extent that these questions can be anticipated, they should be covered in the agreement. For example, §754 contains an election which, if exercised, results in the adjustment of the basis of partnership property in the case of certain current distributions and liquidating distributions. Also, under §743 an adjustment to basis can be made in the case of any transfers of partnership interests. Once made, these elections apply to all such distributions and transfers made during the taxable year for which the election is filed and all subsequent years unless the election is revoked. If there are transfers of interests in subsequent years after the year of organization, should the partnership be required to adjust the basis of its assets to reflect the price paid by a purchaser of such an interest? If the partnership agreement does not provide for such elections, the managing partners or general partners may take the position that they do not wish to be burdened with such adjustments.

(g) Association Status—Remember that if a partnership has more corporate than non-corporate characteristics, it will be classified as an association and taxed as a corporation. In that case, the tax benefits anticipated from the partnership form will be lost. It is essential, therefore, that the partnership agreement be drafted so as to preclude this possibility.

(h) Obligations of General Partner—Since the general partner is normally the organizer of the partnership, the partnership agreement often contains provisions relieving him of virtually all liabilities. However, the limited partners often feel that there are certain minimum requirements which should be fulfilled by the general partner. Accordingly, the agreement should carefully spell out what is, or is not, required of the general partner. Does he guarantee completion of construction of the project? Does he guarantee minimum cash flow distributions for certain periods? If he is required to contribute extraordinary services which were not contemplated when the partnership was organized, is he entitled to be compensated for such services? To what extent does he guarantee the accuracy of financial projections furnished to the limited partners?

(i) Consequences of Deficit Capital Accounts—It is not unusual to provide for disproportionate allocation of tax losses. The consequence of this is that the capital accounts of those partners who are charged with the losses will be debited and ultimately may decrease to the point where they show negative balances, i.e., the losses charged to the capital accounts exceed the amount of the capital investment. What are the conse-

quences of such negative balances, particularly upon the death of a partner or the termination of his partnership interest for any other reason? At least one court has held that upon the death of a partner, his estate is obligated to repay the amount of the negative balance (the negative balance was almost $2,000,000 in the case in question).[37] This will undoubtedly come as a great surprise to many partners who are thinking only in terms of tax losses and a properly drafted partnership agreement can avoid the problem by carefully defining the rights and obligations of partners having such negative capital accounts.

FOOTNOTES FOR CHAPTER THREE

[1]§7701(a)(2) and §761. The terms "trust" and "corporation" are defined and distinguished from partnerships in the Regulations. Reg. 301.7701-2 (Associations), -3 (Partnerships) and -4 (Trusts). *Thomas K. McManus,* 65 T.C. 197 (1975) on appeal by taxpayer.

[2]Regs. 1.761.1(a) and 301.7701-3. Co-owners of an apartment house who delegated all management functions to a management company were only tenants in common. Rev. Rul. 75-374, 1975 -2 CB 261.

[3]*Hyman Podell,* 55 T.C. 429 (1970). See Section 10.5, Chap. 10.

[4]Rev. Rul. 68-79, 1968-1CB 310.

[5]P-H Federal Taxes, ¶28,535.

[6]Reg. 1.752-1(c).

[7]§1223(2). Reg. 1.723-1.

[8]§1223(1).

[9]1245(b)(3) and §1250(d)(3).

[10]Reg. 1.47-3(f)(1).

[11]Reg. 1.47-3(f)(5).

[12]Reg. 1.47-3(f)(2).

[13]Cowan, "Receipt of a Partnership Interest for Services" 32 N.Y.U. Inst. on Fed. Tax. 1501 (1974).

[14]Reg. 1.721-1(b)(1).

[15]*U.S. v Frazell,* 335 F.2d 487, 14 AFTR 2d 5378 (CA5, 1964), cert. denied, on remand 269 F. Sup-885 (WD.LA, 1967).

[16]492 F.2d 286, 33 AFTR 2d 74-852 (CA7, 1974) aff'g 56 T.C.530 (1971).

[17]*Robert D. Fraser,* 64 T.C. 41 (1975). Since the option was granted prior to 1963 the Commissioner did not rely upon Regs.1.61-15(a) and 1.421-6(d) (3) but these Regulations would apply to compensatory options granted thereafter.

[18]*Saunders v U.S.,* 450 F.2d 1047, 28AFTR 2d 71-5989 (CA9, 1971).

[19]Prop. Reg. 1.83-6(a) (1971).

[20]*Jackson E. Cagle, Jr.,* 63 T.C. 86 (1974), aff'd _____ F.2d _____, 38 AFTR 2d 76-5834 (CA5, 1976).

[21]Rev. Rul. 75-214, 1975-1 C.B. 185.

[22]Reg. 1.707-1(c). Edward T. Pratt v Comm., _____ Fd. _____, 39AFTR 2d 77-1258(CA5, 1977)

[23]§704(a); Reg. 1.704-1(a).

[24]Example 5, Reg. 1.704-1.

[25]*S. Rex Lewis,* 65 T.C. 625 (1975).

[26]55 T.C. 395 (1971), aff'd without opinion (CA9, 1973). See McKee "Partnership Allocations in Real Estate Ventures: Crane, Kresser & Orrisch" 30 Tax Law Rev. 1 (Fall, 1974).

[27]*Jean V. Kresser,* 54 T.C. 1621 (1970).

[28]§704(c); Reg. 1.704-1(c).

[29]*Curtis W. Kingbay*, 46 T.C. 147 (1966).

[30]Reg. 1.752-1(e).

[31]Rev. Rul. 69-223, 1969-1 C.B. 184.

[32]Rev. Rul. 72-135, 1972-1 C.B. 200.

[33]Rev. Rul. 72-350, 1972-2 C.B. 394.

[34]*Rodman v. Comm'r.*, 542 F.2d 845, 38 AFTR 2d 76-5840 (CA2, 1976).

[35]Rev. Rul. 75-423, 1975 -2 C.B. 260. Reg. 1.708-1(b)(1)(ii). If the contributed funds or property are used by the partnership to terminate the interests of existing partners, the step transaction rule would apply and the transaction would be treated as a sale of partnership interests. See Reg. 1.731-1(c).

[36]See Freidberg, "Limited Partnerships: A Non-Tax Analysis," 32 N.Y.U. Inst. on Fed. Tax. 1363 (1974).

[37]*Park Cities Corporation v D. Harold Byrd, et al.*, 522 SW 2d 572 (Tex, 1975).

4

SOLVING

PROPERTY

ACQUISITION PROBLEMS

In order to compute depreciation or to determine the amount of gain or loss on the eventual sale of property, the owner starts by computing his "basis" in the property involved. Although real estate is generally acquired by purchase, this is not the exclusive means of acquisition and the amount of basis will be determined according to the form of acquisition. It is also necessary to determine whether the amount due to the seller and the amount of any mortgage on the property is properly included in the purchaser's basis. A number of other problems related to acquisitions also arise. This chapter will analyze these problems. The chapter will be divided into the following sections:

4.1   GENERAL RULES RELATING TO BASIS

The amount of an owner's basis in his real estate depends in the first instance on the method of acquisition.

Property Acquired by Purchase—Where property is acquired by purchase the basis includes the cost of the property to the taxpayer. For purposes of basis, cost includes the amount paid to the seller plus commissions and any other expenses connected with the purchase. §1012. Where the taxpayer constructs a building rather than purchasing it, his basis includes the cost of the labor, materials and applicable overhead.[1] Depreciation on a taxpayer's own construction equipment may not be deducted currently but must be added to the basis of the property constructed.[2]

Certain carrying charges during the period of construction, notably interest and taxes paid or incurred during the construction period, may be either deducted currently or added to basis as the taxpayer elects. §266. See Chapter 7, Section 4.

Property Acquired from a Decedent—Prior to the effective date of the Tax Reform Act of 1976, the basis of property acquired by bequest, devise or inheritance, was the fair market value of the property at the time of the death of the decedent or at the alternate valuation date (six months after death) if the executor elected to utilize the alternate valuation date for estate tax purposes. §1014.

However, the Tax Reform Act of 1976 marks the end of the stepped-up estate tax value basis for most property acquired from, or passing from, a decedent after December 31, 1976. The decedent's basis will in general be carried over. However, in order to accord the estate and the beneficiaries of all decedents dying after December 31, 1976, a "fresh start" the Act provides a step-up (but not a step-down) in basis for purposes of determining taxable gain (but not loss) on all assets which a decedent is treated as holding on December 31, 1976.

Under this provision, contained in §1023, the basis for computing gain on such property is increased by the excess of the fair market value of the property on December 31, 1976, over its adjusted basis on that date. The December 31, 1976 value of real estate (as well as all other property except for marketable bonds or securities) is determined by a special rule introduced into the law in order to avoid the necessity of obtaining appraisals. The rule is applied when the date of death value of the property exceeds its adjusted basis immediately before the decedent's death. The rule assumes that the appreciation in value has occurred at a uniform rate over the holding period, generally commencing with the decedent's acquisition date and ending with his death. If then adds an amount to the decedent's basis to reflect the appreciation in value attributable to the period from acquisition date to January 1, 1977. This special valuation method must be used for all real estate even though the executor can show a different value as of December 31, 1976. For carryover basis property which was subject to depreciation, a special computation is required which has the effect of establishing a basis to the beneficiary which is computed after subtracting the post-1976 depreciation on the property.

An addition for basis is allowed for federal estate taxes attributable to property appreciation. Adjustments are also made for certain state death taxes paid by the transferee of property. However, these adjustments may not increase basis beyond fair market value.

Property Acquired by Gift—The basis to a donee is the same as it would be in the hands of the donor or the last preceding owner by whom it was not acquired by gift. This is referred to as a substituted basis since it is determined by reference to the basis of the property in the hands of another party. However, for purposes of determining loss, the basis is the same as in the hands of the donor or the last preceding owner by whom it was not acquired by gift, or the fair market value of the property at the time of the gift, whichever is lower. §1015(a). Also, the basis of gifts after September 2, 1958 is increased by the amount of any gift tax paid. §1015(a). The adjustment for gift tax paid cannot increase the basis above market value at the time of the gift. Remember that a gift of depreciable real estate results in the transfer to the donee of the potential for recapture of depreciation upon ultimate sale.

Prior to the Tax Reform Act of 1976, the basis of gift property could be increased by the full amount of the gift tax, not just the part attributable to the appreciation at the time of the gift. However, the new law limits the increase in basis to the gift tax attributable to the net appreciation on the gift. §1015(d)(6) effective as to gifts made after 12/31/76.

Basis Equal to Fair Market Value—In a number of situations the basis of property is measured by its own fair market value at the date of its receipt rather than by the value of money or property given for the property received. Some of the more common illustrations are the following: property converted from personal use to business use such as a residence;[3] property received as a dividend by an individual shareholder of a corporation, §301(d)(1); and property received in liquidation of a corporation in a taxable transaction.

Substituted or Carryover Basis—In the following situations, the basis of property to a transferee is measured by the basis to the transferor. Such a substituted basis generally results from exchanges or other transactions which are tax-free. Included in this category are property contributed to a corporation by its stockholders if the conditions of §351 are met; property contributed to a partnership by its partners or distributed by a partnership to the partners; and property transferred between affiliated corporations during a period where consolidated returns were filed.

4.2 INCLUSION OF THE MORTGAGE IN BASIS

We have previously noted that one of the principal advantages of real estate as a tax shelter is the ability to include the amount of a mortgage in the basis of the property, both for purposes of computing depreciation and computing gain or loss on ultimate sale. (Technically, of course, a mortgage is simply security for a promissory note, but in real estate parlance, it has become a shorthand term which includes both the amount payable to a seller or lender and the security therefor.) An understanding of this concept is, therefore, essential to proper evaluation of real estate investments.

(a) The Crane Rule.

In 1947, the U.S. Supreme Court decided the famous case of *Crane v. Comm'r.*[4] which established two important and related principals. First, the amount of the mortgage is included in the tax basis of property acquired subject to a mortgage and this is true whether or not the owner has any personal liability on the mortgage loan. Thus, a taxpayer can take depreciation in excess of his cash investment and this is particularly significant in the early years of ownership if the property is subject to accelerated depreciation. Second, the amount of the mortgage is also included in the amount realized for purpose of calculating the gain or loss on a sale and this is also true whether the buyer assumes the mortgage loan or merely takes title subject thereto.

In the area of partnerships, §752 is generally regarded as a codification of the *Crane* rule for the purpose of determining the basis of a partner's interest in a partnership. An increase of a partner's share of the liabilities of the partnership will be treated as a contribution of money to the partnership, thereby increasing the basis of his partnership interest. §752(a). Conversely, a decrease in a partner's share of the liabilities of a partnership will be treated as a distribution of money to the partner, thereby reducing his basis. §752(b).

Finally, §752(c) adopts the *Crane* rule as to non-recourse liabilities by providing that a liability to which property is subject shall, to the extent of the fair market value of the property, be considered as a liability of the owner of the property (the partnership). In short, between the *Crane* rule and §752, it follows that, regardless of whether property is acquired by an individual or by a group of persons via a partnership, the amount of the mortgage is included in the basis of the purchaser.

Although the Commissioner continues to attack this principle from time to time, particularly in extreme fact situations, the Courts have continued to uphold the doctrine. In a 1973 Tax Court decision IRS argued that depreciable basis cannot include a mortgage for which the taxpayer has no liability in a situation where he has no reason to protect his interest because the property is fully mortgaged and the cash flow is minimal. The Tax Court responded that although the combination of the accelerated depreciation rules and the *Crane* rule may produce a better result for the taxpayer those rules must continue to stand in the absence of contrary legislative action.[5]

(b) Qualifications and Limitations of the Crane Rule.

A 1966 Tax Court decision involved the following facts. Mayerson bought a property for $300,000 paying only $10,000 in cash and giving a 99 year non-amortized mortgage for the balance. There was no personal liability on the mortgage but it could be prepaid at the option of the owner. The price was allocated $200,000 to building and the balance to land. Mayerson later improved the property and was able to obtain institutional financing at which time he prepaid the mortgage. The Commissioner argued that the sale to Mayerson was really a 99 year lease with an option to purchase; that there was no valid debt and depreciation should, therefore, be disallowed. Holding for the taxpayer, however, the Tax Court stated that this was a bona fide arm's length purchase; the mortgage was a valid debt and constituted a part of the basis of the property.[6]

Although IRS has acquiesced in this decision, it has ruled that the *Mayerson* rule is only authority where it is absolutely clear that the property was acquired at its fair market value in an arm's length transaction creating a bona fide debt.[7] For example, where the purchaser routinely defaulted on the mortgage and failed to make interest payments, the debt was held to be illusory for tax purposes and not to constitute a proper addition to basis.[8] Similarly, where the fair market value of the property is less than the mortgage, the courts have refused to recognize the mortgage (or at least the portion of the mortgage in excess of fair market value) for tax purposes.[9] Loans by one of the partners to a partnership are also susceptible to attack, particularly where the loans are on a non-recourse basis and the other partners propose to include the amount thereof in the basis of their partnership interests. See Chapter 3, Section 5(d).

Of course, the taxpayer must acquire a bona fide interest in the property in order to claim the tax benefits of ownership. In a 1976 case, several corporations constructed projects under FHA loans and purportedly transferred title to their stockholders by quit claim deeds. The deeds were never recorded in order to avoid violating the restrictions under the FHA regulatory agreements. The corporate grantors retained ownership of the gross rents and had the duty to make the mortgage payments; all that the individual grantees acquired was the right to receive "surplus cash" permitted to be paid by FHA under the regulatory agreement. The Tax Court concluded that the right to cash receipts retained by the corporate grantors was more than a mere management fee; that the individual grantees had not assumed the risks of ownership and that the operating losses, including interest and depreciation, could not be deducted by the grantees. [9(a)]

In the analagous area of movie production companies, it has been held that third party loans to a partnership upon which no interest was paid and which gave the lender the right to participate in the profits of the venture, would not be recognized as additions to basis for tax purposes.[10] The purported lender is treated as a joint venture participant making a capital contribution.

Similarly, where money was loaned to a partnership engaged in an oil venture and repayment was contingent on the success of the venture, the creditor having an option to convert the loan into a profit participation, IRS ruled that the transaction was not a loan but an equity investment. There was unlimited profit potential and total downside risk due to the non-recourse nature of the debt.[11]

Finally, tax cost does not include obligations which are contingent and therefore not payable in all events, or which are indefinite in amount and not susceptible of present valuation.[12]

(c) Tax Reform Act of 1976: The "At Risk" Provisions.

The Tax Reform Act of 1976 imposes two types of "at risk" limitations on the amount of losses which may be deducted. Significantly, real estate is generally exempted from both provisions. Nevertheless, real estate developers and their advisers should have some familiarity with these new and important concepts.

The first type of "at risk" limitation applies to certain activities whether conducted in the form of partnership, Subchapter S corporation, personal holding company, trust, estate, or direct individual ownership. The activities broadly consist of the following: movies and videotapes, farming, equipment leasing, and oil and gas.

It would appear that the disallowance of losses in excess of the amount at risk is intended to apply at both the partnership and the partner levels, although the Act itself is not entirely clear on this point. There are various effective dates but, in general, all these "activity at risk" provisions apply to the entire calendar year 1976. §465.

The second type of "at risk" limitation is a catchall provision which applies only to partnerships and to any activity conducted by a partnership. Again, a partnership whose principal activity is investing in real estate, other than mineral property, is exempted. This provision applies to all activities other than real estate conducted in partnership form. It would cover general partnerships if nonrecourse financing is used, where the partner is not personally liable as a result of a separate guaranty or other contract. This provision is effective for liabilities incurred after December 31, 1976. §704(d) as amended.

4.3　DEMOLITION OF BUILDINGS

As a general rule, when the owner of a building voluntarily demolishes it, the useful life of the building has been terminated. Accordingly, such demolition will produce a deductible loss. The amount of the loss is equal to the adjusted basis of the buildings which have been demolished increased by the net cost of demolition and decreased by any proceeds from the demolition.[13] This assumes, of course, that the building is business property or property held for the production of income; the demolition of a personal residence or other non-business property would not produce a deductible loss. Since no sale or exchange has occurred, the demolition loss is not subject to the deduction limitations applicable to capital losses.

A different rule applies, however, where real estate is purchased with the intent to demolish the building, either immediately or later. In such cases the regulations provide that no deduction is allowed; the entire basis of the property is allocated to the land only and such basis is increased by the net cost of demolition or decreased by the net proceeds from demolition.[14] Since the question of whether or not a loss is allowable depends upon a subjective condition—whether the intention to demolish existed prior to the date of purchase—most of the controversies in this area involve disputes on measuring this condition. The regulations contain a list of factors for determining the factual question as to whether the plan for demolition was formed subsequent to the date of purchase. For example, a short delay between date of acquisition and date of demolition or evidence of prohibitive remodeling costs suggests that the intention to demolish existed at the time of purchase. Conversely, substantial improvements of the buildings after acquisition or prolonged use of the buildings suggests that the intention was formed subsequent to the date of purchase.

Mere holding of the property for a period of time does not guarantee success. In a recent Tax Court case, the taxpayer held a property for one year before the demolition. The Commissioner alleged that the property was acquired with the intent to demolish notwithstanding this holding period and the renting of the property. The Court agreed and disallowed the demolition loss.[15] Nevertheless in close cases it would appear to be prudent to postpone any actions relating to demolition (or ideally even forming the proscribed intent) until after the property is acquired.

See Chapter 6, Section 2, for a discussion of demolition losses by a landlord incurred to prepare the premises for a tenant.

4.4   APPORTIONMENT OF REAL ESTATE TAXES

It is customary for a buyer and a seller of real estate to agree to apportion taxes between them for the year of sale. Normally the real estate taxes are payable subsequent to the date of closing so the seller pays his share of the taxes by means of a credit to the buyer which is one of the items on the closing statement. The tax law is entirely consistent with this practice. §164(d) provides that where real estate is sold, the taxes for the entire year are apportioned between buyer and seller on the basis of the number of days ownership of the property by each party. That portion of the tax allocable to the real property tax year which ends on the day before the date of sale is considered as imposed on the seller; and the tax allocable to that part of the tax year which begins on the date of sale is treated as being imposed on the buyer. Each party is entitled to deduct the share of the tax which is treated as imposed on him. Furthermore, this allocation formula applies whether or not the parties themselves actually make an allocation of the tax. For example, even if a buyer actually paid the entire tax, his deduction would nevertheless be limited to the portion of the tax allocable to him according to the date of closing.[16] The term "real property tax year" refers to the period which, under the law imposing the tax, is regarded as the period to which the tax relates. Thus, it is entirely a question of state or local law.

> Example: Assume the real property tax year runs from January 1 to December 31 and that a sale is closed October 1. The seller would be entitled to deduct that portion of the tax allocable to the period he held the property (273/365 of the tax) and the purchaser would be entitled to deduct the tax for the balance of the year (92/365 of the tax).

The prior discussion related to the question of how much of the tax is deductible by each party. Another question which must be considered is the proper tax year for each party to claim his deduction. The first step in determining the time for deduction depends on which party was liable for the real estate tax and when the tax was payable. If neither party is liable (for example, when local law provides that the taxes are only a lien against the real estate involved and not a personal liability of the owner) it is assumed that the party who owned the property on the lien date was liable. §164(d)(2)(A). With this rule in mind let us examine the treatment of taxpayers who follow the cash basis of accounting.

Cash Basis Seller—If the seller is on the cash basis and either (1) the purchaser is liable (actually or constructively) for the tax for the real property tax year or (2) the seller is liable for the tax for such year but the tax is not payable until after the date of sale, then the portion of the tax which is treated as imposed on the seller under the general rule discussed above is considered as having been paid by him in the year of sale.[17] In other words, the credit which seller grants the purchaser on the closing statement is equivalent to payment of the tax. In a most liberal approach, however, the regulations provide that such nonpaying seller has an alternative with respect to the year in which he takes the deduction. He may take it in the year of sale or it may be claimed in the year in which the tax is actually paid or an amount representing such tax is paid to the purchaser or to a mortgagee, trustee or other person having an interest in the property as security. This is an obvious tax saving opportunity since it permits the seller to claim the deduction in the year when it will do him the most good. If the seller was liable for the tax himself and it was payable before completion of the sale, then he deducts his share of the tax at the time he actually pays it.

> Example: The real property tax year is the calendar year of 1976. The property was sold on December 1, 1976 which is the 336th day of the year. Purchaser is deemed to be liable for the tax because he held the property on the lien date. Seller is entitled to deduct 335/365ths of the tax and purchaser is entitled to deduct the balance of the tax. The tax was actually paid on March 15, 1977. Assuming a cash basis seller on the calendar year, he can elect to deduct his share of the tax on his 1976 return, the year of sale, or on his 1977 return, the year of payment.

The Cash Basis Purchaser—If the seller was liable for the tax (actually or constructively) the regulations give the purchaser a similar option regarding the time of deduction. He may deduct his share of tax in the year of sale or in a later year when the tax is actually paid or an amount representing the tax is paid to the seller or to a mortgagee, trustee or other person having an interest in the property as security.[18]

> Example: The real property tax year is the calendar year 1976. The seller is liable for the tax. The property was sold on December 1, 1976 and the tax was paid on March 15, 1977. Assuming a cash basis purchaser on the calendar year, the regulations provide that he can elect to deduct his share of the tax in 1976, the year of sale, or 1977, the year of payment.

If the purchaser himself is liable for the tax (for example, where the sale takes place after the lien date) he deducts his share of the tax in his return for the year of actual payment.

The regulations give special rules applicable to accrual basis taxpayers who have not elected under §461(c) to accrue real estate taxes ratably over the period to which they related.[19]

Excess Payment of Taxes. Supposing the contract of sale does not follow the statutory apportionment formula. Assume, for example, that a purchaser or a seller pays a greater amount of taxes than he is permitted to deduct under the rules outlined above. How is such excess payment treated?

As to the purchaser, the non-deductible tax paid by him is a capital expenditure which is added to the basis of the property.[20] If the property is not depreciable it follows that the purchaser loses the tax benefit of such payment until he sells the property when it will enter into the computation of his gain. As to the seller, on the other hand, the non-deductible portion of the tax paid by him may be treated in one of two ways. If he simply pays excess taxes in the year of sale, he adds the excess to his basis for the purpose of computing gain or loss on the sale. However, if in his return for a prior taxable year, he deducted taxes in excess of the amount properly allocated to him, the excess amount, subject to the tax benefit rules in §111, must be included in his income for the year of sale.[21]

> Example: The real property tax year is the calendar year but the tax is due and payable on October 1 of the preceeding year. On October 1, 1975, a cash basis seller pays the tax for 1976 and deducts the payment on his 1975 return. He sells the property on June 30 of the following year and only 180/365ths of the tax for 1976 is considered as being imposed upon him. The excess deduction is includable on his income for the year of sale assuming that he received the full benefit of a deduction in the year of payment.

4.5   LOANS DISTINGUISHED FROM PURCHASES IN SALE-LEASEBACK TRANSACTIONS.

Assume that A sells real estate to B and that A simultaneously leases the property from B under a long term lease. Assume further that A attempts to retain control over the ultimate disposition of the property upon termination of the lease, for example, by including a contractual provision that the property must be sold back to A. The fact that both parties to the transaction have agreed to treat it as a sale is not necessarily binding upon IRS or the courts. The transaction may be treated as a loan from the purported buyer to the purported seller. In that case, only the portion of the rental payments attributable to interest on the presumed loan will be deductible by A although he may be entitled to claim depreciation on the theory that he has, in effect, retained title. No gain or loss will be recognized on the purported sale.

The entire transaction must be examined carefully to determine whether it will be treated as a loan or a purchase by B, but the following factors will normally influence a court to classify the transaction as a loan: long term of the lease, option to renew the lease, option to repurchase particularly at a low price or where the rental payments are credited against the purchase price, and lack of economic substance.[22] In one case, the Tax Court used as a test whether the taxpayer has "retained all the risks, responsibilities and duties of an owner of real property." The Court held the transaction in question to be a mortgage loan rather than a sale-leaseback. The seller had an option to re-purchase at a minimal price, there was a credit for a portion of the rent which was "applied to reduction of principal," an option to renew the lease with rental payments decreasing in subsequent terms and the rent payments abated upon damage, condemnation or other destruction of the property so that the risk of loss would fall on the tenant.[23]

4.6   PROBLEMS OF THE LAND DEVELOPER.

Land developers have some unique tax problems. In a sense, the developer is a manufacturer converting raw land into a finished product—developed lots. For tax purposes, he must determine which of the development costs are to be deducted currently, which are to be capitalized as additions to the basis of the property to be recovered as the lots are sold and which are to be capitalized as the cost of separate assets. The topic is a complex one and we will only attempt to hit some of the more important rules.[24]

Some of the principles discussed earlier in this chapter apply equally to land developers. For example, the basis of land purchased includes the cost of the land whether paid in cash or by means of the mortgage loan, and this is true whether or not the developer is personally liable. The developer is not allowed to deduct currently amounts which are properly allocated to land cost. This includes surveys, legal fees involving title, grading and excavating costs,[25] the cost of demolishing buildings where demolition is required to properly prepare the land, as well as interest, taxes and other expenses which have been incurred by the seller but are paid by the buyer.[26] The sum of all of these items becomes the total basis for the land which must be apportioned among the several parcels on an equitable basis. Equitable does not necessarily mean ratable, and more valuable parcels must be charged with a greater portion of the total basis.

What about off-site improvements? These are often major expenditures which are made either because they are required by local law in order to obtain approval of the subdivision or because the developer feels the improvements will benefit the entire project. Included in this category are such items as access roads, bridges, utility lines and in more recent years parks, golf courses, artificial lakes, etc. The cost of such off-site improvements cannot be deducted but must be allocated to all of the lots in the parcel.

> Example: Developer was required to build a shelter on a parksite in order to obtain approval of his subdivision plat. The improvement added no value to the remaining lots. Taxpayer argued that the cost should be a current business expense, but the Tax Court held that the construction of the improvement was a "capital outlay to be identified with the other costs of the subdivision project" and therefore should be capitalized.[27]

Sometimes IRS will contend that the cost of the improvement cannot be allocated to the lots in the subdivision but must be capitalized as a separate asset to be written off over its useful life. In that event, the developer is better off to divest himself of title by conveying the improvement to a third party such as a homeowners' association or a municipality. In one case, for example, where a developer was unable to get the assistance of the local authorities, he transferred the utility which he had constructed to an operating company which issued deeds granting the homeowners the rights and obligations connected with the system. It was held that the systems' prorata cost was included in the basis of each house.[28] On the other hand, if the developer retains an improvement to operate at even nominal revenue, some case law may preclude the allocation of the cost thereof as an off-site improvement. For example, developers have been compelled to capitalize and depreciate the costs of recreational areas and water supply systems where they retained ownership.[29] Therefore, the developer must chose between two alternatives: Is he better off to divest himself of title and thereby get the tax benefit of allocating the cost of the improvement among the lots or homes being developed or is he better off to retain ownership and thereby get the business benefits of control of the facility and the possible economic benefit flowing from the operation of a revenue-producing project such as a golf course or a utility.

A developer may add to the cost of the property not only his actual development costs but the estimated costs of future improvements as well, provided that he is contractually obligated to make the improvements and the costs are not recoverable through depreciation. In updating the procedures for such estimated costs, IRS has held that after a subdivider has received permission to add prospective costs to the basis of the property sold, a follow-up statement must be filed each year with his income tax return containing certain designated information.[30]

Sometimes a developer charges the buyers of the homes in a subdivision for so-called tie-in fees permitting the buyers to participate in the sewage disposal system. The developer uses such tie-in fees to finance the construction costs of the system. It has been held that such fees constitute taxable income to the developer and cannot be excluded from income on the grounds that they are capital contributions.[31] Similarly, in a 1975 ruling, IRS held that effective February 1, 1976, utility corporations whose rates are subject to regulation must include in gross income amounts received from groups of customers, such as builders, contractors, or potential homeowners in a subdivision, who are called upon to advance funds to aid in the construction of utility facilities.[32]

Finally, a developer should remember that he has an election to either deduct interest and taxes or to capitalize such items under §266. Assuming that he has no outside income during the development period, capitalization of such carrying charges is normally advisable. The election is annual if the real estate is unproductive and unimproved, but once construction of the improvements on a project begins, the election is binding.[33]

FOOTNOTES FOR CHAPTER FOUR

[1]Regs.1.263(a)-1 and -2. In addition, basis may include the purchase price of property demolished. See *W.I. Nash,* 60 T.C. 503(1974).

[2]*Comm. v Idaho Power Co.,* 418 U.S.1, 34 AFTR2d 74-5244 (1974).

[3]*Court J. Beisinger,* 1968 P-H TC Memo ¶68,146. See Reg.1.167(g)-1.For depreciation purposes adjusted basis on the date of conversion must be used if it is less than fair market value.

[4]331 U.S.1, 35 AFTR 776(1947). Although the *Crane* case applied to inherited property, the rule has been extended to include property purchased subject to tax liens, *Blackstone Theatre Co.,* 12 T.C.801 (1949) acq., and purchases without assumption of the mortgage debt, *Woodsam Associates, Inc. v Comm.,* 198 F.2d 357, 42 AFTR 505 (CA2, 1952).

[5]*David F. Bolger,* 59 T.C. 760 (1973), acq. See, however, the discussion relating to the *Davis* case cited at footnote 9(a) in the following section. The Bolger decision was distinguished in *Davis.*

[6]*Manuel D. Mayerson,* 47 T.C. 340 (1966), acq.

[7]Rev.Rul.69-77, 1969-1 C.B.59.

[8]*Leonard Marcus, 1971 P-H TC Memo ¶71,299; Marvin M. May,* 1972 P-H #72,070, (depreciation deduction disallowed on purchase of TV films on the grounds that the buyer never intended to pay the $365,000 purchase price and the seller never intended to require him to pay same.) See also *Mark Bixby,* 58 T.C.575(1972), (sham arrangement involving inflated price on a non-recourse basis).

[9]*Edna Morris, 59 T.C.21 (1972) acq.; Est. of Charles T. Franklin* v. Comm, — F.2d —, 38 AFTR 2d 76-6164 (CA9, 1976) (Purchase price less than fair market value of the property, interest and depreciation disallowed).

[9(a)] *Maclin P. Davis, Jr., et al.* 66 TC260 (1976). In *Arnold L. Ginsburg,* 1976 P-H TC Memo ¶76,199, the Court held that where a prospectus on a cattle breeding limited partnership showed that there would be no economic gain on the investment, only tax savings, the loss would be disallowed on the ground that the arrangement wasn't entered into for profit.

[10]*Carnegie Productions, Inc.,* 59 T.C. 642(1973).

[11]Rev. Rul. 72-250, 1972-2 C.B. 394. See also Rev. Rul. 72-135, 1972-1 C.B. 200, holding that a non-recourse loan by a general partner to the partnership was a capital contribution which the limited partners could not include in their basis.

[12]*Lloyd H. Redford,* 28 T.C. 773(1957) (obligation payable out of future earnings, not payable in all events).

[13]Reg. 1.165-3(b)(1).

[14]Reg. 1.165-3(a)(1).

[15]*William I. Nash,* 60 T.C. 503(1973). Depreciation deductions were limited to the net rental income in view of the intent to demolish.

[16]*Ernest A. Pederson,* 46 T.C. 155 (1966), Reg. 1.164-6(b).

[17]Reg. 1.164-6(d)(1).

[18]Reg. 1.164-6(d)(2).

[19]Reg. 1.164-6(d)(6).

[20]§1012; Reg. 1.1012-1(b).

[21]Reg. 1.164-6(d)(5).

[22]*Helvering v. Lazarus,* 308 U.S. 252, 23 AFTR 778(1939); *Karl R. Martin,* 44 T.C. 731 (1965); *Southeastern Canteen Co. v. Comm.* 410F.2d 615, 23 AFTR 2d 69-1362 (CA6, 1969).

[23]*Paul W. Frenzel,* 1963 PH TC Memo ¶63,276. To the same effect *Frank Lyon v. U.S.,* 536 F.2d 746, 38 AFTR2d 76-5060 (CA8, 1976). See chapter 6, Sec 6. 26 U.S. Supreme Court has granted certiorari in *Lyon*

[24]For a thorough discussion, see Sandison & Waters, "Tax Planning for the Land Developer," 37 J. Tax 80 (Aug, 1972) and 37 J. Tax. 154 (Sept, 1972).

[25]Rev. Rul. 65-265, 1965-2 C.B. 52.

[26]*Broadhead, Est. of, v. Comm.* 391 F.2d 841, 21 AFTR 2d 851 (CA5, 1968) (interest expense); Reg. 1.164-6 (taxes); *Jack T. Foster,* 1966 P-H T.C Memo ¶66,273 (other expenses).

[27]*Lots, Inc.* 49 T.C. 541(1968).

[28]*Willow Terrace Development Co.,* 40 T.C. 889 (1963), aff'd. 345 F.2d 933, 15 AFTR 2d 1108 (CA5, 1963).

[29]*Biscayne Bay islands Co.,* 23 BTA 731 (1931); *The Colony, Inc.,* 26 T.C. 30 (1956).

[30]Rev. Proc. 75-25, 1975-1 C.B. 720.

[31]*State Farm Road Corp.,* 65 TC 217 (1975).

[32]Rev. Rul. 75-557, 1975-2 C.B.33 (Clarified in Rev. Rul, 76-61 1976-1 C.B. 12). The ruling revokes Rev. Rul, 58-555, 1958-2 C.B.25, which held such receipts to be non-taxable.

[33]Reg. 1.266-1(c)(2)(ii)(a).

Part 2

TAX PROBLEMS
IN OPERATING
REAL ESTATE PROJECTS

5

EFFECTIVE

MANAGEMENT

OF DEPRECIATION

From a tax and an accounting point of view, depreciation means distributing the cost of a capital asset over its estimated useful life in a systematic manner.[1] It is obvious that property used in a business gradually wears out and becomes inefficient and obsolete. It would be most unrealistic to postpone recognition of that decline in value for tax purposes until the property was actually disposed of and a loss incurred. Rather, the tax law, as well as good accounting procedure, recognizes that a portion of this loss should be deducted each year as an offset against the income realized from the use of the property. Accordingly, the Internal Revenue Code allows "as a depreciation deduction a reasonable allowance for the exhaustion, wear and tear (including a reasonable allowance for obsolescence) (1) of property used in a trade or business or (2) of property held for the production of income."[2] The previous chapter dealt with the *basis* of property which is used to compute depreciation—the starting point in determining depreciation. This chapter will deal with the methods and techniques of measuring depreciation and the tax consequences arising from the disposition of depreciable real estate. The discussion will be divided into the following sections:

5.1 Real Estate Eligible for Depreciation.
    (a) Trade or Business Use Required.
    (b) Depreciation of Land and Land Improvements.
    (c) Leased Property.

5.1   REAL ESTATE ELIGIBLE FOR DEPRECIATION

(a)   Trade or Business Use Required.

Under the Internal Revenue Code, only property which is used in a trade or business or which is held for the production of income can be depreciated. §167(a)(1) and (2). Accordingly, the following types of property are not eligible for depreciation: property held for personal use such as a residence, although if the same building is used partially for business purposes and partially for residential purposes, depreciation can be taken on the business portion of the property; property which is held primarily for sale; and property that has been abandoned and is no longer used as a trade or business asset.

Note, however, that depreciation is allowable on property which is held for the production of income even though the property is not currently producing income or is operating at a loss. However, there must be a true "profit inspired use" and not merely a use which provides for reimbursement of expenses.[3]

(b) Depreciation of Land and Land Improvements.

In order to be depreciable, property must have a limited life which is capable of measurement. If it has an indefinite life, it is not depreciable. Accordingly, land is generally not depreciable whether it is income producing or not.[4] However, the cost of certain types of land improvements may be subject to depreciation. As a general rule, land improvements are not depreciable if they permanently improve the land but they are depreciable if they improve the land only so long as a particular building or structure remains useful. In the latter case, the land may be thought of as being a part of the building. The following cases and rulings illustrate the treatment of land improvements by the courts and by IRS.

In 1965 IRS ruled that land improvement costs which were incurred after initial clearing and grading (such as excavating, grading and removal costs) are subject to depreciation if they are "directly associated" with buildings rather than "inextricably associated" with the land.[5] The ruling in question involved roads connecting certain facilities which had to be graded at a certain angle because of the weight of the materials that would move over them.

In a follow-up ruling in 1968 IRS made explicit the reasons why the grading costs were depreciable. The roads were so directly associated with the total business complex that if the buildings were retired, abandoned or reconstructed, it would be necessary to modify the construction of the roads.[6]

In a case involving the preparation of land for a mobile home park, IRS disallowed depreciation for the cost of grading and shaping the land, carving out spaces for pads, patios and road beds and providing necessary landscaping and shrubbery. However, the taxpayer prevailed in court on a showing that any other use of the land would require removal of the pads and patios and reshaping of the land.[7]

The cost of designing and constructing lagoons is depreciable over a period of 20 years. However, where the fill produced by dredging the lagoons is used to improve surrounding land, the basis for depreciation must be reduced by the value of the fill.[8] Also, the cost of excavating water canals and dredging channels and slips is depreciable if the "asset is actually exhausting and such exhaustion is susceptible of measurement."[9]

(c) Leased Property.

Both the landlord and the tenant of real estate are entitled to depreciate their respective investments. The landlord claims depreciation on his basis in the property. Also, he may depreciate the cost of any improvements made by the tenant which constitute rental payments to him. However, if the lease requires the tenant to return property of equal value at the expiration of the lease, then the landlord is not entitled to a depreciation deduction.[10]

> *Suggestion:* A lessor would be well advised to protect his deduction by properly wording the lease. It could require the lessee to return the property at the end of the term in the same condition as at the beginning of the term "reasonable wear and tear excepted." Such a clause will protect the deduction for the lessor.[11]

The tenant may claim depreciation on improvements constructed by him. If the useful life of the improvements is less than the term of the lease, he depreciates the improvements over their useful life and may use a method of depreciation as if he were the owner of the property.[12] On the other hand, if the useful life of the improvements is longer than the term of the lease and there is no renewal option, then the tenant's investment is amortized on a straight-line basis over the remaining term of the lease. If he has an option to renew, the tenant may be required to take into account the renewal term. This is covered in Code §178. See Chapter 6, Section 17.

5.2 DETERMINING THE RATE OF DEPRECIATION

Depreciation is recovered over the useful life of the property, i.e., the period over which the property is reasonably expected to be useful to the taxpayer in his trade or business or in connection with the production of income. This useful life determines the rate of depreciation. The taxpayer can determine the useful life in one of two ways. First the government has established guideline lives which reflect the average replacement policy for taxpayers in various industries. Second, the taxpayer can by-pass the recommended guidelines and claim depreciation based on his own experience with similar assets and certain other factors.

(a) Guideline Rates

Following are the useful lives which will be accepted under the government guidelines, i.e., if a taxpayer does not claim depreciation on new buildings at a rate greater than that indicated below, his rate will normally be accepted by I.R.S.[13]

Type of Building	Useful Life
Apartments	40 years
Banks	50 years
Dwellings	45 years
Factories	45 years
Garages	45 years
Grain elevators	60 years
Hotels	40 years
Loft Buildings	50 years
Machine Shops	45 years
Office Buildings	45 years
Stores	50 years
Theatres	40 years
Warehouses	60 years

(b) Bypassing the Guidelines

Where the taxpayer can establish a useful life which is shorter than that established by the guidelines, he is free to do so and compute depreciation at the increased rate. However, he must establish facts and circumstances which justify that his case is an exception to the general rule.[14]

Example: The Tioga Building was hastily constructed at the lowest possible cost in order to meet a sudden demand for bulk office space. It was so substandard in construction and design that it could not be modernized to compete with newer buildings. Recognizing this from the outset, the owners elected not to spend any money on the building. They intended to replace it long before the end of its physical life. So, they claimed depreciation based on a 32-year useful life. The District Court held that useful life is measured by use in the taxpayer's business—not by the physical life of an asset. Accordingly, a 32-year useful life was reasonable under these circumstances.[15]

In a number of recent cases taxpayers have been able to persuade the courts that the economic life of property was less than its physical life and depreciation should be based on the shorter economic life.

Example: The owners of a shopping center claimed a 19-year useful life for their property based on the length of the major tenant's lease. However, IRS claimed that the proper useful life was 33-1/3 years. At the trial, the taxpayer's accountant testified that it was his experience that the length of the major tenant's lease determines the useful life of the buildings in the center. When this lease expires, a new building is normally put up by the major tenant with the satellite stores then following suit. Recognizing the accountant as an expert in the field, the Tax Court approved the 19-year life.[16]

Example: A Holiday Inn motel and restaurant with a 50-year physical life was accorded a 33-1/3-year useful economic life (although the taxpayer failed to show that obsolescence justified a 20 year life).[17]

(c) Component Parts Depreciation

The depreciation rates discussed above, with respect to the recommended guideline lives as well as in the various court decisions, relate to an *entire* building. Of course, a building actually consists of various components such as the roof, plumbing fixtures, electical system, heating system, etc., each of which depreciates at a different rate. Where it is advantageous to the taxpayer to do so, he is permitted to depreciate new construction by determining the useful life of *each component part* and thereby determining a composite rate of depreciation.[18] This composite rate frequently exceeds the rate permitted where the entire building is treated as a single unit.

Example: Here are the useful lives which the Tax Court upheld for the components of a new shopping center.[19] Although the breakdown as well as the useful lives will vary from case to case, you can see that component parts depreciation can substantially increase the amount of the deduction.

Item Depreciated	Yrs. of Life	%
Plumbing		
Bathtubs, lavatories, etc	25	4
Faucets, valves	15	6-2/3
Pipes, iron, cold-water	25	4
Iron, hot-water, steam	20	5
Pumps, suction and pressure	13	7-2/3

Roofs

Asbestos	25	4
Asphalt and tar	15	6-2/3
Tarred felt	10	10
Switchboards, electric	25	4
Telephone equipment	20	5

Suggestion: Where the taxpayer plans to utilize component parts depreciation, it is essential that accurate records be kept detailing the costs of the various components. If a construction contract is granted to a general contractor, it should also contain a breakdown of the contract price *by components*. A breakdown of this type should probably be standard in new or remodeled construction.

Although IRS originally held that component depreciation could not be used by the purchaser of a used building, the courts held otherwise. In a 1970 case, a District Court held that a used building could be depreciated on the component parts method provided that the owner had a reasonable basis for allocating his total cost among the components,[20] and IRS eventually accepted that rule.

Comment: IRS maintains that depreciation deductions resulting from the component method must not differ substantially from deductions available under the composite method. Rev. Rul. 68-4, 1968-1 C.B. 77. However, the Tax Court has refused to adopt this position. In a 1975 case, the Court found that the lives utilized for the component assets were proper and that any difference in the amount of the depreciation deduction which would have resulted if the composite method had been adopted and the guideline lives had been used, was irrelevant.[21] This case contains a determination by the Tax Court of the useful lives of 37 components of a 16-story office building as well as the lives claimed by the taxpayer and by IRS for those same components.

(d) Salvage Value.

Normally, the amount of investment in property on which depreciation can be claimed must be reduced by salvage value, namely, the amount recoverable upon the sale or other disposition of the property when its useful life is exhausted. Net salvage value is defined as salvage value, less the cost of removal. The determination of salvage value and net salvage value of buildings can be quite difficult. Normally, the cost of removing the building and its foundation will exceed any scrap value obtained by the sale of the components of the building. Therefore, net salvage value is normally zero and may even be a negative figure.[22] Also, salvage value need not be taken into account if the guideline lives of Rev. Proc. 62-21 are used or if the declining balance method of depreciation is used. In both situations, however, salvage value continues to serve as a limit on total depreciation allowable; the property cannot be depreciated below its salvage value.

5.3 SELECTING THE METHOD OF DEPRECIATION

After the txpayer has determined whether his property qualifies as depreciable real estate and after he has determined the rate of depreciation to be utilized (guideline or non-guideline and component parts or composite rate), he must select a method of figuring depreciation. The depreciation methods in most general use are the straight-line method, the declining-balance method, and the sum-of-the-year's-digits method.

Consistency is not required. A taxpayer is permitted to use a different depreciation method for each asset or asset account. For example, straight-line depreciation can be claimed on one property or one group of assets and declining-balance depreciation may be claimed on another property or another group of assets. Moreover, it is not unusual for tax depreciation to differ from the depreciation method utilized in preparing financial statements. Many taxpayers elect to take accelerated depreciation deductions on the returns, thereby minimizing income taxes, while taking smaller amounts of depreciation on the books of account, thereby maximizing the earnings reported for non-tax purposes.

(a) Straight-Line Method

The straight-line method of depreciation is probably the most frequently used method because it has the advantage of simplicity. The taxpayer simply spreads the depreciation equally over the useful life of the property until it is fully written off.

> *Example:* Taxpayer constructed an apartment building at a cost of $1,000,000. (This does not include the cost of the land on which the building is located.) The building has a useful life estimated at 40 years, consistent with the guideline rate. Under these circumstances, the taxpayer can claim straight-line depreciation each year equal to 1/40th of $1,000,000, or $25,000 per year.

(b) Accelerated Methods—Residential Property.

§167(j) added to the Code by the Tax Reform Act of 1969 imposed limitations on the use of accelerated methods of depreciation if construction of the property started after July 24, 1969, or if the property was acquired after that date. (The old rules continued to apply if the construction or acquisition was pursuant to a contract for such construction or acquisition or for the permanent financing thereof which was binding on the taxpayer on July 25, 1969, and at all times thereafter.) The type of accelerated depreciation permitted, however, depends on whether the property is residential or non-residential and on whether it was new or used property when the taxpayer acquired it.

(1) New Property—In the case of new residential property the taxpayer is permitted to use the double-declining balance (sometimes referred to as the 200% declining balance) method or the sum-of-the-year's-digits method. These methods permit the acceleration of disproportionate amounts of the deductions in the early years following the purchase or construction of property.

Double-Declining Method—Where property qualifies for accelerated depreciation, the double-declining balance method produces the greatest deductions in the early years. The deductions are progressively smaller in later years. Under this method a uniform rate which cannot exceed 200% of the applicable straight-line rate is applied each year to the adjusted basis of the property (meaning basis as reduced by depreciation previously taken).

Example: Taxpayer constructed an apartment building at a cost of $1,000,000, including his own investment and the construction mortgage proceeds, but excluding land. The building is estimated to have a useful life of 40 years, thereby providing a straight-line rate of 2 1/2% per year. Taxpayer elects to use the double-declining balance method of depreciation. Accordingly, he utilizes a 5% rate (twice the straight-line rate) on the declining depreciation balance. Following are his depreciation deductions and his accumulated depreciation.

YEAR	ANNUAL DEPRECIATION	COMPUTATION FORMULA	CUMULATIVE DEPRECIATION
1	$50,000	5% x ($1,000,000)	$ 50,000
2	47,500	5% x ($1,000,000 - $50,000)	97,500
3	45,125	5% x ($1,000,000 - $97,500)	142,625
4	42,870	5% x ($1,000,000 - $142,625)	185,495
5	40,730	5% x ($1,000,000 - $185,495)	226,225

Note that in the declining-balance method, the *rate* remains constant throughout the computation and only the *basis* on which the depreciation is computed declines.

Sum-of-the-Year's-Digits Method—Under the sum-of-year's-digits method, the depreciation deductions are almost as high as the double-declining method in the early years, and within a few years, the cumulative deductions are actually greater. This method is applied by utilizing a decreasing fraction each year to compute the depreciation deduction. Although the denominator of the fraction is constant, the numerator is reduced each year. For example, assume the taxpayer acquires a piece of equipment with a useful life of five years. In order to compute depreciation, he would utilize a fraction. The denominator is the sum of the number of all the years of useful life of the asset, or 15 in this illustration (5 + 4 + 3 + 2 + 1). The numerator of the fraction for the first year is five, thereby producing depreciation equal to 5/15ths of the depreciable base. Each year the numerator is reduced by one (4/15ths during the second year, 3/15ths during the third year, etc.) so that the amount of allowable depreciation declines in later years.

Illustration: Assume the same facts as above, a $1,000,000 building, excluding land, with a useful life of 40 years. Following are the amounts of allowable depreciation under the sum-of-the-year's-digits method during the first five years.

YEAR	ANNUAL DEPRECIATION	CUMULATIVE DEPRECIATION
1	$48,780	$ 48,780
2	47,560	96,340
3	45,340	142,680
4	45,120	187,800
5	43,900	231,700

The mathematics of this method may become quite complex. Fortunately, most tax services contain charts and tables which give the decimal equivalents of the sum-of-the-year's-digits fractions assuming various useful lives.

(2) Used Property—Used residential property with a remaining useful life of 20 years or more qualifies for the 125% declining-balance method. §167(j)(5). This method is similar to the double-declining balance method except that the permitted rate is limited to 125% of the straight-line rate. Thus, where property qualifies for a 4% straight-line rate, depreciation of 5% can be claimed under this method. Where the useful life of the property is less than 20 years, only the straight-line method is available. §167(j)(4). Of course, if the property was acquired before the July 24, 1969 cut-off date the old rules apply; in that case, used residential property can be depreciated on the 150% declining-balance method.

Normally, if the taxpayer is the owner of a residential building when the first tenant moves in, he qualifies as the first user and may claim 200% declining-balance depreciation. Where property is acquired from a builder-developer, however, occupancy by existing tenants may not be conclusive. If the builder-developer held the property for sale, he is not entitled to claim depreciation even if the building was occupied by tenants.[23] In that event, the ultimate purchaser of the property should be regarded as the first user entitled to claim depreciation.[24]

(c) Accelerated Methods—Non-Residential Property.

(1) New Property—Prior to July 24, 1969, non-residential property such as office buildings, shopping centers, etc., was treated the same as residential property and, therefore, qualified for the double-declining balance and the sum-of-the-year's-digits methods of depreciation. New non-residential property acquired after the cut-off date, however, is limited to the 150% declining-balance method; i.e., the rate of depreciation cannot exceed 150% of the applicable straight-line rate.

(2) Used Property—If acquired after July 24, 1969, all used commercial property is limited to the straight-line method of depreciation.

(d) Definitions of Residential Property and First User Status.

As the foregoing discussion demonstrates, in order to determine the appropriate rate and method of depreciation, it is first necessary to determine whether the property is residential or non-residential and also whether the taxpayer is the first user of the property. Property qualifies as residential property if at least 80% of the gross rental income from the building is from "dwelling units." §167(j)(2). A house or an apartment building used to provide living accomodations constitutes a dwelling unit, but a unit in a hotel, motel or other establishment, more than half of the units of which are used on a transient basis, does not constitute a dwelling unit. §167(k)(3)(C).

The following chart summarizes the maximum write-offs permitted for various types of real estate (residential and non-residential) according to the dates of construction or acquisition.

ALLOWABLE DEPRECIATION

Type of Property	Date of Construction or Acquisition	Maximum Write-off Permitted
Residential Real Estate		
New Property	1954 and subsequent years	200% declining-balance or sum-of-year's-digits methods.

Type of Property Residential Real Estate	Date of Construction or Acquisition	Maximum Write-off Permitted
Used Property	Prior to 7/25/69	150% declining-balance method.
Used Property (useful life of 20 years or more)	After 7/24/69	125% declining-balance method.
Rehabilitation of low-income rental housing	After 7/24/69	Straight-line method, 60-month life.
Non-Residential Real Estate		
New Property	1954 and subsequent years through 7/24/69	200% declining-balance or sum-of-the-year's-digits method.
New Property	After 7/24/69	150% declining-balance method.
Used Property	Prior to 7/25/69	150% declining-balance method.
Used Property	After 7/24/69	Straight-line method only.

(e) Switch to Straight-Line Method

There will always be an unrecovered amount under the declining-balance method since the balance never declines to zero. Also, it is apparent that after a number of years the amount of depreciation is reduced substantially. To avoid these problems, the taxpayer may switch at any time from double declining-balance to straight-line depreciation without the consent of IRS.[25] Once the change is made, the balance of the unrecovered cost is written off through equal annual allowances over the remaining life of the property.

(f) Rehabilitation of Low-Cost Rental Housing.

Under §167(k)(2), expenditures which are incurred after July 24, 1969, for the rehabilitation of a dwelling unit in low-income rental housing may, if the taxpayer so elects, be depreciated under the straight-line method over a five-year period and with no salvage value. This election is available only if the aggregate amount expended per unit exceeds $3,000 in a two-year period, and no more than $15,000 of expenditures per dwelling unit may be depreciated in this manner. The Tax Reform Act of 1976 increased the allowable expenditure to $20,000 per unit effective after 12/31/75. Furthermore, the election is only available with respect to expenditures incurred by the taxpayer. Although this provision was originally scheduled to expire for expenditures incurred after January 1, 1975, it has been extended to January 1, 1978. It is possible, of course, that additional extensions will be passed in the future. A dwelling unit will be considered low-income rental housing while rented to individuals of low or moderate income, or if not rented, the rental indicates that it is held for occupancy by such individuals. The final regulations under this section will determine low or moderate income levels by relying upon the determination of low and moderate income as made by the Department of Housing and Urban Development (HUD). The Tax Reform Act of 1976 makes the test for qualifying under this section the Leased Housing Program under §8 of the Housing Act of 1937. It also provides that expenses under a binding contract for rehabilitation begun on or after January 1, 1978, shall be deemed incurred before that date. Rehabilitation expenditures are defined as amounts chargeable to capital for property or additions or improvements to property or related facilities connected with rehabilitation of an existing building, but do not include the cost of acquisition of the building itself. §167(k)(3)(A)

> *Warning:* In order to obtain the fast write-off, an election must be made under the regulations. The election must be made for the year in which the 60-month period commences, although if the taxpayer does not then qualify because of the $3,000 limitation, he can file a statement of intent to meet the test or subsequently file an amended return. Once the election is made, the 60-month write-off is in lieu of any other method of depreciation for the amount covered by the election including additional first-year depreciation.

> *Warning:* Excess depreciation under this method is a tax preference item subject to the minimum tax under §56. Also, excess depreciation claimed under this method is subject to the depreciation recapture rules of §1250 upon the disposition of the property.

(g)   Comparison of Methods

The schedule on page 95 compares the four common methods of depreciation, the straight-line, 200% declining-balance and sum-of-the-year's-digits methods and the 200% declining-balance with a switch to straight-line in the 21st year.

A number of observations follow from an examination of this schedule.

1. The straight-line method has the advantage of consistency and simplicity. The deduction for depreciation is the same each year. If tax rates increase in later years, either because of a change in law or a change in the taxpayer's level of income, the deduction would be worth more in those years than if the taxpayer were at the declining end of an accelerated depreciation method. Also, the straight-line method eliminates the problem of recapture of depreciation upon the eventual disposition of the property and the tax preference problem. As more taxpayers become aware of these implications, the popularity of the straight-line method is increasing.

2.   The 200% declining-balance method will typically write-off about 40% of the cost of the property in the first quarter of its useful life and about two-thirds of the cost in the first half of the useful life.

3.   Although it is true that the declining-balance method produces the greatest deductions in the first and second years, sum-of-the-year's-digits method produces greater deductions in years 3 through 33. In this illustration, for the first 33 years of useful life, the cumulative depreciation deductions under the sum-of-the-year's-digits method exceeds that under the declining-balance method by approximately $15,000. In the light of this fact, it is surprising how infrequently the sum-of-the-year's-digits method is utilized by taxpayers. The reason probably lies in the fact that many taxpayers instinctively select that method which produces the greatest immediate deductions. This is frequently a short-sighted approach.

4.   Each of the methods illustrated produces total depreciation deductions in the aggregate of exactly the same amount, $100,000 over a 40-year period. The accelerated methods are, therefore, nothing more than their name implies, namely, means of accelerating deductions to earlier years, not means of producing larger deductions over the life of the property. Whether this is desirable will depend upon the facts of a particular case.

SELECTION OF DEPRECIATION RATES AND METHODS—COMPARATIVE TABLES

40-Year Useful Life

Year	*Straight-Line* Annual	Cum.	*Declining-Balance* Annual	Cum.	*Declining-Balance, Switch to Straight-Line $* Annual	Cum.	*Sum-of-the-Year's Digits $* Annual	Cum.
1	$2,500	$ 2,500	$5,000	$ 5,000	$5,000	$ 5,000	$4,878	$ 4,878
2	2,500	5,000	4,750	9,750	4,750	9,750	4,756	9,634
3	2,500	7,500	4,512	14,262	4,512	14,262	4,634	14,268
4	2,500	10,000	4,287	18,549	4,287	18,549	4,512	18,780
5	2,500	12,500	4,073	22,622	4,073	22,622	4,390	23,170
6	2,500	15,000	3,869	26,491	3,869	26,491	4,268	27,438
7	2,500	17,500	3,675	30,166	3,675	30,166	4,146	23,584
8	2,500	20,000	3,492	33,658	3,492	33,658	4,024	35,608
9	2,500	22,500	3,317	36,975	3,317	36,975	3,902	39,510
10	2,500	25,000	3,151	40,126	3,151	40,126	3,780	43,290
11	2,500	27,500	2,994	43,120	2,994	43,120	3,659	46,949
12	2,500	30,000	2,844	45,964	2,844	45,964	3,537	59,486
13	2,500	32,500	2,702	48,666	2,702	48,666	3,415	53,901
14	2,500	35,000	2,567	61,233	2,567	51,233	3,293	57,194
15	2,500	37,500	2,438	53,671	2,438	53,671	3,171	60,365
16	2,500	40,000	2,316	55,987	2,316	55,987	3,049	63,414
17	2,500	42,500	2,201	58,188	2,201	58,188	2,927	66,341
18	2,500	45,000	2,091	60,279	2,091	60,279	2,805	69,146
19	2,500	47,500	1,986	62,265	1,986	62,265	2,683	71,829
20	2,500	50,000	1,887	64,152	1,887	64,152	2,561	74,390
21	2,500	52,500	1,792	65,944	1,792	65,944	2,439	76,829
22	2,500	55,000	1,703	67,647	1,793	67,737	2,317	79,146
23	2,500	57,500	1,618	69,265	1,792	69,529	2,195	81,341
24	2,500	60,000	1,537	70,802	1,793	71,322	2,073	83,414
25	2,500	62,500	1,460	72,262	1,792	73,114	1,951	85,365
26	2,500	65,000	1,387	73,649	1,792	74,906	1,829	87,194
27	2,500	67,500	1,310	74,967	1,793	76,699	1,707	88,901
28	2,500	70,000	1,251	76,218	1,792	78,491	1,585	90,486
29	2,500	72,500	1,189	77,407	1,793	80,284	1,463	91,949
30	2,500	75,000	1,130	78,537	1,792	82,076	1,341	93,290
31	2,500	77,500	1,073	79,616	1,793	83,868	1,220	94,510
32	2,500	80,000	1,019	80,629	1,792	85,661	1,098	95,608
33	2,500	82,500	969	81,598	1,793	87,453	976	96,584
34	2,500	85,000	920	82,518	1,792	89,246	854	97,438
35	2,500	87,500	874	83,392	1,793	91,038	732	98,170
36	2,500	90,000	830	84,222	1,792	92,830	610	98,780
37	2,500	92,500	789	85,011	1,793	94,623	488	99,268
38	2,500	95,000	749	85,760	1,792	96,415	366	99,634
39	2,500	97,500	712	86,472	1,793	98,208	244	99,878
40	2,500	100,000	676	87,148	1,792	100,000	122	100,000

5.4　THE INVESTMENT CREDIT

The investment credit rules permit a taxpayer to claim a credit against his tax for a specified percentage of the cost of certain eligible property. Obviously, a credit against tax is more valuable than a deduction in computing taxable income since the amount of the credit reduces the tax payable dollar for dollar. Although the investment credit is generally not available on buildings, a familiarity with the concept is advisable for those involved in real estate development, first, because certain structures do qualify for investment credit, and second, because there are certain items of personal property involved in the operation of most buildings which may qualify for the credit.

(a)　Amount of the Investment Credit

For eligible property acquired prior to January 21, 1975, the credit is equal to 7% of the qualified investment. §46(a)(1). The portion of total investment which constitutes "qualified investment," however, varies according to the useful life of the eligible property. The full 7% credit is allowed only for property which has a useful life of seven years or more. Property having a useful life of between five and seven years will qualify for two-thirds of the 7% credit while property having a useful life of three to five years will qualify for one-third of the 7% credit.[26] However, the Tax Reduction Act of 1975 increased the maximum investment credit rate from 7% to 10% of the qualified investment in property if the property is acquired after January 21, 1975, and before 1977, and is placed in service before 1977.[27] The Tax Reform Act of 1976 extended the 10% rate through 1980. In short, the amount of the credit is 7% or 10% for property with a long useful life (more than 7 years) depending upon the date that the property was acquired or constructed; and for properties with shorter useful lives the amount of the credit will be a fraction (one-third or two-thirds as the case may be) of this maximum rate.

The Tax Reduction Act of 1975 also introduced a new concept—the 11% credit. Under this rule a corporation may elect to increase its investment credit from 10% to 11% if it agrees to transfer its securities to an Employee Stock Ownership Plan (ESOP).[28] The securities which are transferred must have a value equal to the increase in the credit; that is, 1% of the employer's qualified investment for the year. This provision is also effective through 1980. Cash may also be transferred to the ESOP if such cash is, under the plan, used to purchase eligible securities of the employer corporation. Thus, the corporation can fund the purchase of its securities from its controlling shareholder without the normal redemption rules becoming operative. The securities must be transferred to the plan by the time the credit is claimed or the corporation must agree in writing that such securities will be transferred. Various other requirements are imposed upon a qualified ESOP. Under the Tax Reform Act of 1976 employers may get an extra half percent credit starting in 1977—bringing the total credit to 11 1/2%—if they meet certain conditions. The extra credit is only available if the employer qualifies for the 11% credit and then only to the extent both employer and employees contribute an amount equal to the extra half percent credit to the ESOP.

(b) Property Eligible for the Credit.

The principal problem in connection with real estate and the investment credit revolves around the definition of the eligible property. Eligible property is called §38 Property and the definition of this term is the nub of the credit provision. (In typical tax law logic, the term "§38 Property" is defined in §48.) General speaking, to be eligible for the investment credit, the property must qualify for depreciation or amortization and must have a useful life of three years or more. Further, it must be either (A) tangible, personal property or (B) other tangible property, not including a building and its structural components, which is used in certain specified ways, such as in connection with manufacturing or production. Research or storage facilities used in connection with any of the specified activities are expressly made eligible for the credit as well as elevators and escalators put into use after June 30, 1963.

Since we are primarily concerned with the tax problems of real estate, an examination of the exclusions will be useful.

Buildings—Buildings and structural components (except for elevators and escalators) do not qualify for the investment credit. The definition contained in the Regulations[29] is quite broad and provides as follows:

> Definition of buildings and structural components. (1) Buildings and structural components thereof do not qualify as §38 property. The term "building" generally means any structure or edifice enclosing a space within its walls, and usually covered by a roof, the purpose of which is, for example, to provide shelter or housing, or to provide working, office, parking, display or sales space. The term includes, for example, structures such as apartment houses, factory and office buildings, warehouses, barns, garages, railways or bus stations and stores . . .

Property Used for Lodging—Property cannot be "§38 Property" which is eligible for the investment credit if it is used predominantly to furnish lodging.[30] This is true whether the lodging is furnished by the owner of the property or by another person. Even elevators and escalators which normally qualify for the credit are ineligible if they are used predominantly in connection with the furnishing of lodging.[31]

Property used to furnish lodging includes furniture and fixtures (beds, carpets, air conditioners, kitchen equipment, etc.) used in apartment houses or rental homes.

There are, however, a number of exceptions to this rule. Property used for or in connection with lodging may be eligible for the investment credit (1) if the lodging is provided by a hotel or motel for transients or (2) if the property constitutes a commercial facility in its own right, besides its connection with lodging and is available to the general public on the same basis as to the lodgers. For example, property of a restaurant or a barber shop or pharmacy in an apartment building, is eligible if the general public can use it on the same terms as the tenants. Also, the Revenue Act of 1971 amended §48(a)(3) to provide a further exception for coin-operated vending machines and coin-operated washing machines and dryers. Finally, lodging property is eligible for the credit if it is primarily part of a transportation facility or a medical or convalescent facility such as a hospital or nursing home.[32]

5.5   ADDITIONAL FIRST YEAR DEPRECIATION

Under Section 179 certain property qualifies for a first year depreciation allowance equal to 20% of its cost, unreduced by salvage value, in addition to the regular depreciation allowable with respect to such property, whether straight-line or accelerated. Although, like the investment credit, this deduction relates primarily to personal property, there are instances in which eligible property is involved in real estate projects and a familiarity with this provision is important.

(a)   Eligible Property

The first year depreciation allowance is allowable only for the year in which the taxpayer bought the property. In order to be eligible, the property must meet the following requirements:

> It must be tangible, personal property, whether new or used. This would include items such as refrigerators and window air-conditioners even though under local law such items may be classified as fixtures. However, it does not include structural components of a building such as plumbing, central heating, etc.
>
> The property must have a useful life of six years or more. Remember that "useful life" for the same type of property may vary from taxpayer to taxpayer. Thus, for example, a taxpayer who normally trades his car in every four years or less cannot claim a useful life for his automobile of more than four years and, therefore, it would not qualify for this additional depreciation.
>
> The property in question cannot be acquired in any of the following ways: by gift or inheritance; from the wife, husband, parent, child, ancestor or lineal descendant of the taxpayer claiming the deduction; in a transaction between a partnership in which the acquiring taxpayer has, directly or indirectly, more than a 50% interest; or from a corporation in which he owns, directly or indirectly, more than 50% in value of the outstanding stock. (Certain attribution of ownership rules apply between the taxpayer and members of his family in determining whether his stock ownership exceeds the 50% test.)

(b)   Limitation on the Amount

The taxpayer is limited to $10,000 cost for all qualifying property, although this is increased to $20,000 in the case of joint returns. To put it another way, the maximum tax deduction allowable by reason of this provision is $2,000 (20% of a $10,000 investment) or $4,000 in the case of joint return. In the case of partnerships, prior to the Tax Reform Act of 1976 each partner was considered to have purchased his proportionate share of the qualifying property and the deduction was allocated accordingly. For example, if there were five partners filing joint returns, each of them could claim the maximum $4,000 allowable if the partnership purchased an asset for $100,000. However, under the Act, effective for partnership taxable years beginning after December 31, 1975, the limit applies both at the partnership and the partner level. The partnership will only be able to flow through to its partners their allocable shares of the maximum $2,000 limit.

(c) Claiming the Deduction

A taxpayer who wishes to claim the 20% first year depreciation allowance must show the deduction in his tax return as a separate item, specified as depreciation claimed under §179. The first year allowance must be claimed on a timely filed return in order to be allowable.

Unlike the investment credit, the first year depreciation allowance serves to reduce the depreciation base for subsequent years. In effect, it is another form of accelerated depreciation.

RECAPTURE OF DEPRECIATION

In the good old days, before the enactment of the recapture rules, a taxpayer had nothing to lose by claiming the maximum depreciation allowable. Since depreciation is a deduction against income it reduced tax at ordinary rates while the gain realized on the eventual sale of the depreciable property was normally taxed at only capital gain rates. Thus, to a 50% bracket taxpayer, depreciation deductions produced tax savings of $.50 per dollar of depreciation claimed while the eventual recovery of the depreciated amounts upon a sale of the property was taxed at a maximum rate of only $.25 per dollar. Accordingly, §1245 governing recapture of depreciation of personal property was added to the Code in 1952 and §1250 governing recapture of depreciation of real estate was added in 1964. To further complicate matters, the Tax Reform Acts of 1969 and 1976 amended the recapture rules by applying different recapture rules to residential and non-residential property. In short, as is typical in the development of tax law, what was conceived as a simple concept—recapturing ordinary deductions as ordinary income upon the eventual sale—has developed into a complex maze requiring careful study by one planning the sale of his property.

5.6   RECAPTURE OF DEPRECIATION ON PERSONAL PROPERTY

Recapture of depreciation on personal property is relatively simple. All depreciation claimed subsequent to 1961 is "recaptured" and taxed as ordinary income at the time of the sale of the property. Of course, if the gain on sale exceeds the amount of depreciation claimed during the period of ownership, such excess continues to be taxed as a capital gain.

> *Example:* In 1975, taxpayer acquired a piece of equipment for $30,000. He has claimed $10,000 of depreciation and his adjusted basis is, therefore, $20,000. If he sells this equipment for $25,000 the entire $5,000 gain is taxed as ordinary income since it does not exceed the amount of depreciation claimed. If he sells for $32,000, he would be taxed on $10,000 of ordinary income, the depreciation claimed, and $2,000 of capital gain.

5.7   RECAPTURE OF DEPRECIATION ON REAL ESTATE

Although §1250 extended the recapture rules to real estate, there are a number of significant differences between the two types of property. Briefly, recapture rules relating to real estate are somewhat more liberal than those applied to personal property.

(a)   Depreciation Subject to Recapture

In the case of personal property, all depreciation claimed subsequent to December 31, 1961, is subject to recapture. In the case of real estate, only depreciation claimed subsequent to December 31, 1963, is subject to recapture.

Another distinction between personal property and real estate is that all of the depreciation on personal property is subject to recapture as ordinary income regardless of the method of computation up to the amount of gain realized. In the case of real estate, however, there are two exceptions to the recapture rules which were provided in an attempt to eliminate gain attributable merely to increased price levels from the amount subject to recapture. First, where the property has been held for more than 12 months, there is no ordinary income recapture where the depreciation on the property sold does not exceed the amount which would have been allowable on the straight-line method of depreciation. Such excess will be referred to herein as additional depreciation. Second, the amount of gain subject to ordinary income treatment is reduced according to the holding period of the property—the longer the holding period, the smaller the amount of additional depreciation subject to recapture.

(b)   Effect of Holding Period—Pre-1970 Depreciation.

The holding period rules governing the recapture of pre-1970 real estate depreciation may be summarized as follows:

(1)   Dispositions During the First Year—If real estate is sold within one year of its acquisition, the applicable percentage is 100% and all depreciation claimed subsequent to 12/31/63, including the straight-line portion, is recaptured as ordinary income. For example, if the taxpayer bought a building January 1, 1974 for $100,000, claimed depreciation of $2,500 for the first six months of the year, and sold the building on July 1 for a sum in excess of his basis, all of the depreciation claimed would be recaptured and taxed as ordinary income. To the extent that the sales price exceeded depreciation claimed, it could qualify as a capital gain.

> *Suggestion:* In view of the harsh rule applied to dispositions of real estate within one year of acquisition date, it is generally advisable to postpone the closing of a transaction until this one-year holding period has expired.

(2)   Disposition in Months 13 Through 20—If the real estate is sold before the taxpayer has held it for at least 20 months, the applicable percentage is still 100%. The difference here is that only "additional depreciation" (depreciation in excess of straight-line depreciation) is recaptured as ordinary income. To the extent that the gain is attributable to straight-line depreciation, it is taxed as a capital gain.

Example: Taxpayer acquired a building at a cost of $100,000 on January 1, 1964. He claimed double-declining depreciation utilizing a 5% rate. His depreciation for 1964 was, therefore, $5,000, while the straight-line depreciation would have been $2,500. He sold the building on January 2, 1965, for his original cost, $100,000. Result: 100% (the applicable percentage) of $2,500 (the additional depreciation) is recaptured and taxed as ordinary income; but the balance of the $2,500 gain is capital gain.

(3) Dispositions After a Holding Period of more than Twenty Months—Commencing with the 21st month following acquisition of real estate, the applicable percentage (the percentage of pre-1970 additional depreciation which is taxed as ordinary income) is reduced by 1% for each month that the property is held. Thus, if property is sold after being held for 21 months, the applicable percentage is 99%; if it is sold after being held for 22 months, the applicable percentage is 98%, etc. Note that after the property is held for 120 months or ten years, the applicable percentage has been reduced to zero and the recapture problem has been eliminated.

Example: A building is purchased December 31, 1964, and is sold on January 1, 1968, following 36 full months of ownership. The building cost $100,000. The gain realized on the sale was $10,000. The owner claimed depreciation deductions on the double-declining balance method utilizing a 40-year life. Straight-line deductions would have been $2,500 per year, or $7,500 for 3 years while the total accelerated depreciation was $14,262.50. Under these assumed facts, the "additional depreciation" would be $6,762.50 (accelerated depreciation less straight-line depreciation.) The applicable percentage would be 84%. Therefore, the depreciation subject to recapture is $5,680.50 (84% x $6,762.50). Of course, if the gain had been less than the "additional depreciation" then the applicable percentage would have been applied to the amount of gain only. Thus, if the gain was $4,000, the amount of ordinary income would be 84% of that amount, or $3,360.

(c)   Effect of Holding Period—Post 1969 Depreciation

The Tax Reform Act of 1969 increased the amount of excess depreciation which is subject to recapture. The new rules apply to properties acquired prior to December 31, 1969, as well as to properties acquired after that date; it is the year the depreciation is claimed that is determinative. The amount which is recaptured as ordinary income depends upon the type of real estate involved, residential or non-residential. Residential properties are further divided into low-income housing and other residential property.

Low-Income Housing—For property constructed or acquired before 1975 under certain government assisted programs such as §221(d)(3) or §236 of the National Housing Act, the applicable percentage of recapture income on post-1969 additional depreciation is 100% less 1% per month for each full month the property was held over 20 full months. Thus, the rules in effect prior to the Tax Reform Act of 1969 for all real estate continue to apply to low-income housing.

Other Residential Property—For normal residential property, the applicable percentage of recapture income on post-1969 additional depreciation is 100%, less 1% per month for each full month the property was held over 100 full months. Thus, by the time an apartment building has been held for 200 months (16 years and 8 months), the entire gain on the sale will be long term capital gain.

Commercial Property—For commercial, industrial and other non-residential property, the applicable percentage of recapture income on post-1969 additional depreciation is 100%; all of the accelerated portion of the depreciation is recaptured regardless of the holding period.

> *Example:* The gain on the sale of an office building is $30,000. Additional depreciation after 1969 is $3,000 and additional depreciation for earlier periods was $6,000. The holding period is 30 months. All of the $3,000 of post-1969 additional depreciation is recaptured as ordinary income. Also, 90% of the $6,000 pre-1970 additional depreciation is recaptured. (The 30-month holding period is ten months over the 20-month base which applies to pre-1970 depreciation so the applicable percentage is 100 less 10.) Total recapture income is $3,000 plus $5400 or $8400. The balance of the gain is taxed as capital gain.

(d) Recapture of Depreciation under Tax Reform Act of 1976.

As stated above, for non-residential real estate, all post-1969 additional depreciation is recaptured as ordinary income regardless of the holding period. Under the Tax Reform Act of 1976, this same rule applies to residential real estate with respect to all post-1975 additional depreciation. Thus, all depreciation in excess of straight-line depreciation will be recaptured as ordinary income to the extent of gains realized at the time of sale.

The rules covering recapture of depreciation of low-income housing will be the same as pre-1976 law for residential property. In short, under the Act with respect to depreciation claimed after January 1, 1976, low-income housing will be treated the same as residential real estate under the previous law and residential real estate will be treated the same as commercial real estate under the previous law.

The Tax Reform Act of 1976 also adds a new section relating to foreclosure proceedings. §1250(d)(10). Under this section, once foreclosure proceedings start, reduction of the recapture potential will cease. For example, if foreclosure proceedings start at 130 months, but actual foreclosure sale does not take place until 20 months later, 70% (not 50%) of the gain will be subject to recapture.

(e) Exceptions and Limitations.

In the preceding discussion it has been assumed that the disposition of the depreciable property took the form of the sale. Although this is the most common form of disposition, there are a number of other forms, some of which do not trigger the recapture provisions. Following is a list of some of the most common types of transactions other than ordinary sales and a brief statement as to the treatment of the transaction with respect to the recapture of depreciation.

Transfers at Death—Transfer by reason of the death of the owner of the property is not a taxable event for income tax purposes. Not only is the recapture gain not recognized upon a transfer at death, but the person who inherits the property takes it free of the potential recapture income.

Gifts—A gift is not a taxable event for income tax purposes. Accordingly, no recapture income is realized by reason of the gift. However, the recapture potential carries over to the donee and the recapture income will be realized upon a subsequent sale. (Note that the donor's holding period is tacked to the donee's holding period and this tacking can be of substantial importance where the property is residential real estate since the depreciation recapture is phased out after a specified holding period.)

Charitable Contributions—Although a donor does not recognize any recapture income upon a gift of depreciable property, his charitable contribution is reduced by the amount of recapture income which he would have recognized if the property had been sold for its fair value. §170(e)(1)(A).

Tax-Free Incorporations and Tax-Free Contributions to Partnerships—Where a taxpayer contributes property to a controlled corporation in exchange for stock or securities or where he contributes property to a partnership in which he is one of the partners, the conveyance is normally tax-free and there will be no recapture income. However, the grantee inherits the grantor's potential recapture income. Also, if the transfer is partially taxable—for example, where the grantor receives boot in addition to stock or securities—there may be recapture income to that extent.

> *Comment:* In view of the fact that a sale of depreciable property produces recapture income while a sale of corporate stock does not do so, it may be advisable for a taxpayer to incorporate his property and sell the stock rather than the underlying asset. Beware of the rule relating to collapsible corporations, however.

Distributions by Partnerships to Partners—Such transactions are not a taxable event for depreciation recapture purposes. However, the potential ordinary income will carry over to the grantee to be applied when he disposes of the property.

Like Kind Exchanges—If depreciable real estate is exchanged for like kind property and no gain is recognized under §1031, then no recapture income will be taxed upon the transfer. §1250(d)(4)(A). If, however, the exchange is partially taxed—for example, because of the receipt of boot—then the gain which is recognized will be taxed as ordinary income to the extent of the lower of the recapture gain or the gain recognized without regard to recapture rules.

Corporate Distributions Which Are Normally Not Taxable to the Corporation—Where a corporation pays a dividend in kind or makes a distribution in partial or complete liquidation, or makes a sale of property during the 12-month liquidation period permitted under §337, the corporation normally does not recognize any gain on the conveyance. However, if the property involved in such a sale or distribution is depreciable property having a potential for recapture income, then the distribution or sale can be taxable to the extent that depreciation recapture rules apply.

FOOTNOTES FOR CHAPTER FIVE

[1]Accounting Research Bulletin 1026.23.

[2]§167(a).

[3]*Gerald Melone* 45 T.C.501(1966).

[4]Reg.1.167(a)-2.

[5]Rev. Rul. 65-265, 1965-2 CB 52.

[6]Rev. Rul. 68-193, 1968-1 CB 79.

[7]*Thomas J. Trailmont Park, Inc.,* 1971 P-H TC Memo ¶71,212.

[8]*Tunnell v. U.S.* 512 F.2d 1192, 35 AFTR2d 75-995 (CA3, 1975).

[9]Rev.Rul. 75-137, 1975-1 CB 74. IRS has ruled that the cost of shrubbery and ornamental trees is depreciable over the life of building if the landscaping is so located that it will be destroyed when the building is replaced at the end of its useful life. Rev.Rul. 74-265, 1974-1 CB 56.

[10]*Comm. v. Terre Haute Electric Co.,* 67 F.2d 675, 32 AFTR 468 (CA6, 1944).

[11]*Alaska Realty v. Comm.,* 141 F.2d 675, 32 AFTR 468 (CA6, 1944); I.J. *Wagner v. Comm.,* 518 F.2d 655, 36 AFTR2d 75-5233 (CA10, 1975).

[12]Reg. 1.167(a)-4.

[13]Rev. Proc. 62-21, 1962-2 CB 418, Group One, Guideline Class 4.

[14]See P-H Federal Taxes ¶15,251.

[15]*Hastings v. U.S.,* 279 F. Suppl. 13, 20 AFTR 2d 5633 (D.C., Cal, 1967) appeal not authorized.

[16]*Athenaise M. Hill, v. U.S.,* 63 T.C. 225 (1974).

[17]*Concord Towers, Inc.* 1974 P-H TC Memo ¶74,259. See P-H Fed. Taxes ¶15,267 for an annotation of the cases relating to useful lives of buildings.

[18]*Herbert Shainberg,* 33 TC 241 (1959) (Acq.).

[19]*Herbert Shainberg,* supra. See P-H Fed. Taxes ¶15,395 for additional citations.

[20]*Harsh Investment Corp. v. U.S.,* 27 AFTR 2d 71-706 (D.C. Ore., 1970), (Acq.).

[21]*Merchants Natl. Bank of Topeka,* 1975 P-H TC Memo ¶75,238.

[22]*Portland General Electric Co. v. U.S.,* 223 F. Supp. 111, 13 AFTR 2d 400, (D.C. Ore., 1963).

[23]Reg. 1.167 (a)-2; *John D. Vidican,* 1969 P-H TC Memo ¶69,207; *Camp Wolters Enterprises, Inc.,* 22 TC 737,754 (1954).

[24]See Rev.Rul.60-15, 1960-1 CB 22; Rev.Rul. 69-272, 1969-1, CB 23 (use of an airplane as a demonstrator by the dealer does not preclude the purchaser from treating it as a new property for purposes of claiming the investment credit); and *Points to Remember #1,* The Tax Lawyer, Vol. 28, No. 3, p. 623.

[25]§167 (e)(1). Under the 150% declining-balance-method and presumably the 125% declining-balance-method, the consent of the Comm. to switch to the straight-line method is required. Reg.1.167(e)-1(a). This change can generally be accomplished by complying with the procedure of Rev. Proc. 67-40, 1967-2 CB 674.

[26]§46(c)(2) as amended by the Revenue Act of 1971 applicable to property described in §50 (property acquired by the taxpayer after 8/15/71 or where construction was commenced after 3/31/71 or completed after 8/15/71).

[27]§46(a) (1) (D) (ii).

[28]§46(a) (1) (B).

[29]Reg. 1.48-1(e).

[30]§48(a) (3).

[31]*Klingle Corp.,* 1970 P-H TC Memo ¶70,135, affirmed per curiam.

[32]Reg. 1.48-1(h) (1) (i).

Summary of Recapture Rules

1963-1969

Property	Holding Period	Percentage of Excess Depreciation to Be Recaptured
All types of real property	Less than 12 months	*All* depreciation (not just excess over straight line) is recaptured
	12 to 20 months	100%
	20 months to 120 months	100% reduced by 1% per month of holding period over 20 months
	Over 10 years	None

Property	1970-1975	
	Holding Period	*Percentage of Excess Depreciation to Be Recaptured*
Sold under binding contract in existence before 7/24/69, and government-sponsored projects	12 to 20 months 20 to 120 months Over 10 years	100% 100% reduced by 1% per month of holding period over 100 months None
Residential rental property (other than the above), including § 167(k) expenses	12 to 100 months 100 to 200 months Over 200 months (16-2/3 years)	100% 100% reduced by 1% per month of holding period over 100 months None
Nonresidential, commercial, industrial	Any length of time	100%

Property	Post-1975	
	Holding Period	*Percentage of Excess Depreciation to Be Recaptured*
Residential and nonresidential	Less than 12 months Any length of time over 12 months	All depreciation (not just excess over straight line) is recaptured 100%
Low-income rental* housing	Less than 12 months 12 to 100 months 100 to 200 months Over 200 months (16-2/3 years)	All depreciation (not just excess over straight line) is recaptured 100% 100% reduced by 1% per month of holding period over 100 months None

*Including property on which a mortgage is insured under §221(d)(3) or §236 of the National Housing Act; low-income rental housing that qualifies for the rehabilitation writeoff under §167(k); property covered by §8 of the United States Housing Act of 1937; and property insured under Title V of the Housing Act of 1949.

6

REAL

ESTATE

LEASES

Experience indicates that in negotiating the terms of the landlord-tenant relationship, the parties are invariably concerned with economic and real estate questions. They frequently neglect to consider tax consequences and it is not until the tax return is prepared or audited that the parties wake up to the shortcomings of their agreement. Of course, by then it is too late—the lease cannot be amended retroactively and the interests of the parties are often adverse so that an amendment which is acceptable to one party is probably not acceptable to the other.

In contrast with some previous chapters which dealt with fairly broad areas of tax law, leases generally involve a considerable number of narrow and technical points. This chapter will, therefore, attempt to catalogue the tax problems of the landlord and the tenant and to state the rules governing their receipts and disbursements in connection with the leased property. For ease in locating the discussion of a particular problem we have divided the chapter into four principal categories dealing with landlord's disbursements, landlord's receipts, tenant's disbursements, and tenant's receipts.

Following is an outline of the various topics to be discussed in this chapter.

SECTION A: LANDLORD'S DISBURSEMENTS
The Cost of Acquiring and Keeping Tenants.

6.1 Lease Cancellation Payments to Former Tenant.
6.2 Building Demolition to Prepare Premises for Tenant.

SECTION A: LANDLORD'S DISBURSEMENTS.

THE COST OF ACQUIRING AND KEEPING TENANTS

6.1 LEASE CANCELLATION PAYMENTS TO FORMER TENANT

Where the landlord makes a payment to cancel a tenant's lease for the purpose of reletting the premises to a new tenant, presumable at a higher rental, the landlord has not incurred a currently deductible loss or expense. Rather, the payment constitutes the cost of a property right, a capital expenditure. The problem, of course, is in determining over what period this expenditure should be amortized; the answer depends upon the purpose for which the lease cancellation was obtained.

(a) If the cancellation was incurred for the purpose of acquiring the right to possession for the remaining term of the old lease, the cost is spread over that period. This is true even though the property is subsequently leased to another tenant in a separate transaction.[1]

(b) If the old lease was cancelled so that the landlord could lease the property to a new tenant for an extended term, the landlord may be required to amortize his cost over the period of the new lease.[2]

(c) If the old lease was cancelled for the purpose of erecting a new building or other improvement to be leased to another tenant, the lease cancellation payment is treated as a part of the cost of the improvement to be depreciated over its useful life.[3]

6.2   BUILDING DEMOLITION TO PREPARE PREMISES FOR TENANT

Assume that a property owner demolishes a building in order to prepare the site for a tenant and to realize rental income over the term of a lease. Can the landlord claim a demolition loss based upon his basis for the building? If not, how does he treat the purchase price of the building? The question of demolition losses is generally discussed in Chapter 4, Section 3. We will discuss here the demolition loss of a landlord preparing a site for a tenant.

(a) *Building Acquired with Intention to Demolish*—If the landlord intended to demolish the building at the time he made the acquisition, the regulations provide that he cannot deduct the loss upon such demolition and the cost of the buildings must be allocated to the remaining land.[4]

> *Example:* Taxpayers owned an interest in certain lots leased to a supermarket. When the tenant notified them that the lease would not be renewed unless additional parking space was provided, the taxpayers negotiated for the purchase of adjacent land on which certain buildings were located and then razed the structures and renewed the supermarket lease on terms which compensated them for the cost of the acquisition of the new property. The Court of Appeals, reversing the District Court, held that the Treasury Regulations were a reasonable interpretation of the Code and that in view of the fact that the intention to demolish the buildings existed at the time of acquisition, the entire cost of the real estate purchase must be allocated to the land alone.[5]
> However, when the building is *used* temporarily pending the demolition, a portion of the basis may be allocated to the building and amortized over the period of such use.[6]

(b) *Demolition Required to Construct New Building For Tenant*—If the demolition is for the express purpose of constructing a new building to be leased to a committed tenant, then the adjusted basis of the old building, plus the net cost of demolition or less the net proceeds of demolition, is amortized over the term of the new lease. The courts apparently do not distinguish between the cases where the new lease is longer or shorter than the life of the new building; the lease term and not the building itself is the measure of the amortization period.[7]

(c) *Intent to Demolish Formed After Acquisition*—If the intention was formed by the landlord after he acquired the property and was not required pursuant to the requirements of a lease or any other agreement which resulted in a lease, then under

§165(a) the demolition produces a loss and a deduction is permitted in the year of demolition.[8] However, the courts scrutinize the claimed loss carefully and if it appears that the demolition is for the purpose of erecting a new structure or pursuant to a plan existing at the time of acquisition, the loss will not be allowed.[9]

> *Suggestion:* Some courts have held that although the landlord is not allowed a loss where the lease "requires" the tenant to demolish the landlord's building, this rule does not apply where the lease merely "permits" such demolition at lessee's expense. The drafting implications of this decision are obvious.[10] However, Reg. 1.165-3(b)(2), as amended 12/21/76, rejects this rule and requires that the unamortized portion of the cost be amortized over the remaining term of the lease.

6.3 COMMISSIONS AND OTHER EXPENSES TO PROCURE LEASE

Attorneys' fees, commissions to brokers and similar expenses which are paid by the landlord in obtaining a tenant for his property cannot be deducted when paid or incurred; such expenses must be capitalized as a cost of the lease and amortized over the life of the lease. This rule applies regardless of the accounting method of the taxpayer.[11] There are various exceptions and qualifications to this general rule.

(a) When the tenant abandons or forfeits his lease, or if the lease is cancelled, the landlord is thereupon permitted to write off the unamortized cost.[12]

(b) If the landlord sells the property, the unamortized costs of leasing are added to his basis and reduce the gain realized upon the sale.[13]

It follows that the landlord is normally better off to cancel a lease prior to sale so as to get an ordinary deduction.

IMPROVEMENTS CONSTRUCTED ON LEASED PREMISES

6.4 IMPROVEMENTS CONSTRUCTED PRIOR TO LANDLORD'S ACQUISITION

Sometimes a tenant constructs a building or other improvements on land which he occupies under a long-term lease. Common examples are filling stations and drive-in restaurants, although the practice also extends to larger structures such as department stores. The owner of the land is clearly not entitled to claim depreciation on the building since he has no investment in it. But supposing the property—land and tenant-constructed building—is sold to a new owner. Can the buyer claim that he has an investment in the building and, therefore, qualifies to claim a deduction for depreciation?

The appellate courts have split on this question. One court permitted the deduction, recognizing an allocation of $300,000 to the building out of a total price of $700,000.[14] The court was not disturbed by the fact that the tenant may be depreciating the same building as the landlord (the new owner) since each taxpayer has a separate investment to write off. However, another court rejected this approach, reasoning that since the original landlord had no depreciable interest, he could hardly pass such an interest on to the new owner.[15]

A similar question is whether a "premium value" can be allocated to a desirable lease at the time of the sale of the property, with the purchaser being permitted to amortize, over the term of the lease, such "premium." At least one decision recognized the purchaser's right to such a deduction.[16] Surely, a purchaser would be well advised to claim such a premium if the facts justified it, for example, where the lease provided for an abnormally high rent from a top-rated tenant.

6.5   IMPROVEMENTS CONSTRUCTED BY LANDLORD

The landlord is entitled to claim depreciation based upon the cost or other basis of buildings and improvements on leased property. This rule applies regardless of whether the building or other improvements are in existence at the commencement of the lease or are built pursuant to the requirements of the lease. The useful life for depreciation purposes is determined by the life of the improvements, not the term of the lease.[17]

A lease provision requiring the tenant to make necessary repairs and replacements and to maintain the property in good condition does not preclude the depreciation by the landlord.[18]

However, if the lease requires the tenant to maintain or restore the property to its original condition before surrendering the property at the end of the term, the landlord will lose his right to a depreciation deduction. The deduction is denied on the basis that the lessee's obligation precludes any loss.[19]

> *Suggestion:* Although a requirement that the property be returned to the landlord in its original condition precludes a depreciation deduction, this rule does not apply if the tenant is merely required to return the property at the end of the lease in its original condition "except for ordinary wear and tear." The line is a fine one and it will normally be advisable to draft a provision so as to justify the deduction.

SECTION B: LANDLORD'S RECEIPTS

6.6   GENERAL RULE

Of course rents are taxable to a landlord in the taxable year in which they are received or accrued, depending upon his method of accounting.[20] See Section 25 of this chapter regarding rents received from parties related to the landlord.

6.7   PREPAID RENTS AND SECURITY DEPOSITS

Advance rentals constitute one of the exceptions to the normal rules relating to accrual accounting. Gross income includes advance rentals in the year of receipt regardless of whether the landlord is on the cash or the accrual basis.[21] However, if the payment represents a security deposit rather than an advance rental, the landlord is not required to report income upon receipt. A difficult question, of course, is to differentiate between "advance rentals" and "security deposits." Some of the earlier decisions held that the liability on the part of the landlord to repay the sum to the tenant in a later year precluded its treatment as income in the year of receipt.[22] More recent decisions, which apparently represent the current rule, hold that where the landlord receives a sum under a "claim of right" where there is no duty to segregate the funds or to pay interest on them, the sum constitutes advance rental taxable in the year of receipt, notwithstanding that it also serves as security for the tenant's performance.[23]

> *Suggestion:* In some states a landlord is required to segregate funds held as security deposits under leases. Even where this is not the law, however, actual segregation of the funds appears to be the safest way of avoiding taxation upon receipt.

What is the amount of taxable income realized by the landlord in the year the security deposit is forfeited and becomes the landlord's property? IRS has ruled, contrary to certain earlier cases, that the amount of income realized is the full amount of the forfeited deposit without any deduction for the loss of income which the landlord will incur over the balance of the lease term.[24]

6.8   BONUS RECEIVED FOR LEASE.

A bonus paid by the tenant to the landlord to obtain a lease is treated as the payment of additional rent and is taxable as income in the year received. This rule applies even where the payment is made by the tenant to be relieved of an unfavorable lease provision, such as a restoration clause which existed under the original lease.[25]

6.9   TENANT-CONSTRUCTED IMPROVEMENTS WHICH REVERT TO LANDLORD

Upon the expiration of a lease the tenant's right to occupy the premises terminates and the leased property, including improvements constructed by tenant, revert to the land owner. Must the landlord report taxable income based upon the fair value of the improvements which he thereby acquires? The answer depends upon the intention of the parties with respect to these improvements. The Code expressly provides that "gross income does not include income (other than rent) derived by a lessor of real property on the termination of a lease, representing the value of such property attributable to buildings erected or other improvements made by the lessee."[26]

The U.S. Supreme Court has stated that "even when required, improvements by the lessee will not be deemed rent unless the intention that they shall be is plainly disclosed. Rent is a fixed sum, or property amounting to a fixed sum, to be paid at stated times for the use of property . . . it does not include payments uncertain both as to time and amount made for the cost of improvement . . . "[27]

However, where the improvements are a substitute for rent—for example, where the rent which would otherwise be charged to the tenant is reduced in order to permit him to invest in improvements which will eventually revert to the landlord—taxable income is realized by the landlord in the year the improvements are made, subject to an adjustment to reflect the tenant's right to utilize the improvements for the balance of the lease.[28]

Comment: The form is quite important in this area. If it appears that tenant-constructed improvements amount to rent, either by express language or specific tying of tenant's expenditures to a reduction in his obligations, the landlord becomes taxable. Even the landlord's approval of tenant's plan and specifications for the improvements should be treated carefully to avoid this problem. One way to reduce the likelihood of this problem arising is to specifically grant tenant the right to remove the improvements at the termination of the lease. Where the tenant's improvements are not deemed rent to the landlord and he makes no contribution to their cost, it follows that the landlord cannot claim any depreciation on the improvements. Having no investment he has no basis to depreciate.[29]

6.10   PURCHASE OPTIONS—RENT PAYMENTS DISTINGUISHED

Where the tenant is granted an option to purchase the property and the lease provides that a portion of the rent is to be credited against the purchase price if the option is exercised, there is a question as to whether the amounts received by the landlord actually represent rent (taxed as ordinary income) or sales proceeds (normally taxed as captial gain). This question is covered in Section 24 below.

6.11   AMOUNT RECEIVED TO CANCEL EXISTING LEASE

How does a landlord report the amount received from his tenant as payment for cancellation of an existing lease? The landlord would naturally wish to treat the receipt as a capital gain on the theory that he has sold a capital asset, i.e., a property right. The U.S. Supreme Court has held, however, that in such a case the landlord has not relinquished anything other than the right to collect rent in the future. Consequently, the amount received is merely a substitute for ordinary income and is, therefore, taxable at ordinary income rates.[30] This is consistent with a line of cases holding that a property owner is taxable on all income attributable to his property so long as he retains title. There are a number of possible exceptions to this general rule which may be useful in special situations.

(a) Capital Gain Where Landlord Actually Relinquishes Property Rights—The Tax Court has permitted capital gain treatment in one case where the landlord could demonstrate that he actually relinquished a property right, the right to receive condemnation proceeds in this case.[31] A tenant wanted to demolish a building and erect a new one but this would deprive the landlord of his right to a condemnation award at the time of the taking by the public authority which was anticipated. The tenant, therefore, purchased the landlord's right to a condemnation award whereupon the landlord consented to the tenant's plan. The Court agreed that this involved more than the relinquishment of a right to receive ordinary income in the future, since the condemnation itself would have produced capital gain.

(b) Demonstrating that Payments Are Received for some Reason other than Cancellation of the Lease—A number of cases[32] involved tenant-built improvements which were destroyed by fire. The landlord collected and retained the insurance proceeds although under the lease the tenant could have required the landlord to utilize these proceeds to replace the buildings. The Tax Court held that these proceeds were

not consideration paid by tenants for cancellation of the lease but represented payment to the landlord as compensation for destruction of the buildings. Accordingley capital gain treatment was permitted.

(c) Amounts Received on Sale of Lease by Tenant who was also a Sublessor—The ordinary income rationale does not apply where a tenant who has subleased to another party is paid for cancellation or assignment of his rights, i.e., he steps aside and permits a subtenant to deal directly with the property owner.[33] The tenant then has a reasonably good chance of persuading the courts that he has actually sold a property right and should be allowed capital gain treatment. See Section 22 below.

SECTION C: TENANT'S DISBURSEMENTS

6.12   RENTS PAID—GENERAL RULE

A tenant's deduction for periodic rental payments is expressly permitted by the Code, which allows a deduction for "rentals or other payments required to be made as a condition to the continued use or possession, for purposes of the trade or business of property to which the taxpayer has not taken or is not taking title or in which he has no equity." §162(a) (3). This rule applies not only to payments made to the landlord directly, but also to taxes, insurance premiums, interest and similar payments required under a lease which are made by the tenant to or for the benefit of the landlord.[34] An exception is special assessments which are not deductible when paid but which must be amortized by annual deductions over the remaining term of the lease.

6.13   BONUS TO OBTAIN LEASE

Although the landlord is required to report a bonus as rental in the year of receipt, the tenant is not permitted to deduct the payment that year. The amount of the bonus is treated as a cost of obtaining the lease to be recovered by a deduction for an amortization allowance over the term of the lease.[35] However, the Tax Court has held that higher rental payments in the early years of a lease were fair compensation for use of the premises and, therefore, currently deductible.[36]

6.14   PREPAID RENTS AND SECURITY DEPOSITS

As with bonuses, the tenant is not permitted to deduct prepaid rents in the year of payment but must spread the deduction over the lease term regardless of whether he is on the cash or the accrual basis.[37]

> *Comment:* In view of the inconsistency of treatment between the parties—the landlord is immediately taxed upon receipt of a prepaid rental or bonus while the tenant must spread the deduction over the life of the lease—this appears to be an area which lends itself to negotiation between the parties. Security deposits are not deductible.

6.15   PURCHASE OPTION PAYMENTS AS RENT

If a payment which the parties have labelled as "rent" is actually a disguised payment to apply on the purchase of the property, the rental deduction will be disallowed since the tenant will be treated as the buyer under a deferred payment contract. See Section 24 below.

6.16   PAYMENTS TO MODIFY OR CANCEL LEASE

Since a tenant who pays for the privilege of cancelling a lease no longer has a wasting asset, he can deduct the amount of such payment as a current business expense.[38] This is to be contrasted with a payment for renewal, extension or modification of a lease which must be amortized over the life of the extended lease.[39]

IMPROVEMENTS TO LEASED PREMISES

6.17   PERMANENT IMPROVEMENTS—AMORTIZATION

(a) *Improvements Constructed by Landlord*—If a landlord constructs improvements he will normally depreciate them over the useful life of the improvement, even though this will generally be longer than the lease term. The tenant, on the other hand, can frequently write off his improvement cost over the term of the lease—which may be considerably less than the useful life of the improvement. (Of course, if the useful life of the improvement is less than the remaining lease term, that is the period over which the improvement is depreciated.)[40] In short, by permitting the tenant to construct the improvements, the rate of write-off can normally be increased.

Where it is the life of the physical asset which is the basis for the write-off, the deduction is based on depreciation rather than amortization. Accelerated methods of depreciation can, therefore, be utilized.[41] Moreover, since the landlord is being relieved of the requirement of making an investment in such improvements, he may be persuaded to pass on his savings to the tenant in the form of reduced rents.

> *Warning:* Ordinarily, where the tenant makes improvements which revert to the landlord upon expiration of the lease, there is no taxable event to the landlord. However, where the lease requires the tenant to make the improvements and allows credit to him based on such improvements, the credited rental is deemed taxable to the landlord. See Section 9 above. The drafting implications of this rule are self-evident.

(b) *Improvements Constructed by Tenant—Effect of Renewal Options.* In view of the rule permitting a tenant to write off his improvement cost over the term of the lease, the parties may be tempted to draft a lease which runs for a short term but grants the tenant renewal options, hoping thereby to maximize depreciation deductions. Under §178, objective tests are introduced to determine whether such renewal options must be counted as a part of the basic lease term for purposes of writing off leasehold improvements.

For purposes of computing depreciation and amortization [42] the lease term is generally treated as including the renewal periods unless the taxpayer can establish that it is more probable that the lease will not be renewed. §178(a). If he cannot meet this test the tenant may be required to write the building off over the entire lease term, including the option periods, or over the life of the building if that is less. However, this rule will not apply (and the renewal periods will not be included in the term of the lease for amortization purposes) if the tenant meets one of the following tests:

The 75% Test: In the case of the cost of *acquiring* a lease, if at least 75% of such cost is, as of the time of acquisition, attributable to the remaining portion of the current term of the lease. §178 (a) (2).

The 60% Test: In the case of an improvement *constructed* by the tenant, if the remaining portion of the current term of the lease at the time of completion of the improvement represents at least 60% of the useful life of the improvement. §178(a) (1).

Example: (1) Tenant constructs a building on land leased from landlord. When construction is completed, 15 years remain on the lease with an option to tenant to renew for an additional 20 years. The building has an estimated useful life of 30 years. Since the portion of the term of the lease, excluding renewal options, remaining upon completion of the building (15 years) is less than 60% of the estimated useful life of the building (60% of a 30-year life is 18 years), the renewal period must be counted along with the basic term of the lease in computing the remaining portion of the lease. Accordingly, for purposes of measuring the amortization period, the lease will be treated as having 35 years to run (15 years on the basic term, plus the 20-year option period). However, since the estimated useful life of the building is 30 years, the building is depreciated over its estimated useful life.

(2) If the lease had 21 years to run, plus a 10-year renewal option, the 60% test exception would apply: the remaining portion of the current term of the lease (21 years) would exceed 60% of the estimated useful life (60% of a 30-year life, or 18 years). In that event, the building would be amortized over the 21-year balance of the lease term.

Comment: A comparison of these two examples indicates that from a tax standpoint, it is not always to the tenant's interest to utilize a short lease term. If the term is too short, (example 1) tenant cannot qualify for the 60% test and must count renewal options along with the basic lease term. By using a slightly longer lease term (example 2), the tenant may be able to get larger deductions—a 21-year write-off versus a 30-year write-off in these examples. This is the reverse of what many tenants anticipate.

Suggestion: Using actual useful life of the improvement may be more advantageous than writing the investment off over the current lease term. The reason is that amortization of a leasehold interest does not qualify for accelerated depreciation.[43] The taxpayer may be better off with a slightly longer write-off period which qualifies for accelerated depreciation methods than he will be with a shorter period where he is compelled to utilize what amounts to straight-line depreciation.

Leases Between Related Parties—Under §178(b), where the landlord and tenant are related to each other, tenant-constructed buildings or other improvements must be written off over their useful lives rather than over the shorter lease term. Generally speaking, the relationships which create this situation are a taxpayer and his spouse, ancestors and lineal descendants; a taxpayer and a corporation in which he owns or is treated as owning 80% of the stock; a grantor and trustee of a trust; and a trustee and beneficiary of a trust.

The Reasonable Certainty Test—If the tenant has met the 60% test or the 75% test under §178(a) and if he is not related to the landlord as defined in §178(b), the renewal period will not be included as a part of the lease term for purposes of amortization of tenant's improvements unless the lease has been renewed or there is a reasonable certainty that the lease will be renewed, extended or continued. §178(c). Regulation 1.178-3(c) gives an example of a lease with 29 years remaining when the tenant completes construction of a building with a 40-year life. Thus, the balance of the current term represents more than 60% of the useful life of the improvement. Tenant has two renewal options of five years each at the same rent as in the initial term. The location is particularly suitable for his business, the rent is favorable and there are no facts to indicate that these conditions will not continue. On these facts, the regulation concludes that, despite compliance with the 60% test, the cost of the building should be amortized over 39 years, (including the renewal options) since there is a reasonable certainty that the tenant will renew the lease for both of the option periods.

6.18   TRADE FIXTURES—DEPRECIATION BY TENANT

Of course, the tenant can depreciate his trade fixtures and other improvements which are to be removed by him on the expiration of the lease. The rate of depreciation would be based upon the useful life of the fixtures, not on the term of the lease. On the other hand, if the tenant agrees that his improvements are to become the landlord's property upon expiration of the lease, or if they are of such a nature that they cannot be removed, then the tenant will be permitted to amortize the cost over the life of the lease.[44]

Where the tenant occupies the premises for an indefinite period of time or on a month-to-month basis, the cost of his permanent improvements is not amortizable but can be recovered only under a depreciation allowance based on the useful life of the improvements.[45] If his tenancy is cancelled and he loses the improvements before writing off thier cost, the tenant can deduct the undepreciated balance in the year of cancellation.[46]

6.19   EXPENSE OF ACQUIRING LEASEHOLD INTEREST

Like the landlord, a tenant cannot write off the cost of acquiring a leasehold interest in the year such expenses are paid or incurred. Brokers' commissions, legal fees, expenses of title examination and title insurance and the like must be spread over the term of the lease. This is also true of the purchase price paid by one who acquires the leasehold interest from a prior tenant.[47] Of course, such expenditures would constitute the tenant's basis for his leasehold interest and the unamortized cost would reduce the gain upon a sale of such interest.

6.20   EXPENSES INCURRED IN OPERATING LEASED PREMISES

Of course the tenant can deduct as operating expenses the normal business expenses incurred in operating the leased premises. This includes repairs and maintenance, supplies, etc. Real estate taxes paid by the tenant as additional rent may be deducted as rent (not as taxes) assuming, of course, that the rent is deductible. However, the tenant's deduction for special assessments levied against the property is not allowable in the year paid or incurred; such a non-recurring charge is treated as a bonus or advance rental to be written off over the remaining term of the lease.[48]

SECTION D: TENANT'S RECEIPTS

6.21   AMOUNT RECEIVED TO CANCEL EXISTING LEASE

The amount which a tenant receives from the landlord for the surrender of the lease will normally produce capital gain, the Code recognizing that such a transaction constitutes a sale or exchange of a capital asset. §1241. Of course, if the tenant has a basis for his leasehold interest (for example, where he purchased it from another party), he may have a capital loss if the amount received for cancellation is less than his adjusted basis. This rule does not apply to amounts received for a renewal, extension, or other modification of a lease.[49]

6.22   AMOUNT RECEIVED ON ASSIGNMENT OF RIGHTS UNDER LEASE

A more difficult question arises where the tenant has sub-leased to another party. In such a case, where the tenant receives a payment for cancellation of his lease, thereby permitting the sub-lessee to deal directly with the property owner, IRS has taken the position that the amount so received amounts to a prepayment of future rent and is taxable as ordinary income. The courts have held, however, that this is in the nature of a capital transaction, i.e., a sale or exchange of a property right, regardless of whether the assignment of rights under lease is made from the prime tenant to the subtenant or from the prime tenant to the property owner.[50]

6.23   PAYMENT TO INDUCE TENANT TO LOCATE ON LANDLORD'S PROPERTY

A 1970 case involved the following situation. The owner of a parcel of land wished to construct a shopping center on it. He felt that the development would be helped if Federated Department Stores agreed to construct and operate a store within the center. He, therefore, offered Federated ten acres of land plus $200,000 per year for ten years to locate its store on the property in question. Although IRS felt that the payment constituted income to Federated, the Court disagreed. the amounts received by the tenant were tax-free contributions to its capital under §118. Disagreeing with the government, the Court held that the tax exempt character of the payment was not affected by the fact that it was made by private interest rather than a government unit or civic group or by the fact that it was motivated by the developer's own financial interests.[51] However, payment by Ford Motor Company to one of its dealers to relocate to a more desirable neightborhood was held to constitute taxable income to the dealer.[52]

SECTION E: LEASES WHICH MAY NOT BE RECOGNIZED FOR TAX PURPOSES

6.24   EFFECT OF PURCHASE OPTIONS

Where a lease gives the tenant an option to purchase the leased property, the question often arises as to whether the transaction is truly a lease or whether it more nearly resembles an installment purchase. If the transaction is a purchase, the following tax consequences occur: the tenant's payments are nondeductible capital expenditures rather than deductible rent, but he becomes entitled to depreciation on the property he is deemed to be purchasing; and the landlord's receipts are sales proceeds, presumably taxable as capital gain or loss, not rent which is taxable as ordinary income, and his depreciation deductions are disallowed on the property he is deemed to have conveyed.[53] Aside from the question of whether these are desirable or undesirable results from the standpoint of each party, it is clear that they work major modifications in the tax returns which are frequently not anticipated.

§162 (a) (3) allows a deduction for rent paid only where the tenant "has not taken or is not taking title or in which he has no equity." The Tax Court has stated the rule as follows:

> If payments are large enough to exceed the depreciation and value of the property and thus give the payor an equity in the property, it is less of a distortion of income to regard the payments as purchase price and allow depreciation on the property than to offset the entire payment against the income of one year.***
> *Chicago Stoker Corporation,* 14 TC 441, 445 (1950).

The intention of the parties to the transaction as evidenced by the provisions of the lease and giving effect to the circumstances existing at the time the instruments were executed is the principal criterion. If the rent is reasonable and the option price is a fair measure of future value, the lease should be sustained.[54]

On the other hand the presence of any of the following conditions tends to indicate a deferred purchase transaction and, when weighed with all of the other facts, may require a reformation of the instruments for tax purposes:[55] where the periodic rental payments are to be credited against the purchase price if the option is exercised; where the rental payments exceed the fair rental value of the building; where the option price is unreasonably low, presumably reflecting a credit for earlier rent payments; or where the tenant is required to make substantial improvements to the property, that being consistent with a contemplated acquisition of an equity.

6.25   LEASES BETWEEN RELATED PARTIES

Although there is no outright prohibition on the deduction of rental payments where the tenant and the landlord are related, this is an area which seems to lead to abuses and which has resulted in a considerable amount of litigation. Many of the cases involve professional persons—a typical case involves a doctor who makes a gift of his equipment or an office building to his children or to a trust for his children and simultaneously leases it back. The objective is to give the high-bracket tenant a rent deduction and have the corresponding income taxed in a lower bracket.

IRS will attack these leases on one or more of the following grounds: that the transactions lacks business purpose or is a sham; that the tenant remains in control of the leased property; that the rental is not reasonable; or that where a short-term trust is involved as landlord, the tenant's reversionary interest constitutes an equity in the property so as to disqualify the rents under §162(a) (3). There are numerous decided cases in this area[56] but the following rules should be followed to the extent possible by taxpayers contemplating such a transaction:

1. If a trust is involved as the landlord, it should run for at least ten years. The trustee should be independent, preferably a bank or some other unrelated party.

2. There should be a written lease between the parties.

3. The terms of the lease should be fair and reasonable. Appraisals as to the fair rental value of the property are helpful.

4. A business purpose for the lease should be established if possible.

6.26   SALE-LEASEBACK TRANSACTIONS

In a sale-leaseback transaction, the property is sold on the condition that the buyer lease it back to the former owner. Thus, the seller becomes a tenant paying rent for the use of the property which he originally owned and the buyer becomes an investor-landlord.

Sale-leaseback transactions present a number of benefits to each of the parties. The seller often finds that it is a relatively inexpensive way of raising capital to be employed in its business. The traditional limitations of mortgage loans may be avoided. The seller improves his balance sheet since a fixed asset (real estate) is converted to a current asset (cash) and the balnace sheet reflects no increase in liabilities except in a footnote. (The balance sheet treatment of sale-leasebacks is the subject of a number of studies and reports by the Financial Accounting Standards Board.) Finally, the seller hopes that the rent paid by him under the lease will be fully deductible as contrasted with mortgage payments which represent partially non-deductible payments of principal.

From the standpoint of the buyer the transaction presents other benefits. The buyer has presumably found a satisfactory investment for his available funds. Assuming that there is no repurchase option in the lease, he hopes that in addition to the yield which he well realize on the rents received during the term of the lease, there will be an appreciation factor which will accrue to his benefit as the owner of the property upon the expiration of the lease. Although the rental income is taxable, he will be entitled to a deduction for depreciation on the improvements which will shelter the income and may even produce a tax loss.

The parties must realize, however, that their characterization of a transaction as a sale-leaseback is not binding on IRS. The Commissioner has utilized a number of grounds for attacking sale-leaseback transactions. Chapter 4, Section 5, includes a discussion of the question of loans distinguished from purchases in sale-leaseback transactions. Briefly, the Commissioner sometimes contends that the amount paid for the property by the ostensible buyer is, in fact, a loan to the original owner and that, for tax purposes, title has not passed. Similarly, Chapter 9, Section 7 contains a discussion of cases involving sellers who simultaneously lease the property back for a term of 30 years or more. Such a transaction may constitute an exchange, the seller exchanging his fee interest in the property for a leasehold interest plus cash and notes. Since the leasehold is an interest in real estate, the transaction is sometimes treated as a tax-free exchange rather than a sale, and the seller's loss is not recognized for tax purposes. Similarly, in Section 25 above, we saw that sale-leasebacks between related parties may not be recognized for a number of reasons.

Where the sales price is abnormally low, (thus reducing seller's taxable gain) and the rent payable under the lease is correspondingly reduced (thus reducing buyer's rental income),IRS may contend that the buyer has constructively received advance rental income in the year the transaction is closed. The amount of such constructive income would be the difference between the fair rental value of the property for the entire term of the lease and the amount of rent which is actually payable under the lease.[57] Where there is a repurchase option in favor of the seller, the transaction is particularly suspect because the rental level may be designed to provide a predetermined return to buyer which is significantly less than the fair rental value of the property. Finally, a sale-leaseback which is structured merely for tax purposes, where the buyer assumes no economic risk, will not be recognized.[58] Regardless of the grounds for upsetting the transaction, when the purported lease is not recognized for tax purposes, each of the parties will be required to adjust his returns so as to reflect the true nature of the transaction.

FOOTNOTES FOR CHAPTER SIX

[1] *Henry B. Miller*, 10 BTA 383 (1938); *Harriet B. Borland*, 27 BTA 538 (1933); *Trustee Corp.*, 42 T.C. 482 (1964); Rev. Rul. 71-283, 1971-2 CB 168; *Peerless Weighing & Vending Machine Corp.*, 52 T.C. 850 (1969); P-H Fed Taxes ¶11,304(5).

[2] *Harry Latter*, 1961 P-H Memo T.C.,¶61,067 appeal dismissed (CA5, 1962);*Wells Fargo Bank and Union Trust Co. v. Comm'r.*, 163 F.2d 512, 36 AFTR 53 (CA9, 1947); *The Montgomery Co.*, 54 T.C. 986(1970); P-H Federal Taxes ¶11,306.

[3] *Business Real Estate Trust of Boston*, 25 BTA 191 (1932), non acq.; *Keiler II v. U.S.*, 395 F.2d 991, 21 AFTR 2d 1269 (CA6. 1968); *Houston Chronicle Publishing Co. v. U.S.*, 481 F.2d 1240, 32 AFTR 2d 73-5312.1 (CA5, 1973), cert. den.; P-H Fed Taxes ¶11,307.

[4] Reg. 1.165-3(a); P-H Fed Taxes ¶14,258.

[5]*Bender v. U.S.,* 383 F.2d 656, 20 AFTR 2d 5521 (CA6, 1967), cert. den.

[6]Reg. 1.165-3(a)(2); incidental use of the building is immaterial. *The Montgomery Co.,* 330 F.2d 950, 13 AFTR 2d 1284 (CA6, 1964); *Ryan Motor Sales, Inc.,* 1970 P-H T.C. Memo 70-1301; P-H Fed Taxes ¶14,258(a) (2).

[7]Reg. 1.165-3(b) (2); P-H Fed Taxes ¶14,276(5).

[8]Reg. 1.165-3(b) (1); *Andrew F. McBride,* 50 T.C. 1 (1968); *J.A. Rider,* 1971 P-H T.C. Memo 71-043; *Adolph B. Canelo III.,* 53 T.C. 217(1969), aff'd per curiam (CA9, 1971). Where the land and building were purchased together, it will be important for the taxpayer to show, by some evidence, what portion of the original purchase price was allocable to the improvements.

[9]*Herman Landerman,* 54 T.C. 1042(1970); Rev. Rul. 67-410, 1967-2 CB 93, presumes an intent to demolish where the useful life of the building is less than the unexpired term of the lease but this automatic inference was rejected by the District Court in *Holder* (see footnote 10); *Gerald R. Gorman,* 1974 P-H T.C. Memo 74-72.

[10]*Feldman v. Wood,* 335 F.2d 264, 14 AFTR 2d 5423 (CA9, 1964), non acq; *Holder v. U.S.,* 26 AFTR 2d 70-5693 (D.C. Ga., 1970); P-H Fed Taxes ¶14,276(15); *Hightower v. U.S.,* 463 F.2d 182, 29 AFTR 2d 72-1406 (CA5, 1972).

[11]Rev. Rul. 70-4081, 1970-2 CB 68; Reg. 1.162-11(a); P-H Fed. Taxes ¶11,288 et.seq.

[12]*Manhattan Life Insurance Co.,* 28 BTA 129(1933), rev'd on other grounds, 71 F.2d 292, 14 AFTR 267(CA2, 1934); *Kokjer, Jr. v. U.S.,* 25 AFTR 2d 70-1156 (N.D. Cal, 1970).

[13]*Post v. Comm'r.,* 109 F.2d 135, 24 AFTR 207 (CA2, 1940) dictum; but liquidation in kind by a lessor (without terminating the lease) has been held not to accelerate the deduction of the unamortized balance of the lease expenses.

[14]*World Publishing Co. v. Comm'r.,* 299 F.2d 614,9 AFTR 2d 819 (CA8, 1962); *Barnes v. U.S.,* 34 AFTR 2d 74-5146 (Ct.Cl., 1973) no depreciation allowed to landlord's heirs based on tenant-constructed improvements.

[15]*DeMatteo Construction Co. v. U.S.,* 433 F.2d 1263, 26 AFTR 2d 70-5754 (CA1, 1970). The Court noted that a different result might follow if at the time of purchase the anticipated life of the building had exceeded the term of the lease.

[16]*Comm'r v. Moore,* 207 F.2d 265, 44 AFTR 470(CA9, 1953), cert. den. (1954); Fed Taxes ¶15,357(45). Another court questions the right of a purchaser to the write-off, see *Midler Court Realty Inc.,* footnote 17 infra.

[17]Reg. 1.167(a)-4; *Airport Bldg. Development Corp.,* 58 T.C. 538 (1972); *Midler Court Realty, Inc.,* 61 T.C. 590 (1970), aff'd 36 AFTR 2d 75-5567 (CA3, 1975).

[18]*Alaska Realty Co. v. Comm'r,* 141 F.2d 675, 32 AFTR 468 (CA6, 1944); *The North Carolina Midland Railway Co. v. U.S.,* 163 F Supp. 610, 2 AFTR 2d 5229; *Harry H. Kem, Jr.,* 51 T.C. 455, 460 (1968) dictum *I.J. Wagner v. Comm'r.,* 518 F.2d 655, 36 AFTR 2d 75-5233 (CA10, 1975).

[19]*Comm'r v. Terre Haute Electric Co.,* 67 F.2d 697, 13 AFTR 384 (CA7, 1933); see cases annotated, P-H Fed Taxes ¶15,357(10).

[20]§61(a) (5). An assignment of the right to receive rents is ineffective to avoid taxation without a conveyance of the property. *Iber v. U.S.,* 409 F2d 1273,23 AFTR 2d, 69-1001 (CA7, 1969), *Stedwell Johnston et al,* 1976 P-H T.C. Memo ¶76-636; *J.A. Martin,* 56, T.C. 1259 (1971, aff'd per curiam (CA5, 1972).

[21]Reg. 1.61-8(b); *BJR Corporation,* 67 T.C. _____ No. 11 (1976) and cases cited therein.

[22]*Warren Service Corp. v. Comm'r.,* 110 F.2d 723, 24 AFTR 758 (CA2, 1940); *Clinton Hotel Realty Corp. v. Comm'r.,* 128 F.2d 968, 29 AFTR 758 (CA5, 1942).

[23]*J. & E. Enterprises, Inc.,* 1967 P-H T.C. Memo ¶67,19; *Gilken Corp. v. Comm'r.,* 176 F.2d 141, 38 AFTR 265 (CA6, 1949); P-H Fed Taxes ¶12,310. Labeling the transaction as a "loan" from tenant to landlord will not determine the tax consequences if the facts indicate that a rent prepayment was actually made, *U.S. v. Williams,* 395 F.2d 508, 22 AFTR 2d 5047 (CA5, 1968); see *Clinton Hotel Realty Corp. v. Comm'r.,* 128 F.2d 968, 29 AFTR 758 (CA5, 1942) holding a loan with interest required was recognized as a loan and not taxed as advance rent; *Blue Flame Gas Co.,* 54 T.C. 584 (1976); see generally *Simon M. Lazarus,* 58 T.C. 854 (1972) acq, aff'd 513 F.2d 824, 35 AFTR 2d 75-1191, 35 AFTR 2d 75-1640 (CA9, 1975); *Spa Building Corp.,* 1974 P-H T.C. Memo ¶74,307; P-H Fed Taxes ¶20,310(20).

[24]Rev. Rul. 68-19, 1968-1 CB 42.

[25]*Sirbo Holding, Inc.*, 61 T.C. 723 (1973), aff'd 509 F.2d 1220 35 AFTR 2d 75-568 (CA2, 1975).

[26]§109; Reg. 1.109-1. Neither are the improvements income to the landlord at the time of construction. Reg. 1.61-8(c).

[27]*M.E. Blatt Company v. U.S.*, 305 U.S. 267, 277, 21 AFTR 1007 (1938). *David G. Satterfield*, 1975 P-H T.C. Memo ¶75,203.

[28]I.T. 4009, 1950-1 CB 13; *Isidore Brown*, 22 T.C. 147, aff'd 220 F.2d 12, 47 AFTR 244 (CA7, 1955); *Your Health Club, Inc.*, 4 T.C. 385 (1944). But see *Beechman, Inc. v. U.S.*, 32 AFTR2d73-5916(D.C. Tenn, 1973) (Improvements constructed by tenant at will, rather than by a true lessee, held not to come within the *Blatt* rationale).

[29]§167(g). *Weiss v. Weiner*, 279 U.S. 333, 7 AFTR 8865(1929); *Buzzell v. U.S.* 326 F.2d 825, 13 AFTR 2d 513(CA1, 1964); *Reisinger v. Comm'r.*, 144 F.2d 475, 32 AFTR 1226(CA2, 1944); *Easter v. Comm'r.*, 338 F.2d 968, 14 AFTR 2d 6015 (CA4, 1964), cert. denied.

[30]*Hort v. Comm'r.*, 313 U.S. 28, 25 AFTR 1207(1941); Reg. 1.61-8(b). The same result occurs in respect to a compromise settlement of any obligation of the lessee. See *Sirbo Holding, Inc.*, footnote 25 supra.

[31]*A.L. Trunk*, 32 T.C. 1127, (1959), acq.

[32]*Owen Meredith*, 12 T.C. 344 (1949), acq; *M.N. Tobias*, 40 T.C. 84 (1964) acq.

[33]*Metropolitan Bldg. Co v. Comm*, 282 F.2d 592 6 AFTR 2d 5493 (CA9,1960) rev'g 31 T.C. 971 (1959).

[34]*I.G. Zumwalt*, 25 BTA 566, 575 (1932); P-H Fed Taxes ¶7261 et seq. Reg. §1.61-8(c), payment of lessor's expense may constitute rent and tenant can amortize such payments if they are applicable to an ascertainable period greater than one year.

[35]*Wolan v. Comm'r.*, 184 F.2d 101, 39 AFTR 1025 (CA10, 1950); *Baton Coal Company v. Comm'r.*, 51 F.2d 469, 10 AFTR 270 (CA3, 1931); P-H Fed Taxes ¶11,320.

[36]*Bellingham Cold Storage Co.*, 64 T.C. 51 (1975).

[37]Reg. 1.162-11(a); P-H Fed Taxes ¶11,320; *Steinway and Sons*, 46 T.C. 375 (1966), acq.

[38]*Cassatt v. Comm'r.*, 137 F.2d 745, 31 AFTR 576 (CA3, 1943); Rev. Rul. 69-511, 1969-2 CB 24.

[39]Reg. 1.162-11(a); *Pig & Whistle Co*, 9 BTA 668 (1927); P-H Fed Taxes ¶11,859.

[40]Reg. 1.162-11(b) (1).

[41]Reg. 1.162(b) (1); Reg. 1.167(a)-4; *Kenneth D. Smith*, 1965 P-H T.C. Memo ¶65,169.

[42]See Judge Tannenwald's concurring decision in *Allen M. Early*, 52 T.C. 560 (1969) for a good discussion of the distinction between depreciation and amortization. Essentially, a deduction determined by the useful life of the underlying property calls for depreciation; a deduction determined by the useful life of the taxpayer's interest in the property, without regard to the property itself, calls for amortization; *Cassatt v. Comm'r.*, 137 F.2d 745 (CA3, 1943).

[43]Reg. 1.167(a)-4.

[44]*I.G. Zumwalt*, 25 BTA 566, 575(1932).

[45]*Glazer Steel Corp. v. U.S.*, 388 F.2d 990, 20 AFTR 2d 5921 (Ct Cl, 1968).

[46]See P-H Fed Taxes ¶11,853.

[47]Reg. 1.162-11(a); *King Amusement Co.*, 15 BTA 566, aff'd 44 F.2d 709 (CA6, 1930), cert. den.

[48]See *Mary Evans*, 42 BTA 246, 254 (1929).

[49]Reg. 1.1241-1(b). See *Billy Rose's Diamond Horseshoe, Inc. v. U.S.*, 448 F.2d 549, 28 AFTR 2d 71-5563(CA2, 1971). Rev. Rul. 72-85, 1972-1 CB 234; *Metropolitan Bldg. Co.* footnote 33 supra.

[50]*Samuel D. Miller*,48 T.C. 649 (1967), acq. 1968-1, CB 2 (assignment to subtenant); *Metropolitan Building Co. v. Comm'r.*, 282 Fed 2d 592, 5493 6 AFTR 2d (CA9, 1960) (assignment to lessor).

[51]*Federated Department Stores, Inc. v. Comm'r.*, 426 F.2d 417, 25 AFTR 2d 70-1269 (CA6, 1970), aff'g 51 T.C. 500, non acq. To the same effect see *May Dept. Stores*, 519 F.2d 1154, 36 AFTR 2d 75-5503(CA8, 1975).

[52]*John B. White, Inc.*, 55 T.C. 729(1971), aff'd, 458 F.2d 989, 29 AFTR 2d 72-988 (CA3, 1972).

[53]*Frank Lyon Co. v. U.S.,* 536 F.2d 746 38 AFTR 2d 76-5060 (CA8, 1976), cert. granted by U.S. Supreme Court.

[54]*LTV Corp.,* 63 T.C. 39 (1974); *Estate of Clara Stundon,* 1970 P-H T.C. Memo ¶70,020; P-H Fed Taxes, ¶11,839; *Norman Bake Smith,* 51 T.C. 429 (1969).

[55]*M & W Gear Co.,* 54 T.C. 385 (1970), acq; *D.M. Haggard,* 24 T.C. 1124, aff'd 241 Fed 2d 288,50 AFTR 1035 (CA9, 1956). See Rev. Rul. 55-540, 1955-2 CB 39 for the factors used to classify leases of personal property with purchase options. In Rev. Proc. 75-21, 1975-2 CB 18, IRS set forth the criteria to get an advance ruling on an equipment lease. *Chas Smith,* P-H T.C. Memo ¶76,114 (high minimum rent indicated intent to buy). Drier Real Estate Leasing Transactions, 32 NYU Inst. Fed Tax 1655, 1657; P-H Fed Taxes ¶11,838.

[56]The cases are annotated at P-H Fed Taxes ¶11,832. For recent cases see *Frank L. Butler,* 65 T.C. 327 (1975) (no business purpose present); *Perry v. U.S.,* 520 F.2d 235, 36 AFTR 2d 75-5500 (CA4, 1975) (no business purpose present and the independent bank trustee involvement was not determinative); *Mathews v. Comm'r.,* 520 F.2d 323, 36 AFTR 2d 75-5965 (CA5, 1975) (absence of arm's length bargaining with trustee was indicative of no economic reality); *Brooke v. U.S.,* 468 F.2d 1155, 30 AFTR 2d 72-5284 (CA9, 1972) (gift to guardian for donor's children recognized and rents allowed, no business purpose required).

[57]*Alstores Realty Corp.,* 46 T.C. 363 (1966) See Chapter 7, Section 7.2(c).

[58]*Estate of Franklin v. Comm.,* _____F.2d_____, 38 AFTR 2d 76-6164(CA9, 1976), In the following cases the sale-leaseback was recognized: *Amer. Realty Trust v. U.S.,* 498 F.2d 1194, 34 AFTR 2d 74-5308(CA 4, 1974); and *Sun Oil Co.,* 1976 P-H T.C. Memo, ¶76,040.

7

OVERCOMING TAX PROBLEMS

IN THE OPERATION

OF REAL ESTATE

This chapter is concerned with the tax problems of the real estate operator, one who owns and manages income-producing real estate, whether it be an office building, apartment house, shopping center or commercial property. Although this is essentially the operation of a business and, therefore, involves all of the problems common to business generally, there are certain tax and accounting problems which are peculiar to real estate and which merit special attention. The discussion will cover these major points:

SECTION A: ACCOUNTING METHODS AND PROBLEMS

There are a number of methods of accounting which are acceptable for income tax purposes. All that is required is that the method which is adopted must clearly reflect income. If it does not, the Commissioner may prescribe a method which does.[1] It is not necessary that the same method be utilized for income tax reporting purposes as is utilized in the books of account. For example, the books may be kept on the accrual basis while the business files its tax returns and pays its tax by computing income on the cash basis.[2] Of course, the taxpayer must be consistent and having adopted a method of accounting, he cannot switch to a new method without the consent of the Commissioner.[3]

7.1 CASH METHOD AND ACCRUAL METHOD

The cash receipts and disbursements method of accounting and the accrual method of accounting are both specifically authorized by the Code. Under the cash method, income is recognized for tax purposes in the year in which it is received and expenses are deducted in the year they are paid. Under the accrual method, on the other hand, income is recognized in the year in which the right to receive the income becomes fixed and deductions are allowed when an obligation is definitely established. The principal advantage of the cash method is that of simplicity. There is a minimum of record keeping requirements since accounts receivable and accounts payable are not involved in the computation of income. The bank deposit book which reflects cash receipts and the checkbook which reflects cash disbursements become the basic accounting records. A second advantage of the cash method is that it permits the taxpayer some discretion in controlling the year in which income will be taxed or an expense will be deductible. By accelerating payment of real estate taxes to a high-bracket year, for example, the property owner can accelerate his tax deduction.

The cash method is the method which is most generally utilized in real estate operations. There are some situations, however, where the accrual method is more advantageous, and, of course, where the real estate is merely an incidental part of a larger business which utilizes the accrual method, it is not unusual for that method to be followed in connection with the real estate operation as well.

Combinations of methods—so-called hybrid accounting methods— will be permitted if they clearly reflect income and are consistently used. For example, some taxpayers utilize the cash method for some items and the accrual method for others.

7.2   EXCEPTIONS TO THE GENERAL RULE GOVERNING THE CASH METHOD

The cash method of accounting cannot be blindly followed to the point where it results in a distortion of income. Accordingly, a number of exceptions have developed. Those which are material to the real estate operator include the following:

(a) Assets Having a Useful Life Extending Beyond the Taxable Year—Regardless of the accounting method utilized by the taxpayer, if an expenditure results in the creation of an asset having a useful life which extends substantially beyond the close of the taxable year in which the expenditure is paid or incurred, the amount may not be currently deductible or may be deductible only in part for such year.[4] In short, the taxpayer is normally compelled to write off his investment in long-term property over the life of the property, notwithstanding the cash method of accounting. Examples are:

> Buildings and other fixed assets subject to the allowance for depreciation.
> Leasehold improvements made by a tenant.
> Capital improvements to property which do not qualify as repairs or maintenance.
> Insurance premiums paid on a policy which runs for more than one year.[5]
> Prepaid amounts which represent deposits as distinguished from current business expenses.[6]

(b) Constructive Receipt of Income—The actual receipt of cash is not always essential to produce income for a cash basis taxpayer. Constructive receipt of funds is also a taxable event; a sum may be credited to a taxpayer's account or set apart for him in such a way that he may draw on it freely at any time. In that event, he is taxed on the income whether he chooses to possess it or not.[7] Although revenue agents tend to exaggerate the scope of the constructive receipt doctrine, the courts have held that it is to be sparingly applied. It applies only where the taxpayer's control of the item credited is unrestricted. Thus, a sum is not constructively received if it is only conditionally credited; or if it is indefinite in amount; or if the payor has no funds with which to pay the credited amount; or if it is subject to any other substantial limitation. A property owner who utilizes the cash basis would be required to report as taxable income the receipt of a tenant's check in payment of rent despite the fact that he postponed depositing the check until the subsequent year. Of course, if there are not sufficient funds to cover the check or if the parties have agreed that the landlord is to hold the check for a period of time, then the check is not the equivalent of cash on the date it is received and a contrary result would follow.

> *Warning:* Where a tenant agrees to make bonus or advance rent payments under a lease which are to be spread out over several years, it is dangerous to set up this obligation in a separate negotiable or assignable instrument apart from the lease. It has been held that the promise of a solvent tenant which is unconditional, assignable, not subject to set-offs and of a kind that is frequently transferred to lenders or investors without a substantial discount is the equivalent of cash and taxable the same as cash would have been had it been received by the landlord rather than the tenant's obligation.[8]

Suggestion: Constructive receipt is a doctrine available to the taxpayer as well as to the government. When it is advantageous for a cash basis taxpayer to report income in the year it is constructively received, rather than waiting for the year of actual receipt, he may do so. In fact, he is probably required to do so since the constructive receipt doctrine is not elective.[9]

(c) *Seller's Retained Interest in Cash Flow*—We have commented earlier that often the buyer is more interested in tax benefits resulting from the ownership of real estate, particularly the depreciation deduction, than he is in the cash flow to be derived from the property. Supposing that the buyer and seller agree that the seller may retain the cash flow for a specified period of time even after the closing of the sale and the passage of title to the buyer. The seller has, in effect, increased the amount of cash he will ultimately derive from the property and the buyer has reduced the amount of cash required of him at closing. Will such a transaction be recognized or will the courts hold that the buyer has constructively received the cash flow during the period in question and constructively paid it to the seller?

Example: Under a contract of sale in 1945, taxpayer purchased certain real estate for $40,000. However, seller retained all of the rental income until August 15, 1947. The Commissioner contended that the buyer was liable to pay taxes on the rental income derived during this two year period but the Court held in favor of the taxpayer. The Court pointed out that although the seller retained the income, he specifically agreed to pay property taxes, insurance premiums and all normal maintenance items and expenses so that the property would ultimately be delivered to buyer in the condition it was at closing. In short, the seller took all of the risks of ownership and management and, therefore, should be taxed directly on the cash receipts while the buyer got the depreciation deductions.[10]

Comment: Although the taxpayer was successful in the case described above, a slight change in the form of the instruments can produce the opposite result. If the seller has merely reserved what amounts to a lease of the premises with all of the risks of ownership in buyer, then the buyer will be deemed to have received the rental income.[11]

The courts have said that the following factors normally indicate that the amount in question is part payment of the purchase price and taxable to the buyer: where the amount payable to the seller is limited to a specified amount; where the duration of the payments is limited to a short term; and where interest is to accrue on the entire balance due seller, thus indicating that the amount is a debt running from the time of sale and the periodic payments are simply made in reduction of that debt.[12]

7.3 CARRYOVER OF LOSSES FROM RENTAL PROPERTY

The rental activities of a taxpayer are normally considered to be attributable to his trade or business. Accordingly, any net losses incurred in managing his properties qualify as net operating losses. Net operating losses can be carried back and forward and offset against business income realized in the covered years. This result has been reached in the case of an operator who owned several units as well as in the case of a taxpayer who rented a single property.[13]

Comment: It is not always to the advantage of the taxpayer to claim operating losses. Under §172(d)(4), operating (business) losses cannot be offset against non-business income. Therefore, a taxpayer with non-business income may prefer to claim itemized deductions for the interest and taxes attributable to his rental property.[14]

SECTION B: EXPENSES INCURRED IN THE OWNERSHIP AND MANAGEMENT OF REAL ESTATE

7.4 CARRYING CHARGES

As indicated above, cash basis taxpayers normally claim deductions for expenses in the year they are paid and accrual basis taxpayers normally claim such deductions in the year the liability becomes fixed. In certain circumstances, however, it may be advantageous for a property owner to defer a deduction from the year of payment or accrual to a later year when he expects to be in a higher bracket. The Code grants such an option to the owner of business property.[15] The election to defer the deduction would be useful, for example, where a newly organized business is paying real estate taxes and mortgage interest on an undeveloped parcel of land which may be sold at a later date. Since the business has no income during the early years, tax benefits attributable to such deductions may be wasted, whereas if the deductions are capitalized (i.e., added to the basis of the land) they will reduce the taxable gain in the event of a sale at a later date. Also, a taxpayer who anticipates little or no income while construction of a building is in process may wish to capitalize the carrying charges and taxes until the time when the real estate is in operation, thereby producing larger depreciation allowances to offset against the rental income from the completed project.

Items that may be capitalized include:[16]

(1) Taxes, mortgage interest and other carrying charges on unimproved and unproductive real estate;

(2) Deductible expenditures incurred in developing or building improvements to real estate (such as interest on loans to finance the improvements, social security taxes on wages paid for services in the development and improvement as well as taxes and carrying charges).

Making the elections is relatively simple. The taxpayer files a statement with the original return for the taxable year as to which the election is made setting forth the items to be capitalized.

Normally, consistency is not required. Until an improvement is made on the real estate, the taxpayer may capitalize certain items in one year and deduct them in another year, and if the same type of charges are incurred on two or more projects, they may be capitalized on one project and not the other. However, where a project is being developed "if expenditures for several items of the same type are incurred with respect to a single project the election to capitalize must, if exercised, be exercised as to all items of that type."[17]

7.5 INTEREST EXPENSE

Under §163 for years prior to 1976 interest is deductible in the year it is paid or accrued depending on the accounting method utilized by the taxpayer. This would normally cover all interest paid in connection with the ownership or development of a project, whether the loan is secured by a mortgage or not.

(a) "Points" Paid to Secure a Loan.

A buyer frequently is required to pay a premium in order to obtain a mortgage loan. This charge which is called a loan processing fee or "points" is treated as interest if it is paid to the lender solely for the use or forbearance of money.

> *Example:* Cash basis taxpayer acquires a property and obtains a $350,000 mortgage loan from his bank for that purpose. In addition to paying 8-1/2% interest (the prevailing maximum rate in his area) he agrees to pay two points, or $7,000, at the time of closing. This is in addition to the usual closing costs for title report, escrow fees, etc. Since the fee is paid as compensation to the lender *solely* for the use or forbearance of money, it is deductible as interest.[18]

Moreover, for years prior to the Tax Reform Act of 1976, the payment of such points need not be amortized over the term of the loan, provided the deduction does not produce a material distortion of income.[19] See the discussion at Section 5(b)—*Prepaid Interest under the Tax Reform Act of 1976*—for the treatment of points for years beginning after December 31, 1975. Also see Section 5(f)—*Taxes and Interest During the Construction Period*—which will apply to points paid during the construction period in certain years.

"Points" paid by a seller of property (for example, where the seller arranges for the buyer's mortgage loan) are not deductible as interest. However, the seller may treat these as a selling expense, thereby reducing his gain on the sale.[20]

(b) Prepaid Interest.

Since the interest on a mortgage loan must be paid sooner or later, borrowers will sometimes attempt to prepay a substantial amount of interest so as to accelerate the deduction to a year when it can produce the greatest tax benefit. Since the election as to whether to use the cash basis or the accrual basis is normally made by each taxpayer, it would appear that such prepayments should be permitted. However, under §446 (b) "if the method used does not clearly reflect income, the computation of taxable income shall be made under such method, as in the opinion of the Secretary or his delegate, does clearly reflect income." In other words, in appropriate cases the Commissioner can compel use of the accrual method.

Prepaid interest prior to the Tax Reform Act of 1976—In 1968 the IRS issued a revenue ruling changing its previous long-standing policy (adopted in 1945) of allowing a deduction of interest prepaid for up to five years.[21] The 1968 ruling held that interest prepaid by a cash basis taxpayer for more than 12 months beyond the end of his current taxable year was presumed to materially distort income and the deduction was disallowed. Interest prepaid for a period of up to 12 months following the current taxable year was to be reviewed on a case by case basis to determine whether income was materially distorted. For example, if a taxpayer closed a mortgage loan in July of 1975, he was not permitted to deduct in the year of closing prepaid interest for calendar year 1977 or thereafter; whether the deduction was permitted for 1976 interest depended upon whether there was a distortion of income. Among the factors which were considered in making this determination according to the ruling were the amount of income in the year of payment; the income of previous years; the amount of prepaid interest; the time of payment; the reason for prepayment; and the existence of a varying rate of interest over the term of the loan. Apparently, the most important factor was the reason for prepayment; if the taxpayer established a business purpose for the prepayment as opposed to merely a tax benefit, he had a better chance of justifying the interest deduction.

Although the Courts rejected the arbitrary position of the 1968 ruling that deductibility depended upon a fixed line, with payments of interest for the period beyond the line being automatically disallowed, they generally held against the taxpayers on the material distortion issue where it appeared that the transaction was a sham or was structured in an artificial manner merely for the purpose of creating tax deductions.[22] On the other hand, where taxpayers could establish a reasonable basis for the prepayment, the deduction was sustained.[23]

Prepaid Interest under the Tax Reform Act of 1976—Under the new Act in the case of interest payments made in 1976 and later years, a cash basis taxpayer will be permitted to deduct that interest only in the period to which it relates under the accrual method of accounting. In other words, interest must be amortized over the period of the loan regardless of the date of payment. Points paid to obtain a mortgage loan are also required to be deducted ratably over the term of the loan. However, points paid on home mortgages generally can still be deducted currently.

(c) Investment Interest.

Prior to 1972, investment interest was a tax preference item subject to the minimum tax. Beginning in 1972, however, excess investment interest became an item subject to limited deductibility. As a practical matter most taxpayers need not be concerned with this limitation because the first $10,000 of annual investment interest ($25,000 for years prior to 1976) is deductible each year in any event. Even where investment interest exceeds these limits, the limitation will cause no difficulty if the taxpayer also has investment income (dividends, interest, etc.) since such income can be offset against the investment interest before computing the amount of "excess" investment interest subject to the limitation. There will be many cases, however, where this limitation is relevant and the concept should, therefore, be thoroughly understood by persons dealing in large real estate projects.

Under §163(d) investment interest is defined as interest paid or accrued on indebtedness which is incurred or continued to purchase or carry "property held for investment." It is essential, therefore, to distinguish between property used in a trade or business and "property held for investment." The most common case of property held for investment in the real estate field involves property which is leased to third parties subject to a "net lease." Section 163(d)(4)(A) provides that property subject to a net lease will not be regarded as property used in a trade or business, i.e., the interest paid or accrued on the mortgage on such property will constitute investment interest and will be subject to the limitations referred to above. Property is subject to a "net lease" if it falls under either the expense test or the return test described below.

Expense Test—Property is subject to a net lease if the sum of the landlord's deductions with respect to the property which are allowable solely by reason of §162 is less than 15% of the rental income produced by the property for the taxable year. Note that only §162 expenses are counted in determining whether the landlord can meet this requirement. Hence, depreciation, interest, taxes, amortization and depletion do not count since they are deductible under other Code sections. Also, even the §162 expenses do not count if they are paid or payable by the tenant or any other party other than the landlord unless the landlord is obligated to reimburse the party paying the expenses. In short, where a landlord's expenses in connection with leased property are inconsequential the landlord will fail the expense test, the lease will be classified as a net lease and the interest on the mortgage will be classified as investment interest.

Return Test—Under the return test, a lease is classified as a net lease if the landlord is either guaranteed a specified return or is guaranteed in whole or in part against loss of income. Whether the landlord is guaranteed a specified return or is assured against loss will depend upon the facts and circumstances in each case. It seems clear that the return test is aimed at the the lease which provides that the landlord will receive a stated amount of net return which will not be affected by increases in the overhead expenses attributable to the property. Thus, it is fairly simple to avoid the return test provided that escalator clauses which pass the increased expenses on to the tenant are not included in the lease.

Deduction Limits.—The amount of investment interest which is deductible in a given year equals investment interest paid or accrued reduced by the sum of the following:

(1) $10,000 ($5,000 in the case of a separate return by a married individual) for years beginning after December 31, 1975, and $25,000 ($12,500 in the case of a separate return by a married individual) for years prior to 1976; plus

(2) The total amount of the taxpayer's "net investment income"[24]; plus

(3) The excess of the amount of "out-of-pocket" expanses in connection with property subject to a net lease (interest, property taxes, ordinary business expenses, and non-business expenses incurred to produce income or maintain the net lease property) over gross proceeds from the net lease; plus

(4) An amount equal to the net capital gains for years prior to 1976. (The Tax Reform Act of 1976 does not permit an offset for capital gains); plus

(5) One-half of the amount by which the investment interest exceeds the total of the amounts described above for years prior to 1976. (The Tax Reform Act of 1976 does not permit this offset.)

> *Example 1:* During the taxable year, the taxpayer has $50,000 of net investment income ($60,000 of investment income less $10,000 of investment expenses) and $40,000 of investment interest. Since the amount of the investment interest is less than the net investment income, he can deduct the entire $40,000 interest.

Example 2: During 1977, the taxpayer has net investment income of $10,000 and investment interest of $30,000. He can deduct only $10,000 of investment interest. This is derived by adding the $10,000 base; plus the $10,000 of net investment income; and deducting the $20,000 sum of these items from the investment interest.

The old rules (pre Tax Reform Act of 1976) continue to apply to interest on a specific debt, for a specified term, incurred prior to 9/11/75 or incurred after that date under a binding written contract or commitment in effect on that date and at all times thereafter.

Elections Available to Landlord—The Revenue Act of 1971 added §163(d) (7) which permits certain elections to a landlord, thus providing some flexibility and some avenues of relief from the rules spelled out above. A landlord may elect to treat as a single lease property which is subject to multiple leases. Thus, if the aggregated expenses of the property taken as a whole equal or exceed 15% of gross rental income, the expense test will not result in net lease treatment. The election must be made not later than the time prescribed for filing the return for the year in which the election is applicable. Also, a taxpayer can elect not to apply the expense test at all on property which has been used for more than five years.

Construction Period Interest—A special rule applies to interest paid or accrued during construction. §163(d) (4) (D) provides that interest paid or accrued on indebtedness incurred or continued in the construction of property to be used in a trade or business shall not be treated as investment interest.

Carryover of Disallowed Interest—The amount of investment interest which is disallowed under the rules set forth above can be carried over indefinitely under §163(d (2). However, there are a number of limitations on the amount subject to such carryovers. First, the amount of interest which may be deducted in a carryover year is limited to 50% of the following amounts: the net investment income for the year in question, plus $25,000, less the investment interest paid or accrued during that year. The mathematics can become quite complex but the point is that the amount of investment interest which can be deducted (in excess of $25,000) depends in large part on whether the taxpayer has investment income in the later year which can be utilized to absorb the deduction. A second limitation is that the amount of interest carried over is reduced by 50% of the capital gains deduction to which the taxpayer is entitled for the year. Finally, it should be noted that there is a practical limitation on the amount of the carryover. If the taxpayer had no income against which the interest deduction could have been taken in the year it was paid or accrued, the interest for the year is not subject to being carried over. This follows from the fact that under §163(d) (3) (E) the amount permitted to be carried over is that amount which is not deductible solely because of the limitation formula; if the interest was not deductible anyway—for example, where the taxpayer had no income—the lost deduction cannot be carried over. Carryovers related to years covered by the Tax Reform Act of 1976 are subject to the limitations of the new law.

(d) Miscellaneous Loan Expenses.

The following is a schedule of the most commonly encountered expenses paid by taxpayers in connection with the making of loans and the payment of loans including a list of the tax treatments which the courts and IRS have specified, together with a citation of authorities.

Type of Payment	Tax Treatment	Authority
Points (Loan placement fees)	Deductible as interest but subject to the distortion of income rule.	See Section 7.5(a) above
Standby and commitment fees for availability of construction funds as needed (funds to be drawn in the future)	Not deductible as interest but for the taxpayer engaged in a trade or business, they may be ordinary and necessary business expenses deductible under §162	Rev.Rul. 56-136, 1956-1 C.B. 92
Commitment Fee to FNMA to guarantee purchase of construction loan on completion of project (an existing indebtedness—the construction loan—being covered rather than future funds)	Interest under §163(a) to be deducted over the period of the loan	Rev.Rul. 74-395, 1974-2 C.B. 45 (Rev.Rul. 56-136 cited above distinguished)
Prepayment penalty	Deductible as interest	Rev.Rul. 57-198, 1957-1 C.B. 94
Loan costs (legal fees, printing, brokers fees, etc.)	Amortized over the period of the loan	Rev.Rul. 70-360, 1970-2 C.B. 103; *Julius Stow Lovejoy,* 18 B.T.A. 1179 (1930); *Herbert Enoch,* 57 T.C. 781, 795 (1972).
Discount (interest deducted from face amount of loan but borrower executes note for the full amount).	Not payment of interest by borrower in year of loan, deduction is claimed by cash basis in year(s) of payment of the loan.	Reg.1.461-1(a)(1). Where loan is repaid in installments, discount is amortized prorata, *John R. Hopkins,* 15 T.C. 160(1950); Rev.Rul. 72-100, 1972-1 C.B.122.

(e) Imputed Interest.

Code §483 provides that when a sale or exchange involves the payment of a selling price of more than $3000 over a period of more than one year, then part of that payment must be taxable interest income to the seller. Also, the same amount will constitute an interest deduction to the buyer. Originally, if the parties did not specify at least 4% simple interest, IRS could impute 5% compounded semi-annually. In line with the increase in rates, however, the regulations have been amended. For deferred payment sales made (or contracted to in writing) on or after July 24, 1975, 7% of the price will be interest income if the stated rate in the contract is less than 6% per annum. Therefore, where the parties want the lowest possible rate of interest for tax purposes, they should provide for a 6% rate in the contract; otherwise, IRS has the right to impute a rate of 7% per annum.

(f) Interest and Taxes During the Construction Period.

One of the most significant provisions of the Tax Reform Act of 1976 affecting real estate is the addition of a new section which precludes immediate deduction of interest and real estate taxes during the construction period. §189. Prior to the 1976 Act, cash basis taxpayers could generally deduct construction period interest in the year paid and could also deduct real estate taxes during the year paid subject to the apportionment rules of §164. In appropriate cases, of course, the taxpayer might elect to capitalize such items under §266 but this was optional with the taxpayer. Briefly, the objective of the new section is to require amortization of construction period interest and taxes over a period of ten years. However, in order to ease the impact of the new section, there is a transition period commencing with the year of 1976 in which the new rules are phased in. The situation is complicated by the fact that different rules apply to three categories of real estate: non-residential real estate, residential property other than low-income housing, and low-income housing. Some discussion of the rules is, therefore, essential.

The amortization period commences with the year in which the interest and taxes are paid or accrued; thus, a portion of the capitalized amount is deductible in the taxable year in which it is paid or accrued. The balance of the amount is amortized over a number of years beginning with the later of (1) the taxable year after the year in which such interest and taxes are paid or accrued, or (2) the taxable year in which the property is ready to be placed in service or is ready to be held for sale.

> *Example:* Developer incurs $120,000 of construction period interest in connection with construction of a shopping center in 1977. Therefore, 1977 is the first year of the amortization period. If construction is completed in 1978, then the amortization is completed in a series of years commencing in 1978. However, if delays prevent completion of construction until 1979, then the unamortized balance is written off over a series of years commencing in 1979.

In the case of non-residential real estate, the transition rules are as follows: For 1976, investors will be able to deduct one-half of their construction period interest and taxes; the remaining one-half is capitalized and amortized over three years under the rules discussed above. There is an exception if the construction period commenced prior to 1976. In that case, there is no capitalization required as to any interest or real estate taxes attributable to the construction of the property irrespective of when paid or accrued. §189(f). For 1977, such costs must be spread over five years; for 1978, over six years; for 1979, over seven years; for 1980, over eight years; for 1981, over nine years; and for 1982 and thereafter, over ten years.

In the case of residential real estate other than low-income housing, the rule applies to construction period interest and real estate taxes paid or accrued after 1977. As in the case of non-residential property, there is an increase in the amortization period each year thereafter, starting with a four-year amortization period for 1978 interest and taxes and increasing one year for each year thereafter until the ten-year amortization period applies for such items paid or accrued in 1984 and thereafter.

In the case of low-income housing, construction period interest and taxes paid or accrued prior to 1982 continue to be deducted in full under the old rules. The phase-in commences with 1982 costs and reaches a ten-year amortization period in 1988.

Here is a table that shows the amortization schedule for each type of property:

	Commercial Real Estate	Residential	Low-income Housing
1977	20%	. . . .	. . . .
1978	16 2/3%	25%	. . . .
1979	14 2/7%	20%	. . . .
1980	12 1/3%	16 2/3%	. . . .
1981	11 1/8%	14 2/7%	. . . .
1982	10%	12 1/3%	25%
1983	10%	11 1/8%	20%
1984	10%	10%	16 2/3%
1985	10%	10%	14 2/7%
1986	10%	10%	12 1/3%
1987	10%	10%	11 1/8%
1988	10%	10%	10%

There are two other important points to be considered in evaluating this provision. First, unlike the unamortized portion of the costs of negotiating and obtaining a loan, the unamortized portion of construction period interest and taxes cannot be deducted in the year the property is sold. Instead, the unamortized amounts are added to the basis of the property for purposes of determining gain or loss. §189(c) (2) (B). Second, in the case of a non-taxable transfer or exchange of the property (transfer to a partnership, transfer to a controlled corporation, gifts and like-kind exchanges), the transferor continues to claim the deduction rather than passing the deduction on to the transferor continues to claim the deduction rather than passing the deduction on to the transferee because the deduction is considered to be personal to the transferor. See §189(c) (2) (C)

7.6 TAXES

(a) Real Estate Taxes.

Real estate taxes are a tax deductible item. Where property is held for the production of income, real estate taxes may be included in operating expenses but even in the case of non income-producing property, taxes may be deducted as an itemized non business deduction. Therefore, even a homeowner gets a deduction for real estate taxes if he itemized his deductions.

What is the proper year in which to claim the deduction? Except for taxes paid during the construction period (see Section 5(f) of this chapter) real estate taxes are generally deductible in the year paid or accrued (depending upon whether the taxpayer is on the cash basis or accrual basis for tax purposes). In the case of cash basis taxpayers, real estate taxes are not deductible in the year they are deposited in escrow with the mortgage lender if they are not actually paid to the taxing authority until a later year.[25] In the case of accrual basis taxpayers, each jurisdiction has a date on which the tax liability becomes fixed (normally, the assessment date or lien date) and that date constitutes the accrual date for tax purposes.[26] There are, however, two exceptions to this general rule as follows:

(1) Under §461(c), taxes that relate to a definite period of time may, at the election of the property owner, be accrued ratably over that period. This election, which is limited to accrual basis taxpayers, may be made without the consent of the Commissioner for the first taxable year in which the taxpayer incurs real estate taxes. The election must be made not later than the due date (including extensions thereof) for filing the return for that year. The election may be made for each separate trade or business and for non-business activities if accounted for separately. Special changeover rules prevent double accrual of taxes in the first year of the election and also preclude loss of deductions.

(2) Under §164(d), where real estate is sold the real estate tax must be apportioned between the buyer and seller for the year of sale. This rule applies regardless of whether the parties are on the cash or accrual basis and regardless of whether or not they actually adjust the purchase price between themselves. See Chapter 4, Section 4 for a more detailed discussion of this problem.

Property owners must be careful to distinguish taxes from special assessments. Taxes for local benefits—frequently called "special assessments"—are not deductible to the extent that they increase the value of the property assessed. They are treated instead as capital expenditures.

(b) Sales Tax Deductions.

Sales taxes are deductible by a buyer of items which are subject to such taxes such as materials used in connection with the construction of a project. Thus, for example, a partnership which is formed to construct and operate a rental project may be able to deduct the sales taxes which are imposed on the purchase of materials, thereby increasing the tax losses during the period of construction. However, such taxes would be deductible by the partnership only if (1) state law imposes the tax on the buyer rather than the seller, and (2) the partnership, rather than the general contractor or other third party, is in fact, the purchaser of the material.[27]

Suggestion: It is advisable to make it clear by appropriate contractual provisions that the partnership as buyer is responsible for payment of the sales tax. If the general contractor assumes the obligation to construct the project for a fixed dollar amount, then presumably he is the one entitled to deduct the sales tax. The contract should, therefore, indicate that the general contractor is acting only as the agent of the partnership in purchasing the materials. Of course, there are obvious business advantages to a fixed price contract and this comment relates only to tax considerations.

7.7 REPAIRS AND MAINTENANCE

The amount which a property owner spends for the repair or maintenance of business property is currently deductible in the year the expenditure is paid or incurred, depending upon the method of accounting followed. The amount which he spends for capital improvements to his property cannot be deducted currently, although it normally can be capitalized and recovered through annual depreciation deductions over the life of the improvement. The distinction between the deductible repair and the nondeductible capital improvement is most difficult to draw and has been the course of a considerable amount of litigation between taxpayers and the government.

One of the best definitions of the term "repair" which is frequently cited appeared in an old decision by the Board of Tax Appeals:

> To repair is to restore to a sound state or to mend, while a replacement connotes a substitution. A repair is an expenditure for the purpose of keeping the property in an ordinarily efficient operating condition. It does not add to the value of the property, nor does it appreciably prolong its life. It merely keeps the property in an operating condition over its probably useful life for the uses for which it was acquired. Expenditures for that purpose are distinguishable from those for replacements, alterations, improvement or additions which prolong the life of the property, increase its value, or make it adaptable to a different use. The one is a maintenance charge, while the others are additions to capital investment which should not be applied against current earnings.[28]

The essential characteristic of an improvement which must be capitalized is that the expenditure increases the value of the property, or substantially prolongs its life or makes the property adaptable to a different use. Examples would include lowering of a basement floor to facilitate movement of heavy loads from one building to another or installing a new roof. Of course, a repair may also prolong the life of the property or increase its value to some extent, but this consequence is normally incidental to the primary purpose of the repair which is to arrest a decline in value or to make good deterioration which has already occurred. The following items, although not conclusive either individually or collectively, are normally characteristic of improvements rather than repairs and will tend to result in disallowance of the current deduction:

(1) *Expenditures Substantial in Amount.* Although there is no fixed dividing line between minor items which normally are deductible repairs and major disbursements which are more characteristic of improvements, the fact is that the greater the size of the expenditure, the more apt it is to catch a Treasury Agent's eye and be disallowed on the grounds that it represents a capital improvement.[29]

(2) *Expenditures to Conform the Property to Taxpayer's Use.* Expenditures to make property adaptable to a different use generally are considered to be improvements and the expense deduction is denied. The result is not changed merely because the assessed value, market value or sale value of the property are not increased by the expenditure. The fact that the property has a use to the taxpayer that it did not previously have is sufficient to result in disallowance of the expense. Also, the fact that an expenditure was undertaken involuntarily to comply with building, fire or safety regulations is not sufficient to place it in the category of a repair.

(3) *Repairs Incident to a General Plan of Betterment.* Where the general plan under which the work is performed is one of rehabilitation and permanent betterment, the expenditures incident to that plan, although they might ordinarily constitute deductible repairs, will generally be disallowed as deductions.

Suggestion: In order to obtain the full deduction for repairs, it would normally be advisable not to undertake the repair at the same time as a general plan of improvement; and where the repairs and the improvements are included in one contract, segregation of the two categories of disbursements is always advisable.

(4) *Replacement with Different Materials.* Where a part of a building is replaced with a different material than that which was utilized in the original construction, the expenditure will typically be classified as a non-deductible improvement. This is particularly true where the replacement material is superior to the old material. Examples are replacing of a gravel driveway with a cement driveway or replacing a wood door with an aluminum door. This result normally follows even though the replacement may be required to make good prior wear and deterioration.

Checklist of Deductible Repairs—In an area where the questions are essentially factual and where the possible circumstances are almost unlimited, statements of the rules tend to be mere generalizations. A more helpful approach is to determine how other property owners have been treated in comparable situations. The following check list is based upon numerous decisions and rulings[30] and should serve as a guide in similar cases.

Item	P-H Tax-Service Paragraph	Description	Deduction Allowed or Denied
Heating Systems	11,478(10)	Replacing iron pipes with brass pipes	Denied
	11,478(10)	New gas furnace installed replacing worn-out coal furnace	Denied
Painting and Remodeling	11,477(5)	Repainting exterior of building	Allowed
	11,485(7)	Remodeling building not in disrepair	Denied
Parking Lots and Grounds	11,479(42)	Resurfacing lot to restore to original condition	Allowed
	11,484(35)	Cost of drainage system to settle adjoining property owner's law suit.	Denied
Roofs	11,477(15)	Insulating materials placed on top of roof	Allowed
	11,477(15)	Roof of wood shingles covered with compositions shingles	Denied
Walls	11,477(10)	Tuck pointing and cleaning outside walls	Allowed
	11,481(10)	Partition built to create private office	Denied

7.8　CASUALTY LOSSES

(a) Definition—A casualty is the total or partial destruction of property resulting from an unidentifiable event of a sudden, unexpected or unusual nature. Events listed

in the Code[31] which give rise to casualty losses are "fire, storm, shipwreck or other casualty." Note that progressive deterioration of property is not treated as a casualty; it lacks the suddenness stressed in many of the cases. In line with this standard, the following items have been held to be deductible casualty losses.[32]

Loss due to storm or earthquake;

Loss sustained through bursting of a boiler due to physical forces occuring suddenly and unexpectedly;

Loss by fire;

Damage to property by "mine cave";

Sudden, unusual, unexpected cracking and settling of residence due to excessive rainfall and saturation of subsoil;

Loss caused by sonic boom.

Loss from termite damage will normally not qualify as a casualty loss. Such damage is the result of gradual deterioration through a steadily operating cause and not the result of an unidentifiable event of a sudden, unusual or unexpected nature. The Internal Revenue Service has indicated that it will not follow certain court decisions which took a contrary view with respect to termite damage.[33]

(b) Amount of Loss—Where property used in a trade or business or held for the production of income is *totally* destroyed by casualty, the amount of loss sustained and to be deducted is the adjusted basis of such property less (i) any insurance or other compensation received and (ii) any salvage value.[34] Where a business property is only *partially* destroyed, the amount of the deductible loss is the lesser of (i) the loss in the value of the property or (ii) the adjusted basis of the property. In either case, any insurance recovery or other compensation received reduces the amount of the loss. Seperate computations must be made as to each item of property destroyed, comparing the economic loss resulting from the casualty with the adjusted basis. The lesser of these two figures may then be claimed as the tax deduction.

In some cases the cost of repairs to the damaged property is acceptable evidence of the loss of value. This is true where the taxpayer can show: (1) the repairs are necessary to restore the property to its condition prior to the casualty; (2) the amount spent for such repairs is not excessive; (3) the repairs do not provide for more than the damage suffered and (4) the repairs do not result in an increase in the value of the property.[35]

(c) When is Loss Deductible?—Casualty losses are generally deductible in the year actually sustained. Since the casualty is frequently compensable through insurance or other means, it is sometimes difficult to establish the amount of the loss in the year of the casualty. The rule is that the property owner should take a casualty loss for that part of the damage which will not be covered by any reimbursement and claim the remainder of the loss in the subsequent year when it can be measured.

> *Example:* Fire damage to a building is $10,000, but there is an insurance claim for only $6,000. In the year of fire, it is clear that there will be at least a $4,000 loss and that amount can, therefore, be claimed in that year. In a subsequent year the claim against the insurance company is settled for $5,000. The remaining $1,000 loss can be deducted at that time.[36]

If the reimbursement from the insurance company or other source exceeds the amount of loss claimed in a prior year, the property owner is not required to recompute the tax for the year of the deduction. Rather, he includes the excess reimbursement as income in the year of receipt. Of course, if the loss was not claimed as a deduction in the earlier year the reimbursement is not taxable in the year of receipt under the "tax benefit" rule.

Under a special Code provision if property is damaged by flood, tornado or other disaster between the close of the tax year (say Dec. 31) and the time the tax return is due (normally April 15) the taxpayer may be eligible for speedy tax relief. He can elect to accelerate the deduction to the prior tax year. To qualify for this treatment, however, the loss must have occurred in an area subsequently declared by the President as a disaster area eligible for federal aid.[37]

7.9 MINIMUM TAX ON TAX PREFERENCES

(a) Tax Reform Act of 1969.

The Tax Reform Act of 1969 added a new tax designated as the minimum tax on items of tax preference. §56. This tax applied only to the extent that certain specified tax preference items exceeded the sum of $30,000, plus the federal income tax imposed for the taxable year in question, plus a credit for a seven year carryforward of income taxes paid which were not otherwise utilized to offset tax preferences. One of the items of tax preference is depreciation on real estate to the extent that it exceeds straight-line depreciation. Such excess depreciation is added to all of the other tax preference items. The other tax preference items which are subject to the minimum tax are the following: accelerated depreciation on personal property which is subject to a net lease, the bargain element in tax-favored stock options, the excess of allowable depletion over the adjusted basis of the property, the excluded half of long-term capital gains and certain other items.

The 10% minimum tax was then applied to the total of the tax preference items reduced by the exemptions described above.

> *Example:* Taxpayer constructed new residential property at a cost of $1,000,000 exclusive of land. He utilizes a composite life of 33-1/3 years and depreciates on the double-declining-balance method. In 1975, the first year following completion of construction, he claims $60,000 of depreciation. Since straight-line depreciation would have amounted to only $30,000, he has a $30,000 item of tax preference. Assume that he had a $24,000 capital gain this year and that his deductions and exemptions shelter all of his other income so that his tax is computed only on $12,000 of ordinary income (1/2 of the capital gain). On this assumption, the tax on a joint return would be $2,260. Therefore, the minimum tax would equal $974, 10% of $9740, computed as follows: Tax preference items of $42,000 ($30,000 of excess depreciation plus 1/2 of capital gains), less exemptions of $32,260 ($30,000 flat exemption plus $2260 representing the normal tax on this return.)

(b) Tax Reform Act of 1976.

The Tax Reform Act of 1976 made a number of important changes in this provision effective generally for taxable years beginning after December 31, 1975. First, the new law increases the minimum tax rate from 10% to 15%. Second, for individuals the Act reduces the exemption to $10,000, or half of the regular taxes paid whichever is greater. Third, there are new items of tax preference: itemized deductions (other than medical and casualty loss deductions) in excess of 60% of adjusted gross income; accelerated depreciation in excess of straight-line depreciation on all personal property subject to a lease; and, generally, intangible drilling costs on productive wells in excess of the amount which would have been allowable had the amounts been capitalized and amortized over 10 years. The Act directs the Secretary of the Treasury to issue regulations under which no taxpayer would be subject to minimum tax on a preference item if he received no tax benefit from the preference.

7.10 MAXIMUM TAX ON PERSONAL SERVICE INCOME

Personal service income such as income from salaries, wages, professional fees, etc., is subject to a maximum tax of 50%. However, the maximum tax base is offset by preference items. Prior to the Tax Reform Act of 1976, there was a $30,000 exemption for the preference-income offset and an alternative five-year averaging provision that applied to prior years' preference income. Since the Act reduces the exemptions and expands the definition of preferences, for tax years beginning after December 31, 1975, the benefit of the maximum tax calculation will be reduced for individuals who have tax preference income. §1348.

> *Comment:* The implications of the maximum tax rules on high-bracket individuals under the Tax Reform Act of 1976 are quite significant. There will be many taxpayers who, although they are not subject to the minimum tax because of the exemptions provided under the Act, will lose some of the benefit of the 50% maximum tax rate because of their tax preference income. Remember that the maximum rate on individual incomes can go as high as 70%. Therefore, an individual contemplating an investment in real estate, particularly where accelerated depreciation will be claimed, must calculate the tax consequences of the preference income insofar as it affects his right to utilize the 50% rate; as some of his personal service income is moved up from a 50% bracket to a higher bracket, it follows that some of the benefits of accelerated depreciation are lost. The effect of this rule, together with the new rules on recapture of depreciation, will result in use of straight-line depreciation in many cases.

FOOTNOTES FOR CHAPTER SEVEN

[1]§446.

[2]Rev.Rul. 68-35, 1968-1 C.B. 190.

[3]§446(e). Included in the changes in accounting which require prior approval are changes from the cash method to the accrual method and vice-versa. Reg.1.446-1(e).

[4]Reg. 1.461-1(a).

[5]*Comm'r. v. Boylston Market Assn.,* 131 F.2d 966, 30 AFTR 512 (CA1, 1942). Rev.Rul. 70-413, 1970-2 C.B. 103.

[6]*Bonard G. Stice v. U.S.,* _____ Fed.2d _____, 38 AFTR 2d 76-5931 (CA5, 1976). Rev.Rul. 75-152, 1975-1 C.B. 144.

[7]Reg. 1.451-2.

[8]*Cowden, Sr. v. Comm'r.,* 280 F.2d 20 7 AFTR 2d 1160, 1162 (CA5, 1961).

[9]*Ross v. Comm'r.*, 169 F.2d 483, 37 AFTR 193 (CA1, 1948); P-H Fed. Tax ¶20,165.

[10]*McCulley Ashlock,* 18 T.C. 405 (1952), See 25 N.Y.U. Inst. on Fed. Tax, 636 (1967).

[11]*Alstores Realty Corp.,* 46 T.C. 363 (1966); *Steinway & Sons,* 46 T.C. 380 (1966).

[12]*Bryant v. U.S.,* 399 F.2d 800, 22 AFTR 2d 5375 (CA5, 1968).

[13]*Adolf Schwarz,* 24 T.C. 733, 739, acq. involving several units; *A.I. LaGreide,* 23 T.C. 508,511 and *Reiner v. U.S.,* 222 F.2d 770, 772, 47 AFTR 938 (CA7, 1955) involving one property.

[14]See *Grier v. U.S.,* 120 F.Supp. 395, 398,45 AFTR 1975 (DC Conn), aff'd per curiam (CA2, 1955), (income realized on the operation of rental property may be treated as non-business income).

[15]§266.

[16]Reg.1.266-1(b).

[17]Reg. 1.266-1(c) (1).

[18]Rev.Rul. 69-188, 1969-1 C.B. 54. Compare Rev.Rul. 67-197, 1967-2 C.B. 87, holding that "points" paid for V.A. and FHA insured mortgages were not deductible. Presumably, in those loans the charge is made for a service rendered, not for the use of money.

[19]Rev. Rul. 69-582, 1969-2 C.B. 29. In this ruling a payment of $1,200 in points (6 points, $20,000 loan) was held not to be a material distortion of income.

[20]Rev. Rul. 68-650, 1968-2 C.B. 78.

[21]Rev. Rul. 68-643, 1968-2 C.B. 76.

[22]*A. Douglas Burck,* 63 T.C. 556 (1975), aff'd. 533 F.2d 768, 37 AFTR 2d76-1009 (CA2, 1976). See P-H Fed Taxes ¶13,062 for an annotation of the cases. In *Bernard Resnik,* 66 T.C.74 (1976), it was held that the distortion test is determined at the partnership level, i.e., a distortion of partnership income results in a disallowance of the deduction even though there may be no distortion at the level of the individual partner.

[23]*S. Rex Lewis,* 65 T.C. 629 (1975); *Jackson B. Howard,* ¶75,005 P-H Memo T.C.

[24]Investment income includes nonbusiness interest, dividends, rents, royalties, net short term capital gains from investment property, and recapture of depreciation income. Net investment income is investment income reduced by investment expenses such as ordinary and necessary business expenses, taxes and straight line depreciation. Sec. 163(d) (3) (A).

[25]*Frank J. Hradesky,* 65 T.C. 87 (1975). Aff'd, _____ Fed. 2d, _____ 38AFTR 2d 76-5935 (CA5, 1976).

[26]P-H Fed. Tax Service ¶13,155.

[27]Reg. 1.164-5.

[28]*Illinois Merchants Trust Co., Ex.* 4 BTA 103, 106, acq.

[29]*Cincinnati, New Orleans and Texas Pac. Rwy. Co. v. U.S.,* 424 F.2d 563, 25 AFTR 2d 70-988 (Court of Claims, 1970) permitted taxpayers to deduct all such items of $500 or less.

[30]P-H Tax Service ¶11,471-11,486.

[31]§165(c) (3).

[32]P-H Fed. Taxes ¶14,368.

[33]Rev.Rul. 63-232, 1963-2 C.B. 97. The courts have generally agreed with the position of the IRS in recent years. See *Joseph A. Austra,* ¶66,028 P-H Memo T.C.

[34]Reg. 1.165-7(b) (1).

[35]Reg. 1.165-7(a) (2) (ii).

[36]Reg. 1.165-1(d) (2).

[37]§165(h).

Part 3

TAX PROBLEMS
IN DISPOSING OF
REAL ESTATE

8

SHRINKING

TAXES THROUGH

DEFERRED PAYMENT SALES

An elementary principle of tax planning is that where a substantial gain is about to be realized on the sale of property it is normally advisable to spread the tax on that sale over a period of years. This is true not only because most taxpayers prefer to postpone the payment of taxes but also because graduated income tax rates have the effect of producing a larger tax where there is a bunching of income in a particular year. This is particularly significant since the passage of the Tax Reform Act of 1969 which increased the rate of capital gains tax on gains in excess of $50,000 per year; by holding the reported gain to less than this amount on a large transaction, there will automatically be a tax saving. The same Act introduced the concept of a minimum tax on certain tax preference items. Since the capital gains are included in such tax preference items, spreading the reported gain over a number of years permits utilization of the annual exemptions from this tax and will, therefore, often eliminate the problem of the minimum tax.

There are also other advantages of installment reporting. The seller has temporary use of the funds that would otherwise be utilized to pay the tax and if the installment contract bears a reasonable rate of interest, such funds are income producing for the seller for a number of years. Also, deferment of a capital gain over a number of years gives the seller the opportunity to program capital losses into the same period and, of course, such capital losses may be offset against the capital gains.

Briefly, the installment sale rules provide that where the requirements are met, a gain realized on a sale of property may be deferred for a number of years and reported pro rata as payments are received. Even where such requirements are not met, it is sometimes possible to report the gain on the deferred payment method which may also produce a deferment for payment of tax on the realized gain.

This chapter analyzes the rules governing deferred payment sales including those which are reported on the installment and those which are not. The discussion is divided into the following topics:

8.1   INSTALLMENT SALES: DEFINITIONS AND APPLICABILITY

§453 permits a taxpayer to report a gain, but not a loss, from a sale or other disposition of real estate on the installment method. The gain is reported ratably as payments are received from the buyer. In order to understand the rules, a number of simple definitions are important.

Selling price means the total amount to be paid by the buyer. It includes cash and any other property received by the seller as well as the buyer's promissory notes, whether secured or unsecured, and any other liens on the property at the time it is sold.

Contract price is the total amount to be received by the seller. This normally excludes payments which are to be made by the buyer on existing mortgages except to the extent that they exceed the seller's basis. Such mortgage amounts, although included in the selling price, are not part of the contract price. The contract price is, in effect, the seller's equity in the property in excess of mortgages and liens.

When a sale is reported on the installment basis, the seller's profit is divided by the contract price to determine the profit percentage. This percentage, when applied to each payment received by the seller, establishes the amount of gain which he must report on such payment.

Example: Assume a selling price of $250,000 and a cost basis of $150,000. The buyer assumes an existing $50,000 mortgage, pays $50,000 down at closing and gives his own mortgage note for the balance due, $150,000, payable over a twenty year period. Payments on buyer's mortgage note in the first year amount to $10,000 of which $6,000 represents interest and the balance of $4,000 represents an installment payment on the purchase price. The sale qualifies for installment reporting under the rules discussed below. The seller would report his gain for the year of sale as follows:

Selling price	$250,000	
Cost basis	150,000	
Gain	$100,000	
Payments received (downpayment, plus payments on note)		$60,000
Less interest reported as ordinary income		6,000
Principal amount received		$54,000
Selling price	$250,000	
Less mortgage assumed	50,000	
Contract price	$200,000	
Profit percentage ($100,000 ÷ $200,000	50%	
Reportable gain (50% x $54,000)		$27,000

A number of requirements must be satisfied in order to qualify for installment reporting. These requirements will be discussed in the following sections:

8.2 THE 30% DOWNPAYMENT RULE

The installment election is not available unless payment, if any, to the seller in the taxable year-of-sale do not exceed 30% of the selling price. §453(b) (2) (A). The willingness of a buyer to pay all cash will not disqualify the installment sale provided that year-of-sale payments are, in fact, limited to 30% of the selling price.[1]

In general, any property (other than evidences of indebtedness of the buyer) will be regarded as a payment in the year-of-sale to the extent of its fair market value. Thus, year-of-sale payments include the following items:[2] a downpayment made at closing; a deposit made prior to the year of closing and credited to the buyer at closing; payments made in the year of sale on buyer's deferred payment obligation; evidences of indebtedness issued by any person other than the buyer; cancellation of debt owing from buyer to seller; like kind property received in an exchange; and the fair market value of any other property, tangible or intangible, received by the seller unless expressly excluded from the definition of payment by the Code. A buyer's note or other evidence of indebtedness which is payable on demand may constitute a payment in the year of sale. See the discussion which follows relating to buyer's notes.

There are a number of important exclusions from the definition of payments in the year of sale. Year-of-sale payments will not include the following items:

(a) Mortgages and Other Liabilities

In the sale of mortgaged real estate, the amount of the mortgage to which the property is subject, whether or not assumed by the buyer, is not normally included in the computation of the contract price or the payments in the year of sale.[3]

Comment: A seller may be able to increase his cash proceeds by mortgaging the property prior to the sale.

The fact that a buyer liquidates a portion of the mortgage after the date of sale but within the same year, will be disregarded for purposes of the 30% test.

There is an important exception to this rule, however. To the extent the mortgage which the buyer assumes or takes subject to, exceeds the seller's basis in the property, the excess constitutes a year-of-sale payment to the seller.[4] This presents a difficult problem to many potential sellers of real estate. If the mortgage exceeds the seller's basis by an amount greater than 30% of the selling price, an installment sale election is impossible if the buyer assumes or takes title subject to the mortgage. To avoid this result, the parties can contract that the buyer will not assume the mortgage until a future year, if ever, and that for a period of time—including the year of sale—the seller will retain title to the property or will continue to make the necessary payments on the mortgage. In short, the buyer makes payments to the seller and the seller continues to make payments on the existing mortgage loan. Such a transaction is normally set up in the form of a wraparound mortgage or land contract running from buyer to seller.

Although this technique has been criticized on the grounds that it permits form rather than substance to control tax consequences, the fact remains that this procedure—a sale of the seller's equity in the property without an assumption of the mortgage loan by the buyer—is supported by a number of cases.[5] Accordingly, the wraparound mortgage or land contract have become popular forms utilized to avoid the problem of the mortgage in excess of basis. If the taxpayer proposes to rely on this procedure, however, it must be clear that buyer has not assumed the underlying mortgage. In a 1977 decision, the Tax Court, although affirming the procedure in principle, held that where the buyer had executed a separate guarantee of the underlying mortgage to the mortgage lender, presumably for the purpose of obtaining lender's consent to the transfer, the buyer had, for purposes of this rule, assumed the mortgage loan. The fact that the seller also remained liable on the loan did not change the result. Since the excess mortgage amounted to more than 30% of the selling price, installment sale reporting was not permitted.[5(a)] The implication of the decision is that any documents or conduct indicating an assumption of the mortgage loan by buyer should be carefully avoided.

The rules governing sales of partnership interests are similar. Under §752(d) and the regulations thereunder, a partner's proportionate share of partnership liabilities is deemed to be received on a sale of his partnership interest. Where the partner's share of mortgage debt exceeds the basis of his partnership interest, the excess is deemed to be received in the year of sale and in some cases may disqualify installment reporting by the selling partner.

(b) The Buyer's Note or Other Evidence of Indebtedness.

The buyer's notes, whether secured or not, or other evidence of indebtedness, are not included in computing payments in the year of sale. §453(b) (2) (A) (ii). Once again, there is an important qualification of this rule. In the case of sales after May 27, 1969, the amendment to §453 made by the Tax Reform Act of 1969, disqualifies as an evidence of indebtedness of the buyer—and thus treats as a payment when received—a buyer's note which is payable on demand. §453(b) (3).

(c) Money or Property Held in a Bona Fide Escrow

It is clear that if an escrow deposit stands in the way of receipt by a seller of his sale price, he may not be taxed as if he received the price directly. For example, one ruling involved a case where the sale was originally made with the balance secured by a deed of trust. In a later year the purchaser needed to clear title so he deposited an amount sufficient to recover the remaining balance in an escrow account. The purchaser remained liable for the balance and was required to recognize for tax purposes the income earned on the escrow account. The funds were not available to seller immediately but were to be released only in accordance with the original payment schedule. IRS held that there was no constructive receipt of the escrow amount and installment reporting continued to apply.[5(a)] However, in a number of cases where the buyer was willing to pay cash at closing but the seller insisted on an installment sale and the transaction was closed on deferred payment terms with the buyer creating an escrow deposit of the unpaid balance, the courts, relying on the substance of the transaction, have disregarded the escrow and have refused to recognize the installment election.[6] A similar result has been reached where the seller has the right to demand the balance of the purchase price in the year of sale[7] or where a portion of the price was placed in trust for the benefit of the seller with the annual income from the investments of the trust being credited to seller.[8] In view of the fine line which the courts draw between the bona fide escrow on one hand and constructive receipt by the seller on the other hand, it is advisable where an escrow is contemplated to clearly set forth the business reasons for the escrow (such as to insure compliance with seller's covenants or to clear title for the benefit of the buyer) and to specify that any earnings on the escrow fund will be credited to the buyer.

(d) Payment of Seller's Liabilities

As discussed above, the fact that a buyer liquidates a portion of a mortgage after the date of sale but within the same year will be disregarded for purposes of the 30% test. Generally, this rule also applies to the seller's unsecured debts which are assumed by the buyer in connection with a purchase transaction; the assumption or payment of such debts will not constitute year-of-sale payments. At one time IRS took the position that current liabilities which arose in the ordinary course of seller's business and which were assumed by the buyer, were to be treated as payments in the year of sale if such liabilities were liquidated during that year. The courts disagreed and held that such liabilities were in the nature of a mortgage indebtedness within the meaning of the regulations.[9] IRS, however, has recently ruled that a buyer's assumption of the seller's unsecured liability is not a year-of-sale payment, whether or not such liability is paid in the year of sale.[10]

(e) Disposition of Buyer's Note

The disposition of an installment obligation is a taxable event under §453(d) which is discussed below. However, the proceeds from the disposition in the year of sale of the buyer's note that is due subsequent to that year, is not payment of the note within the meaning of §453 but is a transaction which is independent of the original installment sale. Accordingly, a year-of-sale disposition representing more than 30% of the selling price, does not invalidate an installment election deferring recognition of the gain on the sale.[11]

8.3 INSTALLMENT PAYMENTS REQUIRED

We have seen above that the payments in the year of sale cannot exceed 30% of the selling price. Supposing there is no payment in the year of sale of a parcel of real estate and the entire price is due and payable in a later year. Such an arrangement would not qualify according to IRS which holds that an installment sale must contemplate a payment in each of two years.[12] A number of courts have now accepted this rule.[13]

8.4 THE INSTALLMENT ELECTION

In order to qualify for installment reporting, the taxpayer "must set forth in his income tax return (or in a statement attached thereto) for the year of the sale or other disposition, the computation of the gross profit on the sale or other disposition under the installment method."[14] The Code is silent on the question of when the seller is required to make his election. Originally, IRS took the position that in order for the election to be valid it had to be made on a timely filed return for the year of sale. The courts had some difficulty with this arbitrary rule, however, and to resolve the conflict, pending issuance of revised regulations, IRS has published a new ruling in 1965.[15] The 1965 ruling holds that an election is valid if it is made on a return for the first year in which any portion of the selling price was received or if made on an amended return prior to the receipt of any portion of the selling price. The ruling also gives a number of examples of inadvertent failures to elect installment treatment (for example, where the taxpayer assumed that the gain was not taxable) and the ruling concludes that if in good faith a taxpayer failed to make the installment election on the original return, IRS will recognize the election as being valid where the election was made on an amended return for the year of sale not barred by the statute of limitations or the operation of any other law if the facts indicate no election inconsistent with the installment election had been made with respect to the sale.

The installment method, once elected for a particular sale, may not be revoked whether by way of an amended return for the year of sale or otherwise.[16]

Comment: Where the taxpayer is not sure whether a sale qualifies for installment reporting, it is advisable to make a conditional election in the tax return for the year of sale. In one recent case where the taxpayer attempted unsuccessfully to report a sale on the cost recovery method, it was held that his conditional election in the year of sale was adequate to protect installment treatment. Even though the taxpayer lost the case on the primary issue, he qualified for installment reporting.[17] Of course, there will be cases where a taxpayer would prefer not to flag the return where he is utilizing the open transaction method of reporting. However, in view of the rules limiting the installment election in years subsequent to the year of sale, the more conservative approach would be to make a conditional election on the return for the year of sale.

8.5   FRAGMENTED SALES

Where the sale of an entire project or parcel of land does not qualify as an installment sale because payments received in the year of sale will exceed 30% of the selling price, it may be possible to divide the transaction into two or more individual sale contracts. By proper allocation of the downpayment, it may be possible to qualify one parcel for installment sale reporting.

> *Example:* Taxpayer sold 52.56 acres of land for a selling price of $262,800 of which $118,020 was paid in the form of a cash downpayment and the balance was represented by buyer's notes secured by a mortgage on the remaining 32.89 acres. The buyer was prohibited from disturbing the growing crops on the 32.89 acre parcel. The Tax Court holding for the taxpayer regarded the transaction as two sales, one sale of 19.67 acres for cash of $98,350 and the other a sale of 32.89 acres for cash of $19,670 and buyer's notes for the balance which qualified for installment sales reporting.[18]

However, the reverse does not appear to be true. A multiple-asset sale cannot be treated by the taxpayer as a single sale in order to qualify for installment reporting.

> The Tax Court refused to permit the taxpayer to aggregate, as a single sale, separate contracts of sale of separate parcels of land even though they were contiguous and the sales were made at the same time to the same buyer. If aggregated, the payments in the year of sale from both parcels would not have exceeded 30% of the total selling price. The Court held, however, that the taxpayer failed to carry his burden of proof that the form of the transaction was not representative of its substance.[19] In short, a taxpayer proposing to fragment sales of real estate and have them treated separately for tax reporting purposes must be sure that the agreements between buyer and seller are consistent with that position.

8.6   INDETERMINATE SELLING PRICE

In order to compute the amount of each payment which represents taxable gain and the amount which represents a return of capital, it is necessary to know the amount of the selling price. Where the selling price cannot be computed because it is indeterminate or contingent on subsequent events, it follows that the installment method is not available.

> *Example:* Seller sold oil and gas leases under an agreement in which the seller received a minimum sales price subject to being increased based upon future production. He computed the installment gain as though the minimum consideration under the contract were the selling price. Additional consideration received was then reported in full as taxable gain in the year received. The Court held, however, that installment treatment was not available although the taxpayer could report the contingent additional consideration by utilizing the open transaction method.[20]

> *Example:* Taxpayer sold the stock of a mining corporation. Because local law was not clear as to the amount of any applicable state mine tax, the buyer agreed to pay an additional amount if the tax were less than anticipated. Ultimately, it developed that the seller was entitled to an additional amount under the contract. The Court concluded that the additional consideration was part of the selling price of the stock and that installment treatment was, therefore, not available.[21]

In a 1976 ruling, IRS held that if the price is determined by the end of the taxable year of the sale, then installment treatment is available notwithstanding that the selling price could not be determined as of the date of sale.[22]

8.7 SELLING EXPENSES

It is normally immaterial whether selling expenses are treated as an offset against gross profit or as an addition to basis; the amount of gain to be reported is the same in either case. However, where installment sales are involved, the treatment of such expenses may determine whether or not the taxpayer is eligible for installment reporting. A 1973 case involved a sale of a farm with more than $23,000 of commission and other selling expenses. Because the mortgage exceeded the seller's basis in the property, the excess mortgage constituted a year of sale payment. See Section 2(a) above. The taxpayer treated the selling expenses as an addition to basis. The Commissioner, however, claimed that the selling expenses should be subtracted from the selling price. This had the effect of reducing the selling price and, since the mortgage in excess of basis constituted a year of sale payment, had the further effect of increasing year-of-sale payments to more than 30% of selling price so computed. On this basis, the taxpayer was disqualified from utilizing the installment method. However, the 9th Circuit Court of Appeals held that selling expenses were a proper addition to basis and that installment reporting should be permitted.[23] IRS has announced that it will not follow this decision,[24] and taxpayers should, therefore, proceed with caution in following this rule.

8.8 DISPOSITION OF INSTALLMENT OBLIGATIONS

It is clear that a sale or exchange of an installment obligation will generally result in recognition of gain or loss. §453(d) (1). The amount of gain or loss recognized is the difference between the amount realized on the sale or exchange and the basis of the obligation (the portion which does not represent gain if the obligation were satisfied by the obligor at face value). §453(d)(1)(A). It is equally clear that simply encumbering the installment obligation—a true pledge as collateral for a loan—does not constitute a disposition and results in no recognized gain or loss.[25] The more difficult question, however, involves transactions which fall somewhere between these two rules, namely, cases where the taxpayer attempts to cast the transaction in the form of a pledge but the substance of the transaction approaches that of a sale or exchange.

IRS takes the position that borrowing on the security of installment paper, if the loan and the installment payments are in equal principal amounts and of equal maturities, constitutes a disposition of the installment obligation. In some cases the courts have sustained this approach, particularly where payments on the installment debt are made directly to the creditor-pledgee.[26] Accordingly, a taxpayer is well advised to avoid such transactions. For example, the amount borrowed should differ somewhat from the amount of the installment note and the borrower-pledgor should continue to collect the installment payments from the buyer and make his own payments to the lender.

8.9   DEFAULT AND REPOSSESSION

§1038 covers all repossessions of real estate sold on the installment basis beginning after September 2, 1964, the date of enactment. In order to come under this section, the property must be reacquired in partial or complete satisfaction of a debt for which the real estate represents the security and the debt must have arisen in a sale of that property by the vendor-creditor. Thus, the section does not apply to a bank or other lender in the business of making mortgage loans.

As a general rule the seller does not recognize any gain or loss upon the repossession nor does he have the right to claim a deduction for a bad debt. §1038(a). The manner in which the seller reacquires the property is generally immaterial. The property may be reacquired by agreement such as a voluntary conveyance in lieu of foreclosure or abandonment to the seller, or it may be reacquired by process of law such as foreclosure proceedings.

There are, however, some exceptions to this general rule. If the seller received part payment on the selling price prior to the reacquisition and such part payments exceeded the amount of gain reported by the seller, then tax is imposed at the time of reacquisition. §1038(b). There is, however, a limitation under §1038(b) (2) on the amount of taxable gain. In no event is the gain attributable to payments received before repossession to exceed the potential gain attributable to the initial sale (the amount by which the selling price of the property exceeded its adjusted basis in the hands of the seller) reduced by the sum of (1) amounts received before repossession already reported as income and (2) the amount of money and the fair market value of other property (except purchase money obligations of the buyer) paid or transferred by the seller in connection with the reacquisition. In determining the potential gain under this rule, the gross selling price is reduced by selling commissions, legel fees and other expenses of the sale.

Example: Assume that seller sells unencumbered real estate with a basis of $80,000 at a selling price of $100,000. Buyer pays $10,000 down and signs a purchase money note for the $90,000 balance payable in nine equal annual installments, together with interest at 6% per annum. Seller elects the installment method of reporting. After making the first two payments the buyer defaults and the seller reacquires the property, either by voluntary reconveyance or by foreclosure, in satisfaction of the mortgage. The seller pays $5,000 in connection with the reacquisition. Since the seller has received total payments of $30,000 and has reported a $6,000 gain (20% of the payments represent gain and 80% represent return of captial) the seller has a potential gain on reacquisition of $24,000. However, under the limitation rule described above, the taxable gain on the repossession is limited to $9,000[27]:

Sales price of property		$100,000
Less:		
Basis of property	$80,000	
Previously reported gain	6,000	
Money paid on reacquisition	5,000	91,000
Limitation on gain		$ 9,000

Of course, the seller is compelled to adjust his basis so that the gain which is not currently recognized is ultimately recognized on the disposition of the property. This is accomplished by requiring that the reacquired property take a substituted basis, namely, the basis of the purchase money obligation. This basis is then increased to reflect the gain previously reported on the acquisition as well as any money or other property paid by seller in connection with the reacquisition. §1038(c). Referring to the above example, the seller has a basis in the purchaser's obligation of $56,000 ($70,000 unpaid balance times 80% representing the return of capital portion). This is increased by $9,000 representing the gain on reacquisition and $5,000 representing the sum paid by seller on the reacquisition, producing a basis in the reacquired property of $70,000.

Another exception to the general rule that there is no gain on a reacquisition applies where the seller claimed a deduction for the complete or partial worthlessness of the buyer's obligation prior to the reacquisition. Such a bad debt deduction must be reversed upon the reacquisition. In that case, the seller realizes income on reacquisition equal to the amount of the prior bad debt deduction. §1038(d). However, the adjusted basis of the indebtedness is increased by a like amount. Also, the taxability of the restored income is limited by the tax benefit rule of §111.[28]

8.10   DEFERRED PAYMENT SALES NOT REPORTED ON THE INSTALLMENT METHOD

There are many cases where the installment method is not utilized to report a deferred payment sale. This occurs, for example, where one of the essential elements of installment reporting is absent—for example, where the payments in the year of sale exceed 30% of the selling price—or where the seller fails or declines to elect installment reporting. The tax treatment of such deferred payment sales depends upon whether the transaction is characterized as an open transaction or a closed transaction.

(a) Open Transactions Versus Closed Transactions—Definitions and Tax Treatment

If the buyer's promise to pay has no ascertainable fair market value, the transaction is said to be "open" and the seller is permitted to report his gain on the cost recovery method. This means that the seller is allowed to recover his basis in the property before being taxed: thus, he can defer ultimate reporting of the gain. Even more important, once the seller has recovered his basis, the subsequent payments by the purchaser in liquidation of the note or contract relate back to the original sale and, therefore, qualify for capital gain treatment if the original transaction involved the sale of a capital asset.

Closed transactions, on the other hand, arise where the evidence of indebtedness of the purchaser has an ascertainable fair market value. In such transactions, the taxable event has occurred in the year of sale and the following results take place: If the sale involved a capital asset, the seller has capital gain in the year of sale to the extent that cash, plus the fair market value of the obligation received, exceed his basis; he then has a basis in the buyer's obligation equal to its fair market value in the year of sale (§1012) and he is required to prorate each subsequent payment received on the obligation between return of basis and taxable gain; and the subsequent gains must be reported as ordinary income because the repayment of an obligation does not qualify as a sale or exchange.[29]

(b) Open Transactions Versus closed Transactions—Classification of Buyer's Obligations

It is obvious from the preceding section that it is normally to the advantage of the seller to have the sale qualified as an open transaction. When will this be possible?

First, if the amount of the sale price is contingent or uncertain, the buyer's promise to pay will ordinarily be found to have no ascertainable fair market value. An example of this type of obligation is a promise to pay a price which is determinable in the future based upon future production or future income arising out of the property sold.[30]

Even though the buyer's obligation is not uncertain or contingent in amount, however, it may be found to be one that is not a cash equivalent, thus permitting the transaction to remain open. Unless the facts support a case of constructive receipt, the cases hold that a mere unsecured contractual promise of future payment given by a solvent buyer, if that promise is not embodied in notes, mortgages or other evidences of indebtedness such as commonly change hands in commerce, is not the equivalent of cash and, therefore, does not require a cash basis seller to recognize gain prior to his actual or constructive receipt of the payments.[31] However, the regulations provide that "Only in rare and extraordinary cases will property be considered to have no fair market value."[32] Also, the courts, recognizing that standard land contracts are secured by the property sold, may be marketable and do sometimes change hands in commerce (even though large discounts may be given) have generally held that such land contracts are property having an ascertainable fair market value. Therefore, sales secured by land contracts will not generally qualify as open transactions and land contract sellers will not be permitted to report their gains on the cost recovery basis.[33] Similarly, a buyer's negotiable promissory note represents current payment to the cash method seller to the extent of its fair market value unless the buyer's financial condition is so poor as to render the note unsaleable as collateral.[34] A non-negotiable note, on the other hand, is similar to the mere contractual obligation and is not treated as the equivalent of cash.[35]

Where a seller is uncertain as to whether a sale will qualify as an open transaction, he may file a conditional installment election on his return in the event it is determined that the cost recovery method is not available. In the *Warren Jones* case, cited in footnote 33, IRS did not contest the validity of such an election; although the taxpayer lost on the open transaction issue, he was still able to avoid most of the harsh tax consequences that would have followed if installment reporting had not been available.

FOOTNOTES FOR CHAPTER EIGHT

[1]Rev.Rul. 73-396, 1973-2 C.B. 161. This Ruling also holds that it makes no difference whether buyer's note is secured by a mortgage or whether the real estate is transferred unencumbered with seller receiving unsecured notes.

[2]P-H Federal Taxes ¶20,427.

[3]Reg.1.453-4(c); *Estate of Sam E. Broadhead*, 1966 P-H Memo TC ¶66,026.

[4]Reg. 1.453-4(c); *Burnet v S. & L. Building Corp.* 288 U.S. 406, 12 AFTR 15 (1933); *R.A. Waldrep*, 52 T.C. 640 (1969) aff'd per curiam, 428 F.2d 1216, 26 AFTR 70-5113 (CA5, 1970).

[5]*Stonecrest Corp.*, 24 T.C. 659 (1955), nonacq., 1956-1 C.B. 6, government's appeal dismissed pursuant to stipulation (9th Cir.1958); *United Pacific Corp.*, 39 T.C. 721 (1963), government's appeal dismissed pursuant to stipulation (9th Cir.1964).

⁵(a) Rev.Rul.68-246, 1968-1 C.B. 198, modified by Rev.Rul.73-451, 1973-2 C.B.158.

⁶ *Everett Pozzi,* 49 T.C. 119 (1967); *Hendrix v U.S.,* 32 AFTR 2d 73-6089 (D.C. Ore., 1973); *Williams v. U.S.,* 219 F2d 523, 46 AFTR 1725 (CA5, 1955).

⁷Rev.Rul. 55-694, 1955-2 C.B. 229.

⁸Rev.Rul. 71-352, 1971-2 C.B. 221.

⁹*Irwin, Jr., v. Comm.,* 390 F.2d 91, 21 AFTR 2d 779 (CA5, 1968); *U.S. v. Marshall,* 357 F.2d 294, 17 AFTR 2d 596 (CA9, 1966). The Tax Court originally took a contrary view, *J. Carl Horneff,* 59 T.C. 63(1968).

¹⁰Rev.Rul. 73-555, 1973-2 C.B. 159. However, payment of seller's selling expenses related to the sale and are held to be payment in the year of sale. Rev.Rul. 76-109, footnote 22 infra.

¹¹Reg. 1.453-4(c).

¹²Rev.Rul. 69-462, 1969-2 C.B. 107.

¹³10-42 Corp., 55 T.C. 593 (1971); *Baltimore Baseball Club, Inc. v. U.S.,* 481 F.2d 1283, 32 AFTR 2d 73-5352 (Court of Claims, 1973).

¹⁴Reg.1.453-8 (b) (1).

¹⁵Rev.Rul. 65-297, 1975-2C.B.152. The Tax Court permits a late election to be made where the failure to make a timely election was in good faith, *Estate of Sam Broadhead,* 1972 P-H Memo T.C. ¶72,195, but not where the non-disclosure was a deliberate attempt to conceal the sale, *John Harper,* 54 T.C. 1121 (1970) acq.

¹⁶P-H Federal Taxes ¶20,423.

¹⁷*Warren Jones Co.,* footnote, 33 infra.

¹⁸*Chas. A. Collins,* 48 T.C. 45 (1967), acq.

¹⁹*Richard H. Pritchett,* 63 T.C. 149 (1974), acq.

²⁰Gralapp v. U.S., 458 F.2d 1158, 29 AFTR 2d 72-1066 (CA10, 1972).

²¹*In re Steen et al v. U.S.,*509 F.2d 1398, 35 AFTR 2d 75-623 (CA9, 1975).

²²Rev.Rul. 76-109, 1976-1C.B.125.

²³*Kirschenmann v. Comm'r.* 488 F.2d 270, 33 AFTR 2d 73-317 (CA9, 1973), rev'g. 57 T.C. 524 (1972).

²⁴Rev.Rul. 74-384, 1974-2 C.B.152.

²⁵*United Surgical Steel Co.,* 54 T.C. 1215 (1970), *acq; Town & Country Food Co.,* 51 T.C. 1049 (1969),*acq.*

²⁶Joe D. Branham, 51 T.C.175 (1968); *Ralph Dessauer,* 54 T.C. 327 (1970), rev'd. on another issue, 449 F.2d 562 (CA8, 1971). P-H Fed. Taxes ¶20,451.

²⁷Reg. 1.1038-1(h), example 2.

²⁸Reg. 1.1038-1(f) (2).

²⁹*Osenbach v. Comm'r.,* 198 F.2d 235, 42 AFTR 355 (CA4, 1952). If the obligation is issued by a corporation, ¶1232 may supply the sale or exchange requirement.

³⁰*Burnet v. Logan,* 283 U.S. 404, 9 AFTR 1453 (1931).

³¹P-H Fed Taxes ¶20,466.

³²Regs, 1.1001-1(a); 1.453-6(a) (2).

³³*Warren Jones Co. v. Comm'r.,* 524 F.2d788,36 AFTR 2d75-5954 (CA9, 1975), rev'g. 60 T.C. 663 (1073). The transaction was "closed" despite the fact that the fair market value of buyer's obligations required a discount of over 40% from face value. See also *Kaufman v Comm'r.,* 372 F.2d 789, 18 AFTR 2d 6031 (CA4, 1966), *Heller Trust v. Comm'r.,* 382 F.2d 675, 20 AFTR 2d 5370 (CA9, 1967) and *Howard Perelman,* 41 T.C. 234 (1963).

³⁴*Doric Apartment Co. v. Comm'r.,* 94 F.2d 895 (6th Cir. 1938); *Joseph Marcello, Jr.,* 43 T.C. 168 (1964), *rev'd on other grounds,* 380 F.2d 400 (5th Cir. 1967); *Harry Leland Barnsley,* 31 T.C. 1260 (1959).

³⁵*Hartland Associates,* 54 T.C. 1580, 1588 (1970).

9

TAX-FREE
EXCHANGES

To the property owner with real estate which is ripe for disposition and which has a large potential gain, the possibility of a tax-free exchange often offers the best of all possible worlds. The tax-free exchange avoids the problem of recapture of depreciation and defers that day of reckoning when the ordinary deductions which were claimed in earlier years are converted to recognized income; the piper may be paid eventually but not yet. Most methods of disposing of real estate carry the potential of recognition of gain, particularly where the mortgage exceeds the depreciated basis— even the charitable contribution may have this effect. However, tax-free exchanges continue to be an exception to the rule. It is not surprising, therefore, to find that the sophisticated investor will go to great lengths to structure an exchange of property as opposed to a simple sale followed by a reinvestment of the sales proceeds.

This chapter will analyze the question of tax-free exchanges of real estate and will cover the following principal topics:

9.1 The General Rule; Nature of Qualifying Property
9.2 Exceptions to the General Rule: Treatment of Boot
9.3 Recapture of Depreciation
9.4 Installment Sales
9.5 Three Party Exchanges
9.6 Basis of the Acquired Property
9.7 Exchanges Compared to Sale-Leaseback Transactions

9.1   THE GENERAL RULE; NATURE OF QUALIFYING PROPERTY

Code §1031 provides that no gain or loss is recognized if property which is held for productive use in trade or business or which is held for investment, but not including stock in trade or other property held primarily for sale, is exchanged solely for property of a like kind to be similarly held. Thus, if one piece of investment real estate is exchanged for another piece of investment real estate, there is a complete non-recognition of gain or loss.

The regulations are quite liberal in defining the term "like kind" for purposes of tax-free exchanges. They provide[1] that the term "like kind" refers to the nature or character of the property and not to its grade or quality. The fact that any real estate involved is improved or unimproved is not material, for that fact relates only to the grade or quality of the property and not to its kind or class. Therefore, no gain or loss is recognized if a taxpayer who is not a real estate dealer exchanges city real estate for a ranch or farm or exchanges a leasehold with 30 years or more to run for real estate, or exchanges improved real estate for unimproved real estate. On the other hand, an exchange of land for timber rights is not a like kind exchange since the two properties involved differ in nature and character.[2] An undivided interest as a tenant in common may be exchanged for a fee simple interest and §1031 will apply.

> *Example:* Three parties each own undivided interests as tenants in common in three separate parcels of real estate held for investment purposes. The three parties exchanged their respective interests in these separate parcels for a 100% ownership interest in a single parcel which is also held for investment. This is a tax-free exchange and no gain or loss will be recognized.[3]

Note that in addition to the "like kind" requirement, it is also esesential that the properties involved, both the property conveyed and the property received, qualify as "property held for productive use in trade or business or for investment." On the other hand, stock in trade and property which is held primarily for sale are specifically excluded from the definition of property held for productive use in trade or business or for investment and will not qualify for tax-free exchanges.

> *Comment:* Note that §1031 referring to property held primarily for sale omits the qualifying phrase "to customers in the ordinary course of (the taxpayer's) trade or business" which is found in the Code sections dealing with capital gains. For this reason, property which qualifies for capital gain treatment may not qualify for tax-free exchange treatment. For example, the Tax Court has hald that a taxpayer who exchanged desert land for residential property was required to recognize the gain in the transaction since the acquired property was intended to be held for subsequent sale.[4] Also, the gain on the exchange for farm properties must be recognized where the acquired property was subject to a contract of sale which was executed prior to the exchange.[5]

9.2   EXCEPTIONS TO THE GENERAL RULE: TREATMENT OF BOOT

(a) Receipt of Boot—If, in addition to receiving like kind property, the taxpayer receives money or non-like kind property (commonly referred to as "boot") any gain will be recognized up to the amount of the boot received.[6]

Example: Taxpayer C conveys real estate which has a basis to him of $75,000 and a fair market value of $100,000 and receives in exchange another parcel of real estate having a fair market value of $90,000, plus $10,000 to equalize the difference. The gain on the transaction is $25,000, but the recognized gain is limited to the amount of the boot, or $10,000.

(b) Payment of Boot—Where the taxpayer pays the boot to the other party to the exchange, the transaction may or may not be taxable depending upon the nature of the boot given. If money is given, no gain or loss is recognized. Accordingly, "trade-ins" of equipment or other business assets qualify for non-recognition treatment despite the fact that the taxpayer pays money in addition to transferring his old property. On the other hand, if non-qualified property (boot) which has appreciated or depreciated in value, is paid in connection with the exchange, gain or loss will be recognized to the extent of the appreciation of depreciation thereon.[7]

Example: Taxpayer D exhcanges his real estate, having a fair market value of $75,000, plus marketable securities having a value of $25,000, for other real estate worth $100,000. The $25,000 of securities have a cost basis to him of $15,000. Although the real estate involved in the exchange qualifies for tax-free treatment, the taxpayer is deemed to have realized a $10,000 gain on the disposition of his securities.

(c) Treatment of Mortgages—Where the property conveyed is subject to a mortgage, the amount of the mortgage is deemed to be received by the transferor in the year of the conveyance, and this rule applies regardless of whether the grantee assumes the mortgage or merely takes title to the property subject to the mortgage.[8] In short, the amount of the mortgage constitutes boot and produces a tax in the year of the exchange to the extent of gain realized.

Example: Taxpayer E owns an apartment building which is worth $220,000, subject to a $100,000 mortgage (leaving him an equity of $120,000). His basis in the property is $100,000. He exchanges this building for another parcel of investment real estate with a value of $120,000, the conveyance of the apartment building being made subject to the mortgage. He has a gain of $120,000 (receipt of $120,000 of real estate and $100,000 of boot compared with a $100,000 basis) and the gain is recognized to the extent of $100,000, the amount of the mortgage on the property conveyed.

Where *both properties* involved in an exchange are subject to mortgage liabilities, there is a netting or offset of one mortgage against the other. If the mortgage on the property which the taxpayer conveyed (deemed to be boot received) exceeds the mortgage on the property which he acquired, he is taxable on the difference; if the mortgage on the property conveyed is less than the mortgage on the acquired property, there is no tax assessed in the year of the exchange.[9]

Example: Taxpayer F owns an investment property with an adjusted basis to him of $100,000, a fair market value of $220,000 but subject to a mortgage of $80,000 (leaving an equity of $140,000). Taxpayer G owns another investment property with a basis of $175,000, a fair market value of $250,000 but subject to a $150,000 mortgage (equity of $100,000). The parties exchange properties with the sum of $40,000 in cash being paid to F to equalize the values. Each property is conveyed subject to the mortgage on it. The following are the tax consequences of this transaction to each party:

TAXABLE GAIN	F	G
Value of Real Property Received	$ 250,000	$ 220,000
Plus: Cash Received	40,000	none
Plus: Mortgage on Property Transferred	80,000	150,000
Total Consideration Received	$ 370,000	$ 370,000
Less: Adjusted Basis of Property Transferred	(100,000)	(175,000)
Less: Mortgage on Property Received	(150,000)	(80,000)
Less: Cash Paid	none	(40,000)
Gain Realized	$ 120,000	$ 75,000
Other Property or Money Received	40,000	30,000
Total Gain Recognized	$ 40,000	$ 30,000*

*This sum represents $150,000, less $80,000 and less $40,000.

9.3 RECAPTURE OF DEPRECIATION

Where depreciable real estate is exchanged solely for other depriciable real estate, there is no recapture income recognized since the transaction is entirely tax-free.[10] However, the recapture potential in the old property is carried forward and attaches to the property received. There is also no recapture problem where boot is *paid* in connection with an exchange. But where boot or non-depreciable real estate is *received* in connection with an exchange, there may be recapture income (income taxable at ordinary rates) to the extent of recognized gain.

(a) Receipt of Boot in Connection with Exchange—If a sale of real estate would produce recapture of depreciation, an exchange of such real estate will also trigger recapture income to the extent that gain is recognized.[11]

> *Example:* A building with a value of $95,000 was exchanged for another building worth $85,000 and 10,000 of cash. Assuming that the adjusted basis of the old building was $80,000, the gain realized is $15,000 but only $10,000 of such gain is recognized under the rules governing tax-free exchanges. To the extent there is depreciation which is subject to recapture under §1250, this gain is ordinary recapture income. Any excess is taxed as capital gain under §1231.

(b) Receipt of Like Kind Property which is not Depreciable—Where like kind property is received in exchange for real estate, but the property received is not §1250 property (i.e., real estate which qualifies for depreciation), the situation becomes more complicated. An example would be the exchange of a building for another building (both depreciable properties) and a second parcel consisting of raw land (not §1250 property since it is non-depreciable). In that case, the recapture income is computed as follows: compute the amount of income subject to recapture if the property conveyed had been sold for the values received—assume that such recapture potential equals $20,000; then compute the first and second limits set forth below and the amount taxable as recapture income under §1250 cannot exceed the larger of these two limits.[12]

Example: Taxpyer H exchanges a building having a basis of $70,000 for another building worth $15,000 (§1250 like kind property) a piece of land worth $100,000 (like kind property but not depreciable §1250 property) and cash of $1,000. Based upon the length of time he held the property the recapture potential is $20,000. The recapture income cannot exceed the greater of the following two limitations:

(1) The first limit is the gain that would be taxed if the normal boot rule applied; $1,000 in this example.

(2) The second limit is the normal recapture income ($20,000 on our assumption) less the value of the §1250 property received ($15,000 in this example).

Since the second limitation, $5,000 in this example, is greater than the first limitation, the recapture income is $5,000. The balance of the potential recapture income is carried forward and attaches to the new building subject, of course, to the usual rules decreasing the recapture amount according to the period of time the property is held.

9.4   INSTALLMENT SALES

Assuming that an exchange is partially taxable by reason of the receipt of boot, the question arises as to whether the recognized gain can be reported on the installment method. The answer is that this is possible provided that the transaction otherwise qualifies for installment reporting.[13] This includes the requriement that the amount received in the year of the exchange, except for obligations of the transferee, cannot exceed 30% of the total consideration to be received, and in making this determination the like kind of property received is counted as a receipt in the year of sale notwithstanding that its receipt is non-taxable.[14]

Example: Taxpayer I exchanges real estate with a $100,000 basis for like property worth $200,000 and an interest-bearing note in the amount of $800,000 payable in equal annual installments over an eight-year term. The realized gain is $900,000 but the recognized gain is only $800,000, the like kind property being received tax-free. If no payments are made on the note in the year of the exchange, the transaction qualifies for installment reporting because the payment that year (the like kind real estate) does not exceed 30% of the total consideration to be received ($1,000,000). The recognized gain being 80% of each payment (including the initial payment of like kind property) is included in income each year as received. Hence, $160,000 is included in income the first year (80% of $200,000) and $80,000 is included in each of the following years (80% of the annual $100,000 payments). If the like kind real estate had a value of more than $300,000 and the note was reduced accordingly, the transaction would not qualify for installment reporting.

9.5   THREE PARTY EXCHANGES

Assume that Taxpayer owns a parcel of real estate with which he is willing to part provided that he can do so without incurring a tax on the disposition. A prospective buyer, Mr. B, is willing to purchase the property and the parties have negotiated a mutually agreeable price. Realizing that they must set up a tax-free transaction insofar as Taxpayer is concerned, they have contacted a third party, Mr. X, who owns a parcel of real estate approximately equal in value to Taxpayer's real estate which he would be willing to accept in exchange. There are two possible techniques whereby the transaction can be set up as a tax-free exchange:

(a) Exchange Between Taxpayer and B—One possibility is for B, the prospective buyer, to purchase the property owned by X, the third party; B then enters into an exchange with Taxpayer.

(b) Exchange Between Taxpayer and X—Another possibility is for taxpayer to exchange properties directly with X, the third party, with X then selling Taxpayer's property to B.

Either of these transactions may qualify as a tax-free exchange provided that the necessary formalities are carefully followed. If Taxpayer and B intend to and do accomplish an exchange of real estate, the transaction qualifies as being tax-free despite the fact that B acquired the real estate solely for the purpose of consummating the exchange.[15] Even if the taxpayer first agrees to *sell* his land for cash and subsequently decides that he prefers a tax-free exchange, the transaction is, nevertheless, tax-free, provided that the formalities of an exchange are followed.[16]

Turning to the second alternative—an exchange of property between Taxpayer and third party, X, followed by a sale from X to B—the cases indicate that this technique may also qualify as a tax-free exchange. Although it is preferable that X has not entered into a binding contract with B for the sale of Taxpayer's property, the fact that a party acquired property with the understanding that it could be disposed of elsewhere, did not necessarily mean that he was acting as an agent for the buyer or that the subsequent sale had no substance. In short, the initial exchange transaction qualifies as being tax-free.[17] Similarly, where a taxpayer exchanged his real estate with a tax exempt foundation and on the same day the foundation contracted to sell the property to a corporation controlled by taxpayer, the exchange was sustained as being tax-free and the Commissioner's argument, that the transfer to the foundation should be disregarded, was not sustained.[18] Even utilizing Taxpayer's attorney as the third party for the purpose of acquiring other real estate, exchanging same with Taxpayer and then selling Taxpayer's property to B, the ultimate buyer, has been sustained as being tax-free.[19] The Court found that the attorney was acting for B, rather than for his client, in consummating the exchange transaction.

It is possible in many cases to accomplish the three-party exchange in an escrow closing. For example, in the case of the transaction described in (a) above (B proposes to buy X's property and convey it to Taxpayer in exchange for his property), the transaction could be handled as follows: B pays into the escrow account the agreed purchase price for X's property, same to be released to X upon delivery to B of a deed to Taxpayer's property. Taxpayer deposits the deed to his property running to B, same to be released upon delivery to Taxpayer of a deed to X's property. X deposits a deed to his property running to Taxpayer, to be released to Taxpayer upon delivery to X of B's purchase money. The transaction qualifies as an exchange by Taxpayer despite the fact that he surrendered his property to B in exchange for receipt of like kind property from X; the grantee under Taxpayer's deed need not be the same person as the grantor of the property conveyed to Taxpayer.[20]

> *Warning:* In closing a three party exchange, it is essential that title to the property being conveyed to Taxpayer in fact be transferred in consideration for the like kind property being conveyed by Taxpayer. In one case, B, who was to acquire the like

kind property from X and to convey it in exchange for Taxpayer's property, short-cut the formalities. Instead of conveying title, B simply paid to Taxpayer the stipulated price for the purchase of his property and simultaneously transferred to Taxpayer B's rights to purchase the like kind property from X. The Court held that Taxpayer made a sale, not an exchange. "The very essence of an exchange is the transfer of property between owners, while the mark of a sale is the receipt of cash for the property."[21]

Supposing that Taxpayer proposes to engage in a three-party exchange and B is willing to accommodate Taxpayer's wishes but the parties have been unable to locate the exchange property to be conveyed to Taxpayer. Can the transaction be held open until suitable property has been located? In *Starker v. U.S.*[22] the following facts existed: Taxpayer entered into an exchange agreement with B by which Taxpayer agreed to convey certain timberlands and B agreed to convey to Taxpayer from time to time like kind property acceptable to Taxpayer. The parties had to first agree as to the value of the property being conveyed by Taxpayer. If by April 1, 1972, the value of the property being conveyed to Taxpayer was less than the value of the timberlands conveyed to B, then B could pay the difference in cash. On April 28, 1976, the timberlands were transferred to B and a credit in favor of Taxpayer was entered on B's books for the agreed value. This amount, increased by 6% per annum to reflect the increase in value of the conveyed property, was used to compute the amount payable from B to taxpayer. Between 1968 and 1972, B conveyed eight separate parcels of land to Taxpayer and with the last exchange there remained no credit in favor of Taxpayer. Therefore, no cash was paid. The Court found that Taxpayer did not have control over the cash used by B to purchase the parcels in question and the transaction was held to constitute a tax-free exchange. Taxpayer's gain was not recognized.

9.6 BASIS OF THE ACQUIRED PROPERTY

When property is sold and the proceeds are reinvested in new property, the basis of the new property is, of course, its cost. But where a tax-free or a partially tax-free exchange is effected, the basis of the new property is determined by reference to the basis of the old property, subject to adjustments where boot is involved.

(a) General Rule; No Boot Involved—In a straight exchange where the taxpayer neither gives nor receives boot, the basis of the property received is equal to the basis of the property transferred.

(b) Boot Is Given—Where the taxpayer gives boot to the other party to the exchange, his basis for the property received is the same as his basis in the transferred property, *plus* the amount of the boot given. Thus, conveyance of real estate with a $100,000 basis plus payment of $10,000 cash produces a basis for the acquired property of $110,000.

Where boot other than money is given (marketable securities, for example) and gain or loss is recognized in the transaction, any such gain increases the basis of the acquired property and any such loss decreases the basis.

> *Example:* Taxpayer transfers real estate with a $100,000 basis, plus marketable securities with a value of $10,000 and a basis of $9,000, for the new real estate. There is $1,000 of recognized gain and the basis of the new real estate is $110,000 (the basis

of the property transferred, plus the basis of the boot given, plus the recognized gain).

(c) Boot Is Received—Where boot (other than money or mortgage debt) is received, basis must be first allocated to the boot property to the extent of its fair market value with the remainder of the basis being allocated to the qualifying (like kind) properties received.[23]

Remember that where there is a mortgage on the property conveyed as well as on the property received, both of the mortgages must be taken into consideration in computing basis. This is consistent with the rule providing for an offsetting of the mortgages for purposes of computing gain to be recognized. The mortgage on the property received is added to basis while the mortgage on the property conveyed is subtracted from basis along with any other boot received in the transaction. Referring to the examples involving taxpayers F and G, Section 2 above, basis would be computed as follows for each of these taxpayers:

BASIS OF PROPERTY RECEIVED

	F	G
Adjusted Basis of Property Transferred	$100,000	$175,000
Plus: Mortgage on Property Received	150,000	80,000
Cash Paid	none	40,000
Total Consideration Paid	250,000	295,000
Less: Cash Received	(40,000)	none
Mortgage on Property Transferred	(80,000)	(150,000)
	130,000	145,000
Gain Recognized	40,000	30,000
Adjusted Basis of Property Received	$170,000	$175,000

The foregoing examples involved transactions where boot is received and gain is recognized on the exchange transaction. Of course, there are cases where the taxpayer incurs a loss on the exchange because the fair value of the property received as well as the boot received is less than the adjusted basis of the property conveyed. In such cases, the basis of the newly acquired property equals the basis of the old property, less the amount of boot received, but the loss is not recognized and does not have the effect of reducing basis. §1031(c). In short, gain recognized by reason of the receipt of boot results in a compensating basis adjustment but since the loss incurred in a tax-free exchange is not recognized, no adjustment in basis is called for.

(d) Holding Period—If the property surrendered in the tax-free exchange is a capital asset or a §1231 asset and if the basis of the new property is determined, in whole or in part, by reference to the basis of the old property, then there is a tacking of holding periods; the holding period of the new property includes the holding period of the property surrendered in the exchange. §1233(1). This rule will apply to most real estate exchanges. If the property surrendered does not fall within these provisions (for example, an asset which is used in trade or business but which has not been held in excess of six months), then the holding period of the new property will commence on the date of the exchange.

9.7 EXCHANGES COMPARED TO SALE-LEASEBACK TRANSACTIONS

As indicated above a leasehold with thirty years or more to run is treated as real estate for purposes for the tax-free exchange rules. Therefore, where a taxpayer sells his property and simultaneously leases it back from the grantee for more than thirty years, IRS may contend that the sale-leaseback transaction is actually an exchange of like kind properties with the fee interest in the real estate being conveyed in exchange for a tenant's interest in the same real estate. In that event, IRS will contend that any loss on the transaction is not deductible. Consider the following examples:

> *Example 1:* Taxpayer transferred real property with a basis of $531,000 to a college for $150,000. The parties then executed a 95-year lease. The Court held that the transaction was a tax-free exchange with $150,000 of boot being received by taxpayer and, therefore, disallowed the loss. The Court noted that the property was the taxpayer's primary asset, a foundry; that the property was required for the continued operation of taxpayer's business; and that no business purpose was present in this transaction.[24]

> *Example 2:* Taxpayer was in need of a new plant for its manufacturing operations. It entered into an agreement with the Prudential Insurance Company whereby, in condideration of $2,400,000 or cost, whichever was less, taxpayer would construct a plant of specified quality and upon completion would transfer title to Prudential. Prudential would lease the plant to taxpayer for 30 years at a specified fixed rental or 7.94% of the purchase price, whichever was less. The lease also was to include extensions for an additional 20 years. Construction costs ran well in excess of the estimated amount and taxpayer incurred a loss of $787,000. The Tax Court sustained the right of the taxpayer to deduct the loss in the year in which the transaction occurred. The Tax Court felt that the risk of loss was on the taxpayer who sustained a real loss because the costs of land and construction exceeded the sales price. Both the sales price and rental were at fair market values and the leasehold, therefore, had no separate value of its own.[25]

It is clear that this is an area where the Commissioner will continue to litigate close cases. The courts have held, however, that in the following situations, losses on the sale of real estate will be recognized despite the fact that the sale is accompanied by a simultaneous leaseback of the property:

> Where the taxpayer was found to have realized the fair market value on the sale of the property, the rent to be paid upon the leaseback was reasonable, the duration of the lease was not such as would warrant a conclusion that the taxpayer had not changed its economic position and there existed a valid business purpose for the sale.[26]
> Where there is a systematic liquidation of the taxpayer's real estate holdings and the lease-back is incidental to such sale and did not include a purchase option.[27]
> Where the lease is less than thirty years.[28]

FOOTNOTES FOR CHAPTER NINE

[1] Reg. 1.1031(a)-1(b) and (c).
[2] *Oregon Lumber Co.,* 20TC 192, (1953) acq.
[3] Rev.Rul. 73-476, 1973-2 C.B. 300.

[4]*Ethel Black,* 35 T.C. 90 (1960).

[5]*Brooks Griffin,* 49 T.C. 253 (1967).

[6]Reg. 1.1031(b)-1.

[7]Reg. 1.1031(a)-1(a) (last sentence) and Reg. 1.1031(d)-1(e), example.

[8]§1031(d).

[9]Reg. 1.1031(d)-2, example 2(c).

[10]§1250(d) (4).

[11]§1250(d) (4) (A) (i) and (C).

[12]§1250(d) (4) (A) (ii) and (C).

[13]Rev.Rul. 65-155, 1965-1 C.B. 356.

[14]*Clinton H. Mitchell,* 42 T.C. 953 (1964).

[15]*J.H. Baird Publishing Co.,* 39T.C. 608, acq.

[16]*Alderson v. Comm'r.,* 317 F.2d 790, 11 AFTR 2d 1529 (CA9, 1963) (reversing T.C.).

[17]*Leo A. Woodbury,* 49 T.C. 180 (1967).

[18]*Mays v. Campbell, Jr.,* 146 F.Supp. 375, 17 AFTR 2d 109 (D.C.Tex, 1965).

[19]*Leslie Q. Coupe,* 52 T.C. 394 (1969), acq. in result only.

[20]Rev.Rul. 57-244, 1957-1 C.B. 247. See also *W.D. Hadden Co. v. Comm'r.,* 165 F. 2nd 588, 36 AFTR 670 (CA5,1948).

[21]*Carlton v. U.S.,* 385 F.2d 238, 14 AFTR 2d 1051 (CA, 1967). See also *Antone Borchard,* 1965 P-H TC Memo ¶65,297.

[22]35 AFTR 2d 75-1550 (D.Ore, 1975).

[23]Reg. 1.1031(d)-1 (c), Example. The receipt of boot in the form of money or mortgage debt results in both an increase in basis (gain recognized) and a decrease (for money and debt relief) under §1030(d) so no basis allocation is required.

[24]*Century Electric Co. v. Comm'r.,* 192 F.2d 155, 41 AFTR 205 (CA-8, 1951), cert. den.

[25]Leslie Co. v. Comm.,—F2d—, 38 AFTR 2d 76-5458 (CA3, 1976)

[26]*Jordan Marsh Co. v. Comm'r.,* 269 F.2d 453, 4 AFTR 2d 5341 (CA2, 1959), nonacq.

[27]*City Investing Co.,* 38 T.C. 1, nonacq.

[28]*Standard Envelope Mfg. Co.,* 15 T.C. 41 (1950), acq.

10

QUALIFYING
FOR CAPITAL GAINS
ON REAL ESTATE SALES

There is probably no area of real estate tax law which has produced more litigation than the question of whether a sale qualifies for capital gain treatment. The reason is fairly obvious. Individual tax rates go as high as 70% while the capital gain rates are limited to a 25% maximum in most cases.[1] Such a differential provides an impelling incentive to high-bracket taxpayers to qualify their sales for capital gain treatment. Unfortunately, the line between a real estate dealer who must pay ordinary rates and a real estate investor who qualifies for capital gain treatment is not clear. Moreover, if a dealer holds some property for investment he may qualify for capital gains and an investor may become a dealer under certain circumstances. The cases are confusing and largely based on factual distinctions. This chapter attempts to bring some order out of the maze of decisions and to formulate some guidelines for taxpayers. The chapter will be divided into the following sections:

10.1 STATUTORY BACKGROUND; DEFINITIONS OF DEALERS AND INVESTORS

Surprisingly, the term "capital asset" is not defined in the Internal Revenue Code. Instead, the Code treats all assets as capital assets except those which are expressly excluded from capital gain treatment. Section 1221(1) provides that capital assets do not include "property held by the taxpayer primarily for sale to customers in the ordinary course of his trade or business." The same exclusion appears in §1231(b) (1) defining "property used in the trade or business." (Actually, assets qualify for capital gain treatment whether they are capital assets under §1221 or trade or business assets held for more than six months under §1231. The only difference in tax treatment under these two sections is that in case of a sale at a loss, §1231 assets receive ordinary loss treatment while capital assets are limited to capital loss treatment.)

The terms "dealer" and "investor" are not defined in the Code either. However, these words have become shorthand terms to describe certain categories of taxpayers who hold real estate. A dealer is one who is in the business of dealing in (buying or selling) real estate. He generally makes his living in that activity although he may also engage in other business activities. Thus, property held by him is generally held "primarily for sale to customers in the ordinary course of his trade or business" and, therefore, does not qualify for capital gain treatment. An investor, on the other hand, is not primarily in the business of selling real estate but holds his property for investment purposes or at least for some purpose other than sale. Since he does not fall within the statutory exclusion, an investor will normally qualify for capital gain treatment.

The courts have repeatedly set forth the criteria which they will utilize in distinguishing dealers from investors. The factors to be considered include the following:[2]

1. The purpose for which the property was initially acquired.

2. The purpose for which the property was subsequently held.

3. The extent to which improvements, if any, were made to the property by the taxpayer.

4. The frequency, number and continuity of sales.

5. The extent and nature of the transactions involved.

6. The ordinary business of the taxpayer.

7. The extent of advertising, promotion, or other active efforts used in soliciting buyers for the sale of the property.

8. The listing of property with brokers.

9. The purpose for which the property was held at the time of sale.

After listing these factors, most courts go on to say that no single factor is determinative and that all of the taxpayer's activities must be considered.

10.2   POSSIBILITY OF DUAL STATUS

We saw in the preceding section that property is not excluded from capital gain treatment unless it is held "primarily" for sale to customers. The definition of the term "primarily" is obviously critical in evaluating the possibility of capital gain treatment. Prior to 1965, the courts were not in agreement on the definition of the term. In that year, however, the U.S. Supreme Court decided the important case of *Malat v Riddell,* holding that when the statute excludes property "held by the taxpayer primarily for sale to customers in the ordinary course of his trade or business" the word "primarily" means "principally" or "of first importance;" the fact that the holding of property for sale is a "substantial" reason for acquiring or holding the property is not sufficient to deny capital gain treatment.[3] Thus, one who is in the business of buying and selling real estate may avoid dealer classification as to a particular parcel or category of property if he can demonstrate that his purpose in holding the property was not principally for sale to customers in the ordinary course of his business, although that might have been one of his purposes—even a substantial purpose—for acquiring and holding the property in question. The *Malat* case is important not only because it establishes a test for measuring capital gain treatment—and, fortunately, one which is most favorable to taxpayers—but also because it accepts the principle of dual status, i.e. even one who is a dealer in real estate may hold certain property for investment. Indeed, the taxpayer in *Malat* had a long history of dealings in real estate and a number of his transactions resulted in tax litigation. Nevertheless, on the facts of the case he was held to qualify for capital gains.

10.3   POTENTIAL ARGUMENTS AGAINST DEALER STATUS

Recognizing the statutory setting and the possibility of dual status under *Malat,* a taxpayer has two principle arguments which can be advanced to support capital gain treatment. First and most obviously, the taxpayer may demonstrate that the property in question was not held primarily for sale. A number of post-*Malat* decisions have accepted the lead of the U.S. Supreme Court and have recognized the principle that if real estate is acquired and held as an investment then the gain realized on its ultimate sale qualifies for capital gain treatment.[4] All of the factors listed in Section 1 above are relevant, but it is clear that the longer the holding period and the greater the amount of gain ultimately realized, the better are the taxpayer's chances to prove that the property qualifies as an investment.

> *Example:* Mr. Scheuber was a Milwaukee real estate developer who admittedly held some real estate for sale to customers in the ordinary course of his business. However, he also owned two tracts of unimproved real estate which were in issue in this case. He sold 1/2 of one tract after eight years and the other 1/2 after nine years at a total sales price of approximately 2 1/2 times his cost. This tract was never advertised for sale and the transaction resulted from an unsolicited offer. The second tract in issue was purchased for $10,000 in 1945 and an award of $130,000 was received in 1959 pursuant to a condemnation of the property. The appellate court held these constituted investment properties and Mr. Scheuber qualified for capital gains treatment notwithstanding that he was generally a dealer in real estate.[5]

There is also a second argument which the taxpayer can utilize. Even if the property was held primarily for sale, if the sale was not to a customer in the ordinary course of the taxpayer's trade or business, the sale does not meet the literal statutory exclusion from capital treatment. A classic example is a case decided by the Tax Court in 1973.[6]

> *Example:* The taxpayer, an accountant, made a practice of purchasing real estate which he anticipated would increase in value, intending to resell when he could make a satisfactory profit. The case involved transactions occurring over a period of less than three years involving the sale of nine parcels, with holding periods ranging from less than two months to twenty-two months. A broker was utilized in nine of the transactions. The Tax Court granted capital gain treatment to the taxpayer. It likened his activities to one who speculates in stocks hoping to realize gains on the increases in market values.

On the other hand the fact that property was originally acquired and held as an investment does not necessarily insulate it from ordinary income treatment. A number of recent cases have dealt with fact situations involving taxpayers who were liquidating investment property. There will obviously be some sales activities in the liquidation of any investment and the test of whether property is held for sale should not be determined as of the moment of sale. Even the construction of streets for access to the property, the provision of drainage and the furnishing of access to water facilities will not necessarily produce ordinary income if such improvements are necessary to liquidate an investment in a large tract of land.[7] But at a certain point the level of activities undertaken by an individual to dispose of his real estate will override his original investment purpose and dealer classification will follow. Thus, ordinary income treatment has been imposed where an individual acquired property by inheritance and subsequently sold it[8] and where an individual sold farm land which he had held for a period of more than twenty-seven years.[9] In both cases the level of the taxpayer's activities in subdividing, improving and selling the property indicated that he had substantially abandoned this original intent. In the latter case the court commented, "we refused capital gains treatment in those instances where over time there has been a thoroughgoing change in purpose . . . as to make untenable a claim either of twin intent or continued primacy of investment purpose."

> *Example:* The taxpayer, an accountant, made a practice of purchasing real estate

10.4 SUBDIVIDED REAL ESTATE

Recognizing the difficulties in qualifying for capital gain treatment where the sale involves lots resulting from the subdivision of a larger tract, Congress incorporated §1237 in the Internal Revenue Code of 1954 when it was enacted. This section provides that if a taxpayer other than a corporation meets certain requirements with respect to a tract of real estate subdivided for sale, the lots or parcels sold from that tract will not be deemed to be held primarily for sale to customers in the ordinary course of the taxpayer's trade or business solely because of the fact that the taxpayer subdivided the property for sale or because of any of his activity incident to the subdivision or the sale. In short, a taxpayer who qualifies under this section is afforded a safe harbor to a limited extent.

The basic requirements of §1237 are as follows:

1. The taxpayer must not previously have held the property in question primarily for sale to customers in the ordinary course of his trade or business.

2. The taxpayer must not so hold any other real property in the taxable year in which the sale occurs.

3. No substantial improvement that substantially enhances the value of the property which is sold may have been made either while the taxpayer held the property or pursuant to the contract of sale, with certain very limited exceptions.

4. The taxpayer must have held the property for at least five years prior to sale, unless he acquired it by inheritance or devise, in which case he need satisfy only the six-month holding period required by §1222(3) for long-term capital gain treatment.

The substantial improvements permitted under this section include improvements by a tenant which do not constitute income to the taxpayer, improvements made by government or political subdivision which do not constitute an addition to taxpayer's basis and certain improvements which qualify as "necessary improvements" as described in §1237(b) (3)—primarily the installation of water, sewer or drainage facilities or roads. Even such necessary improvements are permitted only if the taxpayer's holding period with respect to the property is at least ten years and if certain other restrictive conditions are met.

Moreover, even if the property qualifies in all respects under this section, gain is nevertheless treated as ordinary income to the extent of 5% of the selling price in and after the taxable year in which the sixth lot or parcel is sold from the tract. §1237(b) (1). Note that this rule is not necessarily limited to the sixth and subsequent lots sold; if six or more lots or parcels are sold during the first taxable year in which any such lots or parcels are sold from the tract, then all sales from the tract will be subject to the 5% ordinary income rule. However, if the taxpayer maintains a five year interval between sales, then the property as it existed during this five year period shall be deemed to be the "tract" for purposes of future application of the 5% rule so that the counting of the six sales needed to trigger application of the rule will begin anew. Also, when the 5% rule does apply, expenses of sale may be deducted from that portion of the proceeds which constitute ordinary income and accordingly a part or all of the ordinary income may be offset.

> *Example:* Assume the selling price of the sixth lot of a tract is $10,000, the taxpayer's basis of the lot is $5,000 and the expenses of sale are $750. The amount of gain realized by the taxpayer would be $4,250. Because the expenses of sale ($750) exceed 5% of the selling price ($500) the entire gain is reported as capital gain. If the expenses of sale of the sixth lot were only $300 which is less than 5% of the selling price, it would follow that only $4500 would be reported as capital gain and $200 (5% of the selling price or $500 less the expenses of sale or $300) would be reported as ordinary income.[10]

Obviously, the utilization of this section as a practical matter will be quite limited. Fortunately, §1237 is not the exclusive means of qualifying for capital gains on the sale of subdivided real property.[11]

There are, of course, a number of tax and non-tax reasons why a developer may prefer to use a joint venture or a corporation for the development and sale of real estate. Where there is a danger of ordinary income treatment, however, there is an additional advantage in avoiding development and subdividing activities on the part of the original owner; he hopes to qualify for capital gain treatment on the transfer to the third party (the corporation or partnership) and the third party-transferee will then perform the development and subdividing activities. Of course, if the third party is nothing but an agent acting on behalf of the owner (the principal), the arrangement will have no tax consequence since the activities of a principal are attributed to his agent. Typically, however, the entity utilized is not clearly an agent but is a partnership or corporation wherein the original owner is merely one of the participants. The issue is whether the non-dealer partnership or corporation will be recognized as an independent seller of property or whether the dealer status of the original owner will taint the status of the entity.

Probably the cleanest technique is to have the owner sell the land to a corporation. The corporation is entitled to a stepped up basis according to its purchase price and the seller will presumably claim capital gain treatment on this sale. The corporation will then develop the property and eventually sell the lots or other resulting product. Although the corporation will presumably incur ordinary income tax on its profits, the amount of such profits will be minimal in view of the stepped up basis. Such an arrangement has been recognized as valid by the Tax Court.[12] Obviously such transactions require careful planning. The taxpayer should engage in an absolutely minimum amount of dealer activities prior to the sale, the sales price should be at fair market value, an independent appraisal is certainly advisable and if the sale is on terms other than cash the corporation must be sure to meet its obligations to the seller.[13] Finally, it is important that the corporation-buyer be adequately capitalized. If this is not the case the purported sale will be treated as a tax-free transfer under §351 resulting in a carryover of basis, ordinary income to the corporate developer and dividend treatment to the transferor on the corporate distributions.[14]

Some developers have utilized a partnership as the third party. Typically, the developer combines forces with an investor or group of investors to organize a partnership to develop the property and sell the lots. If an independent partnership or joint venture is found to exist, the dealer or investor status of the partnership, viewed as a separate entity, will determine the character of its income; the individual status of the partners or joint venturers is not necessarily determinative.[15] Obviously, under the rule referred to above, if the partnership is merely an agent of the developer, it will not qualify for capital gains and substance will control over form.

Getting the property from the original developer to the partnership is also difficult. If he merely contributes his land to the partnership there will be no gain or loss recognized by reason of §721 but there will be carryover of basis under §723. Consequently, all of the potential ordinary income from the subdividing and development activities will continue to exist at the partnership level, the desired step-up in basis not having been accomplished. A sale of the property to the partnership is also possible. §707(a) provides that a partner may engage in a transaction with a partnership in which he is a member as a separate entity and §707(b) contemplates the application of this rule to the sale of investment property to a dealer partnership. There is an exception, however, if the selling partner owns, directly or indirectly, more than 80% of the capital interest or profits interest in such partnership. §707(b) (2) (A). In determining whether this 80% test is met attribution rules are utilized. §707(b) (3). The regulations under this section expressly provide that the substance of the transaction will govern rather than its form[16] and taxpayers should attempt to avoid a principal-agent relationship between the developer and the partnership, and to see that the partnership is properly capitalized, that the sales price is reasonable, that the terms of any partnership obligations are met and that, to the extent possible, the relationship between seller and buyer is at arm's length.

FOOTNOTES FOR CHAPTER TEN

[1]The Tax Reform Act of 1969 amended sec. 1201 to increase the maximum rate of tax on long-term capital gains to 35% for individuals, where the gains exceed $50,000 per year, and to 30% for corporations. Also, capital gains of individuals are subject to the minimum tax on tax preferences which include one-half of the excess of long-term capital gains over short-term capital losses.

[2]See, for example, *Maddux Construction Co.*, 54 T.C. 1278(1970), although a number of decisions have listed these criteria.

[3]*Malat v. Riddell*, 383 U.S. 569, 17 AFTR 2d 604 (1966).

[4]*Wm. B. Howell*, 57 T.C. 546 (1972); *Maddux Construction Co.*, 54 T.C. 1278 (1970); *Albert W. Turner v. Comm.*, ____ F.2d ____, 38 AFTR 2d 76-5741 (CA4, 1976).

[5]*Scheuber v. Comm.*, 371 F 2d 999, 19 AFTR 2d 639 (CA7, 1967).

[6]*Robert L. Adam*, 60 T.C. 996 (1973).

[7]*Barrios Estate v. Comm.*, 265 F 2d 517, 3 AFTR 2d 1126 (CA5, 1959).

[8]*U.S. v. Winthrop*, 417 F 2d 517, 24 AFTR 2d 69.5760 (CA5, 1969).

[9]*Biedenharn Realty Co., Inc. v. U.S.*, 526 F 2d 409, 37 AFTR 2d 76-679 (CA5, 1976) (en banc) rev'g 509 F 2d 171, 35 AFTR 2d 75-1019 (CA5, 1975). There were 5 dissents and one concurring opinion in the decision.

[10]Reg. 1.1237-1(e) (2).

[11]*Ralph E. Gordy*, 36 T.C. 855, 860-861(1961); Reg. 1.1237-1(a) (4).

[12]*Ralph E. Gordy*, 36 T.C. 855 (1961), acq.

[13]e.g. *Robert A. Boyer*, 58 T.C. 316 (1972). For a discussion of the cases see *Brown* "Individual Investment in Real Estate" 34 N.Y.U. Inst. on Fed. Tax (1976) 189, 213-218.

[14]See, e.g. *Burr Oaks Corp. v. Comm.*, 365 F 2d 24, 18 AFTR 2d 5018 (CA7, 1966), cert. den.

[15]*Hyman Podell*, 55 T.C. 429, 433 (1970); *Riddell v. Scales*, 406 F 2d 210, 23 AFTR 2d 69-541 (CA9, 1969). In the *Podell* case the entity concept worked to the disadvantage of the taxpayer because ordinary income treatment was imposed at the partnership level while he would not have been classified as a dealer individually. *Thomas K. McManus*, 65 T.C. 197 (1975).

[16]Reg. 1.707-1(a).

11

RULES
GOVERNING
CORPORATE LIQUIDATIONS

There are a number of reasons why stockholders might wish to withdraw real estate from their corporation. Sometimes they belatedly recognize that incorporation of the project was ill-conceived in the first place, and they wish to reverse that decision and take the remaining tax losses and cash flow personally. In some cases the corporation has served its purpose—executing a mortgage note, for example—and can be dispensed with. Frequently, by reason of mortgage amortization or appreciation in value, a substantial equity exists in the property which can produce tax-free cash by means of refinancing; transferring title to their own names permits the stockholders to realize such amounts personally rather than having them flow through a corporation. In other cases the property is about to be sold and leaving it in corporate form precipitates a double tax, one tax at the corporate level on the gain on sale and another tax at the stockholder level on the gain resulting from the liquidating dividend.

Selecting the proper method of withdrawing property from a corporation is a tricky business. The Internal Revenue Code permits various forms of liquidations, each producing considerably different tax consequences. As usual, each alternative must be thoroughly analyzed before the proper one can be selected. This chapter examines the options available in liquidating a corporation which holds real estate and also reviews the principles of collapsible corporations which cut across the entire area of corporate liquidations. In all cases we shall assume that the parties contemplate a complete liquidation of the corporation; no attempt will be made here to discuss partial liquidations or redemptions of stock of one or more stockholders with the corporate entity remaining in existence. The chapter will be divided into the following sections:

11.1   NORMAL CORPORATE LIQUIDATIONS

Let us examine first the tax consequences of liquidating the corporation which either has not elected or does not qualify under the special provisions discussed later in the chapter. In the normal liquidation the corporation simply conveys all of its property to its stockholders in redemption of their shares. The stockholders have, in effect, sold their stock back to the corporation for undivided interests in the corporate assets subject to the mortgages, liens and possibly to unsecured corporate liabilities which may be assumed by the stockholders. What are the tax consequences to the corporation and to the stockholders?

(a) Tax Consequences to Stockholders.

The tax treatment of the stockholders is governed by §331 of the Code. Under this section, a stockholder who received cash or other property having a value in excess of the tax basis of his shares recognizes taxable gain to the extent of such excess. Conversely, if he receives cash or property in an amount less than the tax basis of his shares, he has a deductible loss. Because the stockholder has made a sale or exchange of his shares, the gain or loss will normally be capital gain or loss so if the stock was held for the requisite holding period (9 months in 1977 and 12 months in 1978 and later years), he will qualify for long-term capital gain or loss treatment.

> *Example:* A owns all of the outstanding stock of X Corporation. His basis for the stock is $10,000 representing the basis of property which he conveyed to the corporation in exchange for his shares 10 years ago. The corporation now owns an office building which is free and clear and has a value of $100,000. The corporation adopts a plan of liquidation and conveys the building to A in redemption of his shares. A realizes a long-term capital gain in the amount of $90,000 in the year of liquidation.

What happens when the property is subject to a mortgage or other lien or where the shareholder assumes corporate liabilities, either by agreement or by operation of law? It is clear that such mortgages or liabilities reduce the fair value of the distribution and thus decrease the recognized gain, or increase the recognized loss, on liquidation.

Comment: In view of the fact that dividends are normally taxed as ordinary income while liquidating distributions are normally taxes as capital gain, and then only to the extent that they exceed basis of the redeemed stock, it is important that a liquidating dividend be clearly identified as such. This means, for example, that before the first liquidating distribution is made, the directors and stockholders should adopt resolutions authorizing the corporate liquidation, a plan of liquidation should be put into effect and the necessary forms should be timely filed with state and federal authorities including form 966 which should be filed with the IRS within thirty days of the adoption of the plan of liquidation.

(b) Tax Consequences to Liquidating Corporation.

Under §336, the liquidating corporation realizes no gain or loss by reason of distributing its assets in liquidation. Although the stockholder is treated as though he has made a sale of his stock, it does not follow that the corporation has made a sale of the assets distributed in liquidation.

There are, however, a number of statutory exceptions to this general rule. One exception relates to a distribution of installment obligations; the corporation is normally required to report the deferred profit on the installment sale which has not previously been taxed. §453(d) (1). An important exception for corporations which own real estate is that the depreciation recapture rules are ordinarily fully applied on a distribution of assets in liquidation. §1245(d), relating to personal property, and §1250(i), relating to real estate. The real property recapture rules operate to add back to income a part or all of the depreciation claimed subsequent to December 31, 1963, to the extent it exceeds the straight-line depreciation assuming, of course, that the value of the real estate exceeds its adjusted basis on the distribution date. In short, for recapture purposes the distribution is equivalent to a corporate sale of the property. Where the real estate is being sold by the stockholders shortly after liquidation, establishing market value presents no problem. However, where the stockholders propose to retain the property which they will receive in liquidation it is incumbent upon them to have appraisals made or to utilize some other method to establish fair market values even though the distribution qualifies as a tax-free liquidation. Finally, if the property distributed in liquidation was used in claiming an investment credit, then a part or all of the credit may be recaptured depending upon the corporation's holding period of the property. §47(a) (1).

In addition to these statutory exceptions, there are a number of judicial exceptions to the general rule that a corporation realizes no income on a liquidation. No attempt will be made here to discuss these principles in detail but a brief listing may serve to alert you to some of the problem areas. The liquidating corporation will normally be compelled to recognize income to the extent that is has a reserve for bad debts; the liquidating corporation may be required to report earned income which was not previously reported because of the corporate tax accounting method, such as income from partially completed contracts where the corporation utilizes the completed contract method or income which has accrued but has not been reported because the corporation uses the cash receipts and disbursements method for tax purposes; a liquidating corporation may realize taxable income by distributing in kind assets such as small tools or supplies which were expensed when they were originally purchased; and a corporation may be held to realize taxable income if it uses appreciated assets to pay debts to its stockholders or to other creditors.

11.2 THE TWELVE-MONTH LIQUIDATION

The twelve-month liquidation rules of §337 are intended to avoid a double tax where a corporation sells its property in connection with a plan of liquidation. The problem may be best illustrated by an example.

> *Example:* A owns all of the stock of X Corporation. His stock has a basis of $100,000. The sole corporate asset is an apartment building with an adjusted basis of $200,000 but a fair market value of $400,000. If the corporation sells this property, it will have a gain of $200,000 which will be recognized for tax purposes. For sake of simplification, we will assume that the tax is 25% of the recognized gain, or $50,000. If the remaining $350,000 is distributed to A in liquidation, he will have a gain of $250,000 which will also be subject to tax. Thus, two taxes are payable, one at the corporate level and one at the stockholder level, on what is essentially a single transaction.

To make matters more complicated, a famous decision of the U.S. Supreme Court, the *Court Holding* case,[1] held that a sale by the stockholders after the liquidation may be deemed to be made by the corporation and, therefore, subject to a corporate tax where the sale was negotiated by the stockholders in anticipation of the liquidating dividend. In that case, negotiations for the sale of the corporate property, an apartment building, were conducted while the corporation still existed and held legal title to the property. An oral agreement was reached as to the terms and conditions of sale but before the agreement was reduced to writing the corporate attorney realized the tax consequences of a corporate sale. To avoid the potential double tax, the corporation declared a dividend in complete liquidation of its assets and the sale contract was then drawn showing the stockholders individually as sellers. The down payment, which had been originally paid to the corporation, was credited to the purchase price. The Court held that the sale was, in substance, a sale by the corporation, not its stockholders, and, therefore, the double tax applied.

Several years later the Court recognized that the constructive corporate sale rule could not be applied universally and that where the stockholders negotiated in their individual capacities, rather than as corporate officers, a stockholder sale should be recognized even where negotiations commenced prior to the liquidation.[2]

Recognizing the taxpayer's dilemma in walking the line between these two lines of decisions, Congress included §337 in the 1954 Code for the express purpose of avoiding the double tax on sales made in connection with corporate liquidations. Because of this background, §337 is sometimes referred to as the "anti-Court Holding Co." rule.

The rule of §337 may be summarized as follows: No gain or loss will be recognized to a corporation on sales of property made by it within a 12-month period commencing on the date of the adoption of a plan of liquidation, if the corporation distributes all of its assets (except those retained to meet claims) in complete liquidation within that 12-month period. Since the timing is so critical—sales within the 12-month period are exempt from tax and those beyond the 12-month period are taxable—the following sequence of events should be carefully followed. First, a plan of liquidation must be adopted. This normally means that the stockholders and the directors pass resolutions authorizing the liquidation of the corporation. A statement of intent to dissolve is normally filed shortly thereafter with the secretary of state or other appropriate authority setting forth the date of adoption of the liquidation plan and Form 966 should be filed with IRS, also setting forth such information.[3] Second, the corporation proceeds to sell its assets during the 12-month period; sales could be for cash or on terms but closings should occur prior to the expiration of the deadline. Third, all of the remaining assets (the proceeds of the sales as well as assets which were not sold) are distributed to the stockholders in liquidation except for assets which are retained to meet claims of creditors.

> *Comment:* Because of the inflexibility of the 12-month rule, taxpayers may be tempted to avoid application of the rule where sales will be made at a loss. Thus, taxpayers may attempt to close the loss sales before the adoption of the liquidation plan and sales which produce gains thereafter. Although taxpayers have been successful in some cases in utilizing this technique, the regulations will recognize the date of the shareholders' resolution as controlling only if the corporation sells substantially all of its property before that date or after that date; but where the corporation attempts to split its sales (a so-called straddle transaction) IRS will refuse to accept the purported resolution date.[4]

The 12-month liquidation rule has a number of important exceptions and limitations. First, it does not apply to collapsible corporations, nor does it apply to one calendar month liquidations. Both of these concepts are discussed later in this chapter. Second, §337 is inapplicable to sales of a corporation's stock in trade or inventory unless the inventory is sold to one person in one transaction (so-called bulk sales), and the section is also inapplicable to most installment obligations. Third, the normal exceptions under §336 (see discussion at §11.1(b) above) apply to a corporation liquidating under §337 as well as to all other corporations. Recapture of depreciation, recapture of investment credit and the judicially created exceptions to the tax-free nature of corporate liquidating dividends will, therefore, apply. Moreover, the courts have expanded these concepts in connection with 12-month liquidations creating an impressive and confusing list of cases where gains will be recognized to the corporation notwithstanding the 12-month rule. For example, the sale of accounts receivable by a cash basis taxpayer or the sale of expensed items under the tax benefit rule may produce recognized gains. Despite these limitations, however, the fact remains that the 12-month liquidation rule is one of the most useful tools available to a liquidating corporation. Although caution is obviously required to insure compliance with the technical requirements, this provision is used frequently by liquidating corporations which hold appreciated real estate.

11.3   THE ONE CALENDAR MONTH LIQUIDATION

Under §333, a corporation which has no earnings or profits and which has no cash may liquidate and distribute its property to its shareholders without the recognition of gain by them. Real estate corporations are obvious candidates for such tax-free treatment, particularly where they hold property which has substantially appreciated in value. Such corporations often have no earnings or profits since the depreciation on their property produces tax losses, although for tax years beginning after June 30, 1972, corporations can use only straight-line depreciation in computing earnings and profits. §312(m). Also such corporations often have little or no cash since the cash has been utilized to construct the buildings or to amortize the mortgage loans. This section is particularly useful where there has been an inadvertent or ill advised conveyance of a real estate project to a corporation, where the parties contemplate refinancing a project, or where for some other reason they wish to withdraw the property from the corporate form.

(a) Amount of Gain Recognized.

As indicated above, the gain on a liquidating distribution is tax-free where the corporation has no earnings or profits and no cash or securities. However, an electing stockholder who is not a corporation must recognize gain at three different levels as follows: First, the portion of the gain which is not in excess of his ratable share of earnings and profits is treated as an ordinary dividend distribution. §333(e) (1). The balance, if any, of his gain is treated as capital gain (long term or short term, as the case may be) to the extent that cash and stock or securities acquired by the corporation after December 31, 1953, exceed his ratable portion of the earnings and profits of the corporation. The balance of his gain is **tax-free**.

> *Example:* Stockholder organized a corporation in 1970 with an investment of $25,000. The corporation utilized this amount, together with a $175,000 mortgage, to acquire a parcel of land and construct an apartment building. The building now has a value of $300,000 and the mortgage has been reduced to $140,000, leaving an equity of $160,000. The corporation also has $1,000 of cash and $4,000 of stock and securities, or a total of $165,000 of net assets available for distribution. It has only $1,000 of earnings or profits because of depreciation deductions. The corporation adopts a plan of liquidation under §333 and distributes all of its assets to Stockholder. Although he has a realized gain of $140,000 ($165,000 of assets received, less his $25,000 investment) he has a recognized gain only to the extent of $5,000. This is taxed as ordinary income to the extent of $1,000 (earnings and profits) and as capital gain to the extent of $4,000. The balance of the gain resulting from the receipt of title to the real estate in exchange for the capital stock, $135,000, is not taxed at the time of the liquidation.

(b) Basis of Property Received in Liquidation.

Not surprisingly, one of the consequences of a tax-free liquidation is a carryover of basis; the basis of the property received in liquidation is the same as the basis of the stock surrendered, less any money received and plus any gain recognized. §334(c). Thus, referring to the above example, the stockholder's basis for the property received in liquidation equals the original basis of his stock, or $25,000, less $1,000 of money received and plus $5,000 of gain recognized, for an adjusted basis of $29,000. This amount is allocated among the assets received in proportion to their fair market values. It follows, of course, that the tax which was not recognized upon corporate liquidation will be recognized at the time of ultimate sale of the property. At that time, of course, the owner may qualify for an installment sale, a tax-free exchange or a number of other techniques which were not available to him upon liquidation.

(c) The Statutory Requirements.

In order to qualify under this section, it is essential that the parties comply with each of the statutory requirements. First, the corporation must qualify. Generally speaking, this does not present any difficulty except for the caveat that the corporation may not be a collapsible corporation. Second, the stockholders must qualify. In the case of non-corporate stockholders this means that elections have been filed by at least 80% of the voting shares owned by the non-corporate stockholder group. If elections have not been filed by the requisite percentage, then no individual stockholder may utilize the optional treatment. On the other hand, if the requisite percentage of non-corporate stockholders have properly ratified the plan, it is still necessary for each individual to file his election in order to be entitled to receive the elective treatment.[5] Third, the distribution must be made pursuant to a plan of liquidation adopted before the first distribution occurs. Since a plan of liquidation is normally adopted by the stockholders, this requires stockholder action and it is advisable to properly document such action in the corporate minute book, by documents filed with the secretary of state or other appropriate authority, and by forms filed with the IRS which are discussed below. Fourth, the election to qualify under this section must be filed on Form 964 within thirty days of the adoption of the plan. This is in addition to the requirement relation to Form 966 which must be filed in connection with all corporate liquidations and the simplest procedure is to file the two forms simultaneously. Fifth, §333(a) (2) requires that the transfer of all of the corporation's property under the liquidation must occur "within some one calendar month." Note that it is not sufficient that the distributions are made within thirty days of each other if they occur in different calendar months. In short, if there is more than one asset, whether real estate or not, be sure that the documents of transfer occur during the same month. Since a corporate dissolution under state law has the effect of terminating the corporate existence and transferring the assets to the stockholders, it is generally advisable to formally dissolve the corporation by filing the articles of dissolution or other appropriate forms, even though dissolution under state law is not required for this section to apply.[6] Although cash may be set aside for payment of corporate liabilities and expenses, including the expenses of liquidation, the best practice is to distribute all of the assets within the single calendar month and to have the stockholders assume payment of such liabilities and expenses. This avoids a contention by an examining agent that the amount of cash retained was excessive or was not held in good faith. If a stockholder cannot be located, his interest can be transferred to a trustee in liquidation. In such cases, however, it is advisable that the trustee be an independent person, not a director or corporate officer, and that he have limited powers so that it cannot be asserted that he is merely a continuation of the corporation.

(d) Some Pitfalls to Avoid.

In addition to careful compliance with all of the technical requirements described above, the following two recent developments should be particularly noted. They both involved unsuccessful one calendar month liquidations and they highlight the extremely technical nature of corporate liquidations.

A 1975 Tax Court decision involved the following facts: A corporation owned a tract of undeveloped land which it agreed to sell at a profit under a contract dated February 18, 1969. On October 1 of that year, the corporation adopted a one calendar month liquidation plan under §333 and its stockholders filed the proper elections. The land was then distributed to the stockholders and they closed the sale to the buyer. The corporation reported no gain and the sellers, the former stockholders, reported the sale on the installment basis. The Court held, however, that since the corporation had agreed to make the sale prior to its liquidation, the gain was taxable to it under the *Court Holding* rule discussed above. Not only did this produce a tax at the corporate level, but the constructive sale by the corporation also resulted in a creation of earnings and profits. Since distributions of such earnings and profits are taxable as a dividend, even under a one calendar month liquidation, the liquidating distribution was not tax-free as the parties had assumed. Further, the parties could not avoid the double tax under the 12-month liquidation rule of §337 because that section cannot apply where the one calendar month election has been made.[7]

A 1976 ruling involved a case where the same individual was both a stockholder and a creditor of the corporation. He had invested $50,000 in stock and had made a $300,000 loan to the corporation. The corporation had $1,000,000 of assets on hand, land which was worth $900,000 and machinery which was worth $100,000. However, the basis of such property to the corporation differed from the fair market values, the land being worth more than its basis and the machinery being worth less than its basis. The corporation was liquidated under §333 and the property distributed to the individual stockholder-creditor. IRS ruled that he received the property both in exchange for his stock and in satisfaction of his note. Since a corporation is required to recognize gain when it pays a loan by use of appreciated assets, the corporation realized a gain on the transfer of land (value in excess of basis) and this had the effect of increasing earnings and profits. Further, since a corporation is not permitted to deduct a loss on a sale to a related taxpayer, the loss on the transfer of machinery (basis in excess of value) was not deductible. Accordingly the corporation had to pay a tax on its gain and the stockholder-creditor had ordinary income to the extent of the newly created earnings and profits.[8]

> *Comment:* This result would seem to be avoided where the stockholder cancels his indebtedness as a contribution to corporate capital before liquidating.

11.4 COLLAPSIBLE CORPORATIONS

The collapsible corporation provisions are perhaps the most complex in the entire body of tax law. Unfortunately, real estate corporations are particularly vulnerable to collapsible treatment and an understanding of the rules in this area is, therefore, essential. Once a corporation is found to be collapsible the following consequences occur. The corporation cannot utilize the 12-month liquidation provisions or the one calendar month liquidation provisions discussed above; a distribution from the corporation to its shareholders in liquidation or otherwise results in ordinary income rather than capital gain even though the distribution may not be from earnings and profits; and a sale of stock at a gain by any of the stockholders produces ordinary income rather than capital gain unless one of the statutory exceptions applies.

(a) Definition and Exclusions.

(1) *Definition*—A collapsible corporation is defined by §341(b) (1) to mean a corporation that is formed or availed of:

(i) Principally for the construction or production of property (or for the purchase of certain categories of property);

(ii) With a view to (a) a sale, liquidation or distribution before the corporation has realized a substantial part of the taxable income to be derived from the property, and (b) a realization by the shareholders of the gain attributable to such property.

The definition is quite broad but contains a number of terms, all of which must be met for collapsible treatment to be imposed. Therefore, a corporation which does not meet one or more of the elements of the statutory definition is not a collapsible corporation and is exempt from the rules of §341. The following discussion covers various elements of the statutory definition which the corporation may attempt to avoid.

(2) *Manufacture, Construction, or Production of Property*— The corporation must be formed principally for "manufacture, construction or production of property." Therefore, a corporation which is collapsed early in the game—before any construction or production activities are commenced—may be exempt. It is true that very little activity has been required to find that the construction activity started. For example, rezoning of land from residential to commercial was held to be construction[9] and a corporate taxpayer which leased land to an unrelated party for the purpose of constructing a shopping center with the lessor being obligated to merely subordinate its interest to a construction mortgage, was held to be involved in construction even though it did not participate in the physical construction of the center.[10]

It is also necessary that the corporation be formed or availed of "principally" for the manufacture, construction or production of the property in question. To meet this requirement, however, it is not necessary that the corporation be formed for the purpose of collapsing it; so long as it was formed "principally" for the construction of property the requirement is met.[11]

(3) *Purchase of §341 Assets*—Even if the corporation does not construct its own property, if it purchases certain types of assets, the asset test will be met. §341(b) (3). Included in the prohibited categories of such assets are depreciable or real property used in the trade or business, other than such property used in connection with the manufacture, construction, production or sale of inventory. Real property which is held for rental purposes constitutes a §341 asset but a factory building or warehouse which is used in the taxpayer's manufacturing or mercantile business does not. Property held by a corporation primarily for sale to customers in the ordinary course of business is also included in this category. Notwithstanding these rules, however, the Tax Court has held that collapsible corporation treatment does not apply where the real estate is held as an investment rather than primarily for sale to customers in the ordinary course of trade of business. Although the corporation's only activity was

holding the property as an investment, the Court held that this was not sufficient to cause the property to be held for sale to customers in the ordinary course of business and the corporation, therefore, was not collapsible and qualified for the non-recognition provisions of §337.[12]

(4) *The Prohibited View*—Of course, many corporations are formed for the purpose of constructing property or purchasing real estate to be used in a trade or business. Obviously, all of such corporations are not subject to the collapsible corporation rules. The major issue in many collapsible corporation cases is whether the requisite "view" was also present. In order to be collapsible, the corporation must be formed or availed of with a view to collapsing the corporation prior to the realization of corporate profits. Note that it is not essential that the motivating view be one of saving taxes; all that is required is that there be a view or intention to make one of the collapsible acts (such as sale of stock or liquidation of corporation) before the corporation has realized its income.[13] When must the prohibited view exist? The interpretation most favorable to the taxpayer would be that the view to collapse must exist at some time during the construction process. For example, if a corporation constructs a project and forms the view to collapse after completion, collapsible treatment would not apply under this interpretation. Although some of the early cases held to the contrary, in 1972 IRS accepted this interpretation by filing acquiescences in two Tax Court decisions where taxpayers were successful on this point.[14]

There is one avenue of escape specifically sanctioned by the Regulations which has been successfully utilized by corporations in a number of cases. If it can be demonstrated that the decision to sell, liquidate or distribute was "attributable solely to circumstances which arose after the manufacture, construction, production or purchase (other than circumstances which reasonably could be anticipated at the time of production or purchase)" collapsible treatment will not apply.[15] Thus, for example, the illness of an active shareholder, unexpected changes in the law, dissension among the shareholders, unanticipated changes in the value of the property or a sudden need for money to enter or expand another business, have all been treated as circumstances which could not have been anticipated during the construction period.

(5) *Realization of a Substantial Part of the Taxable Income from the Property*—Even if all of the other requirements are met, in order for collapsible treatment to apply, it is necessary that the corporation be collapsed prior to the realization by it of a substantial part of the taxable income to be derived from the property which was constructed. To put it another way, if the corporation realized the potential taxable gain to be derived from a project, the statutory penalty should not apply. The difficulty arises because the statute does not require that all of the gain be realized at the corporate level, merely that the corporation realize a "substantial part" of the potential gain. Most of the courts have concluded that if a corporation realized one third of the total gain the "substantial" test has been met[16] and IRS now acquiesces in that rule.[17]

(6) *Stockholder Realization of Gain Attributable to the Property*—Finally, in order for collapsible treatment to apply, a stockholder must realize the gain which is attributable to the property constructed by the corporation. Such realization can result from a corporate distribution or from a sale of capital stock but the gain must arise from the proscribed collapsible activity of the corporation. Some taxpayers have

argued that despite construction activities by the corporation the gain which they realized upon a corporate distribution was not attributable to such construction but, generally, this approach has met with little success. For example, sometimes a corporation has excess mortgage loan proceeds not required for the construction of the project or cash flow from rents which are in excess of earnings or profits because of depreciation deductions. Where such surplus funds are distributed to the stockholders and the corporation is collapsible under the statutory definition, the collapsible corporation rules will apply and the distributions will be taxed at ordinary rates notwithstanding the fact that the distributions are not out of corporate earnings and profits.[18] Similarly, in the case of real estate improvements, an increase in the value of the land resulting from a building project constitutes collapsible gain as well as the gain on the improvements themselves. The taxpayers cannot assert that the buildings are worth only their actual cost and that all of the gain represents appreciation in land values not necessarily resulting from the construction activity.[19]

Where the stockholder recognizes no taxable gain, collapsible treatment is inapplicable. For example, if the stockholder exchanges his stock in the collapsible corporation for stock in another corporation and the exchange qualifies as a tax-free reorganization, then the collapsible rules will not apply because no gain was recognized.[20]

(b) Statutory Exceptions to Collapsible Corporation Treatment.

Even though a corporation meets all of the "collapsible" requirements discussed in the previous section, there are a number of statutory exceptions to the rules of §341. Some of these exceptions are contained in §341(d) which exempt certain stockholders from collapsible treatment and some are contained in §341(e) and (f) which exempt certain corporations from collapsible treatment. We will make no attempt to analyze these rules in depth but will merely list the basic principles.

(1) *The 5% Stockholder Rule*—Collapsible treatment will not be applied to a stockholder if he does not own, at any time during the construction process or thereafter, more than 5% in value of the corporate stock. §341(d)(1). In determining whether he qualifies, you must consider not only the stock directly owned by the individual but also stock attributed to him from certain other parties. For purposes of the attribution rules, a person is considered to own the stock owned by members of his family which includes his spouse, ancestors, descendants and brothers and sisters as well as spouses of brothers or sisters and of descendants.

(2) *The 70%-of-Gain Rule*—A stockholder will not be penalized with ordinary income treatment unless more than 70% of his gain is attributable to collapsible property. To put it conversely, if 30% or more of his gain can be traced to non-collapsible property, his entire gain will qualify for capital gain treatment even though the corporation is collapsible. §341(d)(2). As indicated in the prior section, however, gain is attributable to the construction of a project even though the gain in question does not directly flow from such construction. Examples would be the appreciation in land values resulting from the construction of improvements thereon and the distribution of excess mortgage proceeds or cash flow from rentals related to the construction of a project. If the 70-30 test cannot be met and no other exemption applies, all of the gain is

taxed as ordinary income; the stockholder cannot prorate his gain between ordinary income and capital gain.

Note that this exception, as well as the 5% stockholder rule, is applied on stockholder-by-stockholder basis. Thus, some stockholders may qualify for relief while others do not.

(3) *The Three Year Limitation*—Even though a corporation is otherwise collapsible, collapsible treatment will not be applied to a stockholder's gain which is realized after the expiration of three years following the completion of the construction process or the purchase of the property. §341(d) (3). We saw in a previous section that IRS and the courts have given a very broad interpretation to the question of when construction has commenced. A similarly broad intrepretation has been given to the issue of when construction is completed. The regulations provide that the three year period does not commence until final completion of the property; substantial completion is not enough.[21] With some planning, however, this rule presents an obvious and fairly simple escape from collapsible treatment. Following completion of construction the stockholder can simply wait for three years before disposing of his shares. Even entering into an executory contract of sale is not fatal so long as the closing does not occur within the three year period.[22]

> *Comment:* Note that the foregoing three exceptions relate only to the stockholders, not to the corporation itself. Therefore, even if one of these exceptions applies to a particular stockholder, the corporation does not qualify for the special treatment of §337[23] nor do other stockholders of the same corporation necessarily enjoy the exemption.

(4) *The Exception of §341(e)*—In 1958, §341 was amended by the addition of the §341(e) exception. This section was intended to provide an escape hatch where there was no more than a modest appreciation in collapsible type assets. Unfortunately, the wording of the exception itself became unbelievably complex (the first sentence is 643 words long) with a separate set of definitions and tests and with a number of different standards depending upon whether the section is being applied to a stock sale or a corporate liquidation and depending further upon the type of property involved. Briefly, however, the theory of this provision is that the collapsible corporation provisions will not be applied if the net unrealized appreciation in a corporation's "Subsection (e) assets" amounts to less than 15% of corporate net worth. The term "Subsection (e) assets" covers property which would produce ordinary income if it were sold by the corporation itself, or by any of its principal shareholders. A principal shareholder is one who owns, actually or constructively, more than 20% of the stock of the corporation, although if the corporation wishes to utilize the one calendar month liquidation then the class is expanded to include stockholders who own more than 5% of the outstanding stock.

It therefore becomes necessary to determine whether the corporation or any of its principal shareholders are dealers in real estate because if that is the case their status will taint the corporation, the §341(e) exception will not apply and collapsible treatment will follow. Note that a principal shareholder will taint the corporation and the other shareholders irrespective of the attribution of ownership rules. A prospective investor, therefore, who is involved in a project with potential collapsible corporation problems must carefully review the business histories of all of the principal shareholders to determine if any of them might be classified as real estate dealers.

Although this section provides an important safe harbor for many business corporations, it is of only limited application to real estate corporations. Increases of value amounting to more than 15% of net worth are the rule rather than the exception in such corporations, particularly where maximum leverage (and therefore, minimum equity contribution or net worth) is utilized.

(5) *Waiver of Collapsible Corporation Treatment*—The last statutory exception was added in 1964. §341(f) permits a stockholder to sell his stock on a capital gain basis, without the threat of collapsible treatment, if the corporation consents to recognize gain on its "Subsection (f) assets" (primarily real estate and ordinary income assets) when and if the corporation disposes of them in a transaction that would otherwise qualify for non-recognition of gain. Thus, a consenting corporation will not be eligible for tax-free treatment on a later sale of its assets pursuant to a 12-month liquidation plan and the corporation would recognize gain on the distribution of a dividend or in liquidation despite the exemptions of §331 and §336. Once it is filed, the consent under this section is binding on the corporation and applies to all dispositions of subsection (f) assets regardless of how long they occur after the date of the stock sale. In short, the Code exacts a high price to qualify for the waiver of collapsible treatment under §341(f) and the section has been of limited applicability in actual practice. Certainly, in any business purchase where the transaction takes the form of a purchase of capital stock, the buyer should require, as a part of the seller's representations, a warranty that no §341(f) election was ever filed by the corporation.

FOOTNOTES FOR CHAPTER ELEVEN

[1]*Comm. v. Court Holding Co.,* 324 U.S. 331, 33 AFTR 593 (1945).

[2]*U.S. v. Cumberland Public Service Co.,* 338 U.S. 451, 38 AFTR 978 (1950).

[3]Failure to file form 966 may not be fatal to the plan, *Alameda Realty Corp.,* 42 T.C. 273 (1964), acq. 1964-2 C.B.3. However, IRS is likely to contend that a failure to file is evidence that the Plan was not timely adopted.

[4]Reg. 1.337-2(b).

[5]Reg. 1.333-2(b).

[6]Regs. 1.333-1(b) (1) and (b) (2).

[7]*Aaron Cohen,* 63 T.C. 316 (1974).

[8]Rev.Rul. 76-175, IRB 1976-19,2.

[9]Rev. Rul. 56-137, 1956-1 C.B. 178.

[10]Rev.Rul. 69-378, 1969-2 C.B. 49.

[11]Reg. 1.341-2(a) (2); *Weil v. Comm.,* 252 F.2d 805, 1 AFTR 2d 1096 (CA2, 1958).

[12]*Sam B. Ginsburg,* 1974 P-H Memo TC ¶74,191.

[13]*Gelfand v. U.S.,* 375 F.2d 807, 19 AFTR 2d 1195 (Ct.Cl., 1967).

[14]*Chas. J. Riley,* 35 T.C.848 (1961); *Maxwell Temkin, 35 T.C. 906 (1961).*

[15]Reg. 1.341-2(a) (2).

[16]*Comm. v. Kelly,* 293 F.2d 904, 8 AFTR 2d 5232 (CA8, 1961); *George W. Day,* 55 T.C.257 (1970) (56% held sufficient). Some courts hold that the gain remaining to be realized should be measured to see if it was "substantial" (a much more difficult test for taxpayers to meet) but that rule was rejected by IRS in favor of the more liberal approach. See footnote 17.

[17]Rev.Rul. 72-48, 1972-1 C.B. 102.

[18]*Gelfand v. U.S.*, footnote 13, supra. Where excess FHA mortgage proceeds are distributed, earnings and profits are automatically created and ordinary income treatment follows. §312(j).

[19]*Benedek v. Comm.*, 429 F.2d 41, 26 AFTR 2d 70-5049(CA2, 1970).

[20]Rev.Rul. 73-378, 1973-2 C.B. 113.

[21]Reg. 1.341-4(d).

[22]Rev. Rul. 67-100, 1967-1 C.B. 76. An installment sale will not qualify where the 3 year period has not run on the date of the sale even though the payments are received after the three year period. Rev.Rul. 60-68, 1960-1 C.B. 151.

[23]*Leisure Time Enterprises, Inc.*, 56 T.C. 1180 (1971).

12

ESCAPING

FROM

A LEAKY SHELTER:

Sales, Gifts and Foreclosures
of the Property

In earlier chapters we saw that real estate is an attractive tax shelter largely due to the advantages of leverage. A relatively small investment combined with a large mortgage, aside from the economic benefits, can produce substantial tax savings to the owner, particularly in the early years. The day of reckoning comes, however, when the mortgaged property must be sold or otherwise conveyed. The sale may occur because the tax benefits are running out or simply because economic or other considerations call for a disposition of the property. What are the consequences to the owner resulting from the disposition and what techniques are available to minimize the tax problems? This chapter will analyze these questions. It will be divided into the following sections:

12.1 The Problem of the Excess Mortgage; Shortcomings of Standard Techniques

12.2 Determining the Amount of Gain

12.3 Mortgage Foreclosures, Conveyances in Lieu of Foreclosure and Settlements with the Mortgage Lender

(a) Foreclosures and Conveyances in Lieu of Foreclosure

12.1 THE PROBLEM OF THE EXCESS MORTGAGE; SHORTCOMINGS OF STANDARD TECHNIQUES

A typical case might involve an investor who purchased a real estate project several years ago investing $100,000 and taking title subject to a $900,000 mortgage. Although his basis in the property at that point was $1,000,000, that basis has been substantially reduced due to accelerated depreciation, high mortgage interest and points during the early years and possibly start-up losses if new construction was involved. Accordingly, his basis has now been reduced to $600,000. Unfortunately, the mortgage balance normally does not decline as rapidly as tax basis and the mortgage loan has a balance of $800,000. At this point, the owner has a problem of mortgage in excess of basis. If he sells the project for the amount of the mortgage and no more, he will have realized a taxable gain of $200,000. This gain is sometimes referred to as phantom gain because the seller recognizes a gain for tax purposes although he receives not cash.

Various techniques for disposing of property have been discussed elsewhere in this book but generally they do not provide satisfactory solutions to the excess mortgage problem. For example, the installment sale technique is often utilized for sales of real estate. However, in determining the payments received in the year of sale, the excess mortgage is included to the extent that it exceeds the basis of the property. In the illustration outlined above, for example, the $200,000 excess mortgage will be deemed to have been received in the year of sale and, therefore, taxable despite the fact that it is not reflected in a cash receipt. In more extreme cases, the mortgage may be so much in excess of basis that the constructive year of sale payments exceed 30% of the selling price and the installment election is not available. A number of cases have held that the excess mortgage amount is not treated as a payment in the year of sale where the seller does not transfer title or is not relieved of the liability in the year of sale. This is accomplished by use of the land contract or wraparound mortgage. See Chapter 8 Section 2(b). Of course, it is not always possible to structure the transaction in this form and in any case the rule has been narrowed in recent cases.

Another technique often utilized to dispose of real estate is the tax-free exchange. Here again, the excess mortgage presents a serious problem. When real estate is conveyed subject to a mortgage, the amount of the mortgage is considered to be boot received in the year of the transfer. This rule applies whether the grantee takes title subject to the mortgage or assumes the mortgage debt. Where the acquired property is also subject to a mortgage, the mortgage on one property is offset against the mortgage on the other; only the excess, if any, on the property conveyed is treated as boot. See Chapter 9, Section 2. Aside from the practical problems of structuring tax-free exchanges, the implications of these rules are obvious. Where the property is subject to a mortgage substantially in excess of basis, it is often impossible to set up a satisfactory tax-free exchange.

Incorporation of a tax shelter is equally unsatisfactory. Generally, the transfer of property to a corporation in exchange for stock or securities is tax-free, even though the transferred property is subject to a liability. There are two important exceptions to this rule, however, which have particular application to the incorporation of tax shelters. First, under §357(b), if the corporate assumption of the mortgage is for the purpose of avoiding taxes, or at least has no business purpose, the transfer results in the receipt of taxable income. Second, under §357(c), even if the transfer is for a legitimate business purpose, it results in taxable income to the extent that the mortgage exceeds basis. See Chapter 2, Section 4. Once again, there are techniques available to minimize the problem. For example, other property in addition to the real estate may be transferred to the corporation since the determination of whether the liabilities exceed the basis depends on the basis of all assets transferred and is not limited to those assets to which the liability relates. Nevertheless, the difficulties inherent in avoiding the excess mortgage problem will be self-evident.

In the good old days before passage of the Tax Reform Act of 1976, death was always a solution to the negative basis problem. The beneficiaries of a decedent were entitled to a stepped up basis upon the death of the decedent and the recapture of depreciation problem, to the extent that it existed as of the date of death, was eliminated. While death is not a solution which is accepted enthusiastically by owners of property, it was a fact that many sales of tax shelter property were deferred for this reason, particularly in the case of elderly taxpayers. However, the 1976 Act has largely eliminated this technique by the new rules under §23 requiring a carryover of basis from decedent to beneficiaries. There is an exception which applies in the case of property held on December 31, 1976, where the date of death value exceeds its adjusted basis immediately before the decedent's death, permitting a "fresh start" to reflect the December 31, 1976 value. For this purpose it is assumed that appreciation has occurred at a uniform rate over the holding period of the property and this special valuation method must be used for all real estate, even though the executor can show a different value as of December 31, 1976. Accordingly, as time passes and more and more appreciation is attributable to the period December 31, 1976, the benefits of the "fresh start rule" will be diminished.

12.2 DETERMINING THE AMOUNT OF GAIN

Under the *Crane* rule discussed in Chapter 4, Section 2, the amount of the mortgage is included in the tax basis of property acquired regardless of whether the owner has personal liability on the mortgage loan.[1] Similarly, a limited partner is permitted to include his pro rata portion of nonrecourse debt in his basis for his partnership interest.[2] The corollary of this rule, also established in the *Crane* case, is that upon a sale or other conveyance of property the seller is deemed to have realized the amount of the mortgage as well as the amount of cash or other consideration received. As explained above, this often means that the net cash proceeds of a sale will be less than the amount of recognized gain and in some cases the amount of cash received is even insufficient to cover the tax liabilities arising from the sale.

Supposing the fair market value of the property is less than the amount of the mortgage loan. Assume, for example, that the mortgage has a balance of $1,000,000 while the property is worth only $900,000. How much does the owner realize upon a disposition of the project whether such disposition is in the form of a sale, a mortgage foreclosure or otherwise?

It has long been clear that if the owner is personally liable on the mortgage loan, the amount realized upon disposition equals the mortgage debt. This is the general rule established by *Crane* and also has been held to apply in the case of a mortgage foreclosure, even where the mortgagee fails to procure a deficiency judgment within the period prescribed under state law.[3]

Where the mortgage secures a nonrecourse loan the result, until recently at least, has not been as clear. For many years taxpayers took the position that the amount realized could never exceed the fair market value of the property surrendered. This position was based, first, upon the common sense approach that there is no direct benefit to the owner of property upon being relieved of a debt in excess of value ($100,000 in our example) where he is not personally liable to pay the amount in question. The position was further supported by an often quoted footnote (footnote 37) in the *Crane* decision itself which indicated that the Supreme Court was not expressing an opinion on the case where the value of the property was less than the amount of the mortgage, a situation which was not before the Court in the *Crane* case. Although there was undoubtedly some merit to this position of the taxpayers, the Commissioner took the opposite approach, asserting that the amount realized was the balance due on the mortgage irrespective of the personal liability of the mortgagor, and there was some authority subsequent to the *Crane* decision which supported the Commissioner's approach.[4]

The commentators in tax journals debated this issue for some years. However, in a 1976 ruling IRS expressly rejected footnote 37 of the *Crane* case and held that where a debtor transfers the property securing a nonrecourse obligation to the secured creditor in consideration of the cancellation of the obligation, the amount realized by the debtor is the full amount of the cancelled debt, regardless of the fair market value of the property transferred.[5] In a 1977 decision the Tax Court reached the same result, expressly commenting that the value of the property was immaterial.[6] Some taxpayers will probably continue to resist this position and attempt to distinguish these authorities, particularly if they contemplate litigating the issue in a forum other than the Tax Court. Conservative practitioners, however, will probably conclude that the issue is now settled and that the amount realized upon a sale or foreclosure of mortgaged property equals the balance due on the mortgage irrespective of the personal liability of the mortgagor.

12.3 MORTGAGE FORECLOSURES, CONVEYANCES IN LIEU OF FORECLOSURE AND SETTLEMENTS WITH THE MORTGAGE LENDER

(a) Foreclosures and Conveyances in Lieu of Foreclosure

It is clear that the foreclosure of property by a mortgagee constitutes a sale of the property to the mortgagee for tax purposes, whether or not the debtor is personally liable on the mortgage note.[7] Although some old cases raised a question as to whether a voluntary conveyance in satisfaction of a nonrecourse mortgage constituted a sale or exchange where there was no consideration passing to the grantor of the deed, this issue appears to be settled. Both the 1976 ruling and the 1977 Tax Court decision discussed in the preceding section concluded, without discussing this issue expressly, that a sale or exchange had occurred. This result is particularly important where the foreclosure or the conveyance produces a gain because it permits the owner of the property to qualify for capital gain treatment and to offset the unrecovered portion of his basis, a result which might not be possible on a straight cancellation of indebtedness.

Where the mortgagor is a partnership the results are virtually the same. Under Code §752, any decrease in a partner's share of the liabilities of the partnership is treated as a distribution of money to the partner. In a 1971 decision it was held that cancellation of indebtedness of a partnership resulted in a constructive distribution to the partners to the extent that they were deemed to be relieved of partnership liabilities.[8] Note that the cancellation was not a realization event at the partnership level; rather, the event creating the tax consequences was the constructive distribution. This is important because it normally means that the amount of the gain is determined under the rules of §731, i.e., each partner recognizes gain only to the extent that the constructive distribution exceeds the basis of his partnership interest. This is, of course, preferable to having the amount of income determined at the entity or partnership level because under the conduit principle, such income would flow through to the partners without giving them the opportunity to utilize the basis of their partnership interests as an offset. In short, the decision works to the advantage of the taxpayers.

(b) Settlement With the Mortgagee

If the mortgage lender agrees to cancel part of the debt represented by the mortgage, a solvent property owner will generally realize ordinary income to the extent of the discharge.[9] As indicated above, a different rule may apply where the mortgagor is a partnership.

(c) Exceptions and Limitations

It is clear that the problem of the excess mortgage normally cannot be solved by a foreclosure or a conveyance in lieu of foreclosure any more than it can be solved by a sale of the property. However, there are a number of limitations on the foreclosure rules where they would otherwise result in recognition of a taxable gain.

First, it may be possible to restructure the mortgage debt. The mere extension of the maturity date of a note will not be treated as an exchange of one obligation for another and, therefore, will not produce a taxable gain or loss.[10]

Second, an insolvent debtor does not realize income upon the cancellation of indebtedness unless he is solvent after the discharge of the mortgage debt.[11] Of course, even if income is not recognized by the discharge the cancellation can have collateral tax consequences. For example, a cancellation or credit which is treated as a reduction of the purchase price results in a reduction of the basis of the purchased property and this, in turn, will normally reduce the depreciation deductions in subsequent years and also will affect the amount of gain or loss on ultimate disposition. The taxpayer is permitted to make an election under §108 which is discussed in the following section to claim such an adjustment to basis.

Finally, it may be impossible for the investor to utilize another party or entity to purchase the mortgage note at a discount, thus avoiding the recognition which would otherwise result from foreclosure or cancellation. A purchase of the note by a separate taxpayer can defer or avoid the adverse tax consequences relating to the debt.[12] Supposing the purchaser of the discounted note is a shareholder of the debtor corporation. One case has held that contributing the discounted note to the capital of the debtor corporation does not result in recognition of the amount of the discount as taxable income.[13]

12.4   EXCLUSION FROM INCOME UNDER SECTION 108

Under §108 where a mortgagor discharges the mortgage debt at a discount, he may exclude from his gross income the amount attributable to the cancellation of indebtedness provided that he consents to adjust the basis of the property pursuant to §1017. By excluding the amount of cancellation from his income and by reducing the basis of the property by a like amount, the tax on the discounted amount is, in effect, deferred until the property is sold or the reduced basis is fully recovered by depreciation.

However, if the investor, instead of retaining the property, loses it through foreclosure or a conveyance in lieu of foreclosure, the reduction of basis rules are difficult to apply. First, the regulations under §1017 provide that the amount of cancelled debt which may be excluded from income is limited to the adjusted basis of the taxpayer's property; any excess is treated as income.[14] Second, the regulations provide that the basis of the property which was purchased with the discharged debt, or against which the debt was a lien, must be reduced first.[15] Finally, if the property is owned by a partnership, the reduction of the liability that was excluded from the partnership's gross income is considered to be a distribution of money to the partners by the partnership. Such distribution, therefore, will reduce the basis of each partner's interest in the partnership and if the distribution exceeds his basis, may produce taxable income.[16]

12.5   GIFTS

(a) Charitable Gifts.

Can a property owner with an excess mortgage problem avoid the potential gain by simply donating the property to his favorite charity? Aside from the question of whether a charitable organization would agree to accept the conveyance of a real estate project, it seems clear that this technique will not avoid the problem.

In a 1970 ruling, IRS held that gain can be realized on a charitable gift of mortgaged property. The charitable transfer involves both a sale and a gift. A charitable contribution may be available to the extent that the fair market value of the property exceeds the balance of the loan; but to the extent that the loan exceeds the taxpayer's basis, a taxable gain is produced on the transfer.[17] The transfer covered in this ruling occurred before the effective date of the Tax Reform Act of 1969. Presumably, IRS would reach the same result under current law although the gain would be somewhat higher because §1011(b), added by the 1969 Act, requires a partial allocation of the donor's tax basis to the gift in the case of a bargain sale to a charitable organization. This section applies only where a charitable contribution deduction is allowable in connection with a bargain sale to a charity. Thus, where no charitable deduction applies (for example, where the property has no value in excess of the mortgage) §1011(b) is inapplicable.

In a 1975 ruling IRS held that a charitable gift of a partnership interest with a negative capital account resulted in taxable income to the donor.[18] The partnership had liabilities for which none of the partners had assumed personal liability and based on this fact, the ruling reaches two conclusions. First, the limited partner's share of such nonrecourse liabilities is realized on the transfer; and, second, since the liabilities are realized, the bargain sale provisions of §1011(b) are applicable. The position of IRS is supported by the Tax Court.[19]

(b) Gifts to Family Members.

Gifts of the property or of the partnership interest to the donor's child or other relative have also been unsuccessful. In *Joseph W. Johnson* the taxpayer borrowed $375,000 from a bank, pledging stock having a value of $500,000 as collateral for the loan. His basis for the stock was approximately $11,000. The notes were marked "without personal liability." Several days after taking out the loans, he transferred the pledged stock to a trust for the benefit of his children and the trustees substituted their own notes for those of the taxpayers whose notes were marked "paid." It was held that to the extent the loan exceeded the taxpayer's basis in the property transferred, it constituted a sale and he realized income subject to capital gain taxes.[20] However, the Tax Court has refused to follow this rule in cases of net gifts, i.e., gifts where the donee agrees to pay the gift tax due from the donor.[21] It is doubtful whether these cases have any application to the foreclosure cases, however.

12.6   UTILIZATION OF GRANTOR TRUSTS

The term "grantor trust" refers to a trust where the grantor (the party creating the trust) is taxed on part or all of the trust's income as though he still owned the property outright. For example, a revocable trust is a grantor trust and he must report the taxable income of the trust just as if the transfer had not occurred. Depreciation and depletion pass through to the grantor, assuming he is also the trust beneficiary.[22] However, when the beneficiary's interest terminates there is no realization of gain and no recapture of depreciation. Accordingly, if the grantor is also the trust beneficiary for a period of years, a part of the tax loss can pass through to him during those years but when his interest terminates, there appears to be no recognition of gain. In recent years, therefore, some practitioners have utilized the technique of taking title to the tax shelter investment in the name of a grantor trust, passing through the depreciation during the early years followed by a transfer of the beneficial interest to a charity or to a low-bracket taxpayer, such as a child of the grantor. Where this technique is utilized it is best to avoid having the grantor act in any fashion after the initial transfer; rather, the terms of the trust instrument itself should provide a specified date for the termination of the grantor's interest as beneficiary and a designation of the successor beneficiary.

> *Example:* Dr. X is a high-bracket taxpayer who is planning on investing in a real estate project. He is 40 years old and has a child who is one year old. The financial projections for the project indicate that there will be substantial tax losses during the first six years after which the project will begin to produce taxable income. Rather than purchasing the interest in the project in his own name, Dr. X creates a revocable trust and makes an initial contribution of the amount of money required to purchase the investment. The trust provides that Dr. X will be the sole beneficiary for six years at which time his son will become the successor beneficiary and the trust will become irrevocable. During the initial six year term, Dr. X reports losses resulting from the depreciation allocated to the trust. Thereafter, his son, who will then be 7 years old and presumably in a low bracket, will become the trust beneficiary. Trust income will thereafter be taxable either to the trust or to the son as successor beneficiary.

Although a number of commentators have discussed the merits of this plan,[23] there are no cases or rulings specifically in point and the limits of this technique remain to be explored.

12.7   RAISING CAPITAL BY ADMISSION OF A NEW PARTNER

Supposing that the problems with the partnership creditors, including the mortgagee, can be solved by the infusion of additional capital and a new partner or group of partners is found who are willing to make such capital contributions. Presumably, the new partners hope to derive some of the tax benefits resulting from the tax loss and they may also feel that in time the partnership property will increase in value and their investment will prove to be profitable. Assume further that, as an inducement to the new investors, the partnership agrees to allocate to them a specified share, say 60%, of partnership profits and losses.

Unfortunately, the benefits which are allocated to the new investors produce tax problems for the old partners. The allocation of profits and losses to the new partners also requires a similar allocation of nonrecourse partnership liabilities to them. This produces a concomitant decrease in the old partners' share of such liabilities. Thus, in the example outlined above, 60% of the partnership liabilities will be deemed to be allocated to the new partners and the old partners will be left with only 40% of such liabilities. Under §752(b) such a decrease in liabilities is considered a distribution of money by the partnership to the old partners. Assuming partnership liabilities of $1,000,000, there would be a $600,000 constructive distribution to the old partners, notwithstanding the fact that they received none of the cash invested.

Although a cash distribution by a partnership to a partner does not necessarily produce taxable income, it does result in a reduction of the basis of his partnership interest. Of course, to the extent that the constructive distribution exceeds basis, taxable income follows. Moreover, the non-recognition rule is superseded to the extent provided under §751(b). This section relates to certain inventory items and unrealized receivables of the partnership and the latter term is defined to include depreciation recapture income.[24] Referring again to our example, therefore, assuming that the partnership had claimed $100,000 of depreciation in excess of straignt-line depreciation and that all of such excess was subject to the recapture rules of §1250, then the constructive distribution would produce taxable ordinary income to the old partners. Accordingly, whether the admission of new partners is advisable from a tax point of view will depend in large part on the amount of unrecovered basis of the old partners and whether the partnership has been claiming accelerated depreciation.

FOOTNOTES FOR CHAPTER TWELVE

[1]*Crane v Comm'r.*, 331 U.S. 1, 35 AFTR 776 (1947).

[2]Reg. 1.752-1(e).

[3]*R. O'Dell & Sons*, 169 F.2d 247, 37 AFTR 173 (CA3, 1948).

[4]*Woodsam Associates, Inc.*, 16 T.C. 649 (1951), aff'd 198 F.2d 357, 42 AFTR 505 (CA2, 1952). This decision, however, cited an earlier Tax Court decision, *Mendham Corp.*, 9 T.C. 320 (1947) containing language indicating the Court was relying on cash realized from borrowings, not tax benefits from depreciation. See also *Parker v. Delaney*, 186 F.2d 455, 40 AFTR 89 (CA1, 1950) where the first circuit indicated it would have followed footnote 37 of *Crane* had the value of the property been less than the debt.

[5]Rev Rul. 76-111, 1976-1 C.B. 214.

[6]*Gavin S. Millar*, 67 T.C. 656 (1977).

[7]*Helvering v. Hammel*, 311 U.S. 504, 24 AFTR 1082 (1941).

[8]*Stackhouse v. U.S.*, 441 F.2d 465 27 AFTR 2d 71-1211 (CA5, 1971).

[9]§61 (a) (12).

[10]Rev.Rul. 73-160, 1973-1 C.B. 365.

[11]*Lakeland Grocery Co.*, 36 BTA 289 (1937); *Main Properties, Inc.*, 4 T.C. 364 (1944) acq.; Reg 1.61-12(b).

[12]*Plantation Patterns, Inc. v. Comm'r.*, 462 F.2d 712, 29 AFTR 2d 72-1408 (CA 5, 1972).

[13]*Peter Pan Seafoods, Inc. v. U.S.*, 417 F.2d 670 24 AFTR 2d 69-5819 (CA9,1969). But see Rev.Rul. 72-464, 1972-2 C.B. 214 holding that a merger of the debtor and creditor corporations results in recognition of discount as income to the creditor.

[14]Reg. 1.1017-1(b) (5) and (6).

[15]Reg. 1.1017-1(a) (1), (2).

[16]Rev.Rul. 72-205, 1972-1 C.B. 37.

[17]Rev.Rul 70-626, 1970-2 C.B. 158.

[18]Rev.Rul 75-194, 1975-1 C.B. 80

[19]*Magnolia Development Corp.*, 1960 P-H TC Memo ¶60,177.

[20]*Joseph W. Johnson*, 59 T.C. 791 (1973), aff'd 495 F.2d 1079 33 AFTR 2d 74-1102 (CA6, 1974). This case relied on *Malone v U.S.*, 326 F.Supp. 106,27 AFTR 2d 71-1565 (N.D. Miss., 1971), aff'd per curiam by 5th Circuit, a similar fact situation except that taxpayers were personally liable for the debt in question.

[21]*Richard H. Turner,* 49 T.C. 356 (1968), aff'd 410 F.2d 752, 23 AFTR 2d 69-1352 (CA6, 1969); *Edna B. Hirst,* 63 T.C. 307 (1974), on appeal to 4th Circuit.

[22]§167(b) and §611(b) (3). See *Glen E. Edgar,* 56 T.C. 717 (1971).

[23]Cowan "Use of Grantor Trusts to Escape a Tax Shelter Without Detrimental Tax Effects" 41 J. Tax 346 (Dec., 1974). Another commentator votes against the grantor trust technique, Ginsburg, "The Leaky Tax Shelter" 53 *Taxes* 719, 724 (Dec., 1975).

[24]§751 (c); Reg.1.751-1(c) (4). The amount of potential recapture income is treated as an unrealized receivable with a basis of zero. Reg 1.751-1(c) (5).

TABLE OF CASES

REVENUE RULINGS

TABLE OF SECTIONS

TABLE OF REGULATIONS

INDEX